I think the nurses are stealing my clothes...

THE VERY BEST OF
LINDA SMITH

ABOUT THE AUTHORS

Warren Lakin was Linda Smith's lover and constant companion for 23 years, first in Sheffield and then in London. He was a local newspaper reporter before embarking on a 30 year 'career' in arts and entertainment, working as producer, promoter, agent, manager, fundraiser, tour booker, venue programmer, occasional performer, compere and DJ. He is currently writing a biography of Linda Smith entitled *Driving Miss Smith* to be published by Hodder and Stoughton in Autumn 2007.

Ian Parsons is currently working on further projects with Warren Lakin. Deprived forever of the joy of tipping out of Ronnie Scott's at 3 a.m. in Linda's company and not merely because of the recent lamentable changes to the club, he is now retired from a life touring the UK as 'The Amazing Mr. Find-o'. A schema of his life is available from all good jazz record stores. He lives in a huff, north of the Thames.

I think the nurses are stealing my clothes...

THE VERY BEST OF
LINDA SMITH

**Compiled and Edited by Warren Lakin
and Ian Parsons**

HODDER &
STOUGHTON

Introductions:
© Jo Brand; © Ann Lavelle; © Mark Steel; © Hattie Hayridge; © Mark Thomas;
© Steve Gribbin; © Richard Morton; © Stuart Maconie; © Henry Normal;
© Chris Neill; © Michael Rosen; © Tim Brooke-Taylor; © Barry Cryer;
© Claire Jones; © Nicholas Parsons; © Simon Hoggart; © Corrie Corfield;
© Jeremy Hardy; © David Quantick; © Andy Hamilton; © Sandi Toksvig.

Illustrations:
© Phill Jupitus; © Martin Rowson; © Steve Bell.

First published in Great Britain in 2006 by Hodder & Stoughton
A division of Hodder Headline

A Hodder & Stoughton book

2

A CIP catalogue record for this title is
available from the British Library

ISBN 978 0 340 93846 1
ISBN 0 340 93846 3

Typeset in 11.25/14.75pt Plantin Light by
Servis Filmsetting Ltd, Manchester
Printed and bound by
Mackays of Chatham Ltd, Chatham, Kent

Hodder Headline's policy is to use papers that are natural,
renewable and recyclable products and made from wood grown in
sustainable forests. The logging and manufacturing processes are
expected to conform to the environmental regulations of the
country of origin.

Hodder & Stoughton Ltd
A division of Hodder Headline
338 Euston Road
London NW1 3BH

This book is dedicated to Barbara and Terry Giles, Debra Reay, Claire Jones and all the other family members and friends who were there for Linda and I when it most mattered.

Warren Lakin

CONTENTS

FOREWORD
Jo Brand, comedian and writer

Dear old Linda.

Since Linda's sad and unfair death, she has been eulogised in so many ways, by those who knew her and those who didn't, that it seems an impossible task to pick my way through without repeating or paraphrasing others. So I won't try. I'll just say what I feel.

Linda has been deemed a 'radical', a 'wit' and 'unique', words that are often liberally sprinkled by those left behind when someone is lost so young. But the words don't really seem adequate, sat there on the page. They are not really enough to describe the essence of Linda and her spirit. Because Linda really was unique. If you travel the length and breadth of this self-deprecating, weird, conservative, unpredictable nation of ours, she seemed to be the one and only genuinely funny, female, political comic. Well, think about it. Who else is there?

As women stand-ups still struggle against the irritating ubiquity of media articles about the scarcity of female comics, the lack of talent of female comics and a waterfall of spiteful bilge about their looks, from the (mainly female) nasty tabloid-press types, Linda seemed to stand above these attacks, I suspect because many of these old bags hadn't any idea what she was talking about or what she stood for. I always envied the ease with which Linda turned weighty and unfathomable political topics into something warm, funny and fit for consumption by Joe Public, who didn't have to have a degree in PPE from Oxbridge to know what she was on about. Linda had that knack which very few people possess, of taking the piss out of our political landscape in an entirely palatable and female way, but with an extremely low knob-joke count. She wasn't prissy in any way, she was just funny. Her material seemed effortless in its easy-on-the-ear-ness, but it was clever, perceptive, politically sharp and above all very funny. Why wasn't she on the telly more then, I hear you ask. Well, the simple answer is I don't know. She was on the radio all the time and the listeners adored her. I think that perhaps TV viewers, with their insatiable appetite for easily consumed middle-of-the-road stuff, might have found Linda an uneasy companion. Certainly audiences on the comedy circuit found her an amiable and entertaining mate to spend time with.

The early comedy circuit was pure joy for me. I found it hard to wake up every morning and actually believe that was what I did. That I went on stage and people laughed and I got money for it. Linda struck me as similarly pleased about this, but one would never have known it from her sardonic dismissal of any pretensions to an art form for her comedy. She just got up and talked about things that she was interested in.

She was not what I would call a Hattie Jacquesian matron of comedy who looked after everyone, referred them to analysis, listened to their problems, made tea and took a back seat. Linda liked to be at the heart of sociable things; she liked to have a drink, she had a hard heart when one was required, and could often be heard slagging off promoters, acts, TV producers, anyone who deserved her wrath – and believe you me, there were a few.

Linda was so kind too. Today, kindness is a virtue not often acknowledged. Let's be honest, how many very left-wing people do you meet who are horribly unpleasant? And who are not practising what they preach? Linda did not suffer fools gladly. But she did not suffer fools gladly in a nice way.

The early comedy circuit for women was in some ways easy and in other ways hard. Audiences varied from the vegan, hemp-clad lovelies of the only comedy club that was a veggie restaurant to the Neanderthal city boys bathed in sick who came alive at the late show and killed you, mainly with their breath. And we all had to deal with them, man and boy (and about fifteen women).

Linda didn't say 'Fuck off' every two seconds like myself, Jenny Eclair and some others did. And her natural home wasn't the *Comedy Store* late show and its gladiatorial atmosphere, fuelled with alcohol, testosterone and the sort of pre-menstrual, male irritability you get on a Friday night after a swaggering, shouty week at work. I always thought Linda's material was far too intelligent to be thrown to the swine that snuffled into the late show because what Linda produced were little comedy pearls . . . jokes imbued with some knowledge and some wisdom and much wit. Why waste those on a pissed-up arsehole whose command of the English language normally only extends to ordering beer, heckling someone or commenting on the size of certain breasts with the very imaginative lexicon of swear words available in the English vernacular?

Politically speaking, I envied the clarity with which Linda was able to organise her thoughts. She seemed very sure of herself, well informed and faithful to her own ideology. Sadly, some of us aren't quite so grown-up, and I felt I could never live up to Linda's standards. However, she wasn't one of those far-lefters you suspected were condemning you to death in a secret kangaroo court made up of your closest mates while you were at the bar getting them all a beer. We didn't really argue about politics much because we broadly felt the same, except I was slightly more weedily liberal and populist. I appreciated Linda laying off me.

I often wonder how people who write autobiographies, or who speak about incidents in their lives that occurred years ago, manage to remember minor events which couldn't possibly be called to mind by a normal brain. Do they have detailed egocentrically constructed diaries which describe every waking minute? Do they cobble it together with some help from friends? Or do they just make it up? Well, you would, wouldn't you? Faced with a blank page and a sense of rising panic, it's a reasonable step to take, because, apart from a few people who were there, who might quibble with some of the detail, very few people are going to gainsay their version of history.

But perhaps I'm judging everyone by my own standards. I am the woman whose memory erases faster than a speeding bullet or doesn't even work in the first place. My head is and always has been so crowded with stuff that I have to offload events and facts almost as soon as I have heard them. Or I have to not listen to things that are being said to me, in an attempt to retain some current idea I am wrestling with or remember something I have to do later.

All this is a very roundabout way of telling you that I do not have chapter and verse on every single encounter I have ever had with the lovely Linda. So my memories of her follow a rather random scatter-gun path. I am however loath to get someone with a proper brain to fill in the gaps because then it wouldn't be a fair representation of Linda and me.

I first met Linda when she was living in Sheffield at the end of the eighties, running and performing at a working men's club comedy night, and I know that I immediately warmed to her because she was the sort of woman I like. First of all she was a really good laugh, her humour sharp and sardonic and laced with strong opinions and much what I can only call piss-taking, because she was a piss-taker, and I liked that. I remember (vaguely of course) doing a night there with her. I think John Shuttleworth was on and I remember being surprised that Linda put up with what I considered in my London hoity-toity feminist way to be the rather misogynist rules of the club. But Linda was more accepting and grown-up about it than I was, I suppose.

Over the next few years Linda moved down to London and we saw slightly more of each other. We both worked on the circuit and as we women were a scarce resource and had to be divided evenly around comedy club bills along with the other minority groups, we very rarely worked on the same bill as each other. The only time we all worked together was on all-women bills or International Women's Day gigs. *City Limits*, that erstwhile opponent of *Time Out* which I loved, because it was so much less slick and contained loads of misprints (yes, this is a sad attempt at a joke), once listed an all-women night as starring Hattie Hayridge, Donna McPhail, Linda Smith and Bernard Gilhooley. (Brenda, of course.)

I do have an enormous amount of regret that I let many meet-ups with Linda slip through my fingers due to laziness, forgetfulness, pressure of work, domestic issues, the distance between our homes, the temperature, menstrual issues . . . now I'm being silly, but you know what I mean. Much of the time we never saw each other and when we did, we compared notes, got drunk, had a laugh and retired back to our individual lives in different areas of London.

The best times I had with Linda were not what an editor wants to read because they weren't that entertaining. We didn't snort cocaine off fourteen-year-old boys' backs or have lazy drunken fivesomes behind the stage in an Assembly Rooms venue in Edinburgh. We just had a laugh and a nice time together. We compared notes about our careers, talked about people on the circuit and what they were up to, sat in the garden in Linda and Warren's house on long sunny days and drank tea and smelled the flowers. We said brief, drunken hellos in Edinburgh bars, knowing that arrangements to meet for coffee would be overtaken by hangovers; we wished each other luck as one strolled on stage at a show, as the other left for the next gig, and we kept in touch pathetically seldom.

Many years ago I met Kirsty MacColl at a benefit show in London and we got talking in the green room after the show. I really liked her and I identified with a lot of what she said. She was a laugh and seemed so relaxed and friendly. She gave me her number. Time moved along and before I knew it, six months had elapsed and I wondered if she would remember me. The upshot of this is I never called her. She died a tragic death at such a young age and I was filled with sadness and regret for having been so apathetically lazy.

This was how it was with Linda too, except that I knew Linda much better. I liked seeing her. She made me laugh. She was ordinary (and yet of course extraordinary), so normal to be with, and she swore brilliantly.

We were very different too. I've always thought of Linda as travelling along that political road that Billy Bragg sums up so beautifully in 'Waiting for the Great Leap Forward'. Linda was unflinching in her dedication to her political beliefs and changed not a jot over all the years I knew her. Her idealism, even though she was such a cynic at times, didn't seem to desert her, whereas

many of us are pragmatists at best and at worst . . . well, let's say we allow life to pull us politically out of shape, like an old jumper.

Much of Linda's career was separate from mine and we swam in different ponds. I marvelled at her ability to do shows like the *News Quiz* because they terrified me to bloody death. And then when I heard she had been voted the wittiest person in the world by Radio 4 listeners I was so pleased for her because it finally meant – and this doesn't happen very often – that a democratically conducted survey had crowned her Queen of Wit; which was so apt as Radio 4 listeners are very intelligent and they know what they are talking about, Linda would have told me to say.

Linda was a quiet comedy genius, getting on with it and thrilling a perfectly formed band of fans. She was a lovable person with a warm, cheeky smile and a great brain. The Linda-shaped hole is a very big one indeed. She left behind some lovely witty work for us to remind ourselves of her. In this book you'll find some reminiscences from Linda's friends and colleagues but mostly you will find Linda in her own words – from her earliest appearances on stage in the early eighties to her dazzling appearances on TV and radio. I would like to think that reading this might make you want to look up some old friends you haven't seen for a while, because you don't really know how long everyone is going to be here.

Jo Brand, 2006.

PART ONE

'My Real Name is Wanda Starbright'

1984–1988

THE SHEFFIELD YEARS
Ann Lavelle, television producer

I first met Linda at Sheffield University in 1980 when we were both studying English and Drama. Linda was in the year above me. She had a striking personality and really stood out from the crowd. Sheffield was a bit of a cultural hot spot at the time and the now famous film and theatre director Stephen Daldry was in the same year as Linda. We both went up to the Edinburgh Festival to appear in one of his productions – *The Diggers*. That was our first time performing together but not the last.

The early eighties' burgeoning comedy scene had by now spread to the North, and for some reason I got up and did a try-out at a Sheffield pub. I managed to stay on stage for about three minutes and somehow got a few laughs. A few days later I was walking past a famous Sheffield landmark, the second-hand bookshop Rare and Racy. I bumped into Linda and told her about my three minutes of fame. Linda said that she had always fancied the idea of being a comedian and there and then we agreed to have a go together, to give each other moral support.

If only we'd looked up at the name of the bookshop, Rare and Racy, we might have had a decent name, but instead we called ourselves Token Women. This truly awful name, which we thought ironic, didn't stick. Fortunately Linda's love of jazz and blues, especially her passion for fifties' singers such as Etta James, led to us changing our name to Tuff Lovers, the title of an Etta James song. We used to play ourselves on to this track at the start of the set to get us in the mood.

We weren't really a double act. We would come on stage together for about thirty seconds. I would say that I wasn't feeling well and go off again! Then Linda would do about ten minutes, then I'd come back on to do my bit and we'd finish together with a song. It was a really terrible piss-take of 'Goodbye, Norma Jean'. I have no idea now why we thought Elton John was a fitting target for our vitriol, but we did and it seemed to go down well.

In truth, I don't remember that much about our act – it's over twenty years ago now. When I think of my own part I find it incredibly cringe-worthy and I am so glad that I retreated into the world of TV production. But for Linda it was different and it was clear from the start that she had a raw talent and a duck-to-water flair for cutting-edge comedy.

Despite the fact that I certainly wasn't a natural talent, we took to our new careers with gusto. We went on to the legendary Enterprise Allowance Scheme that meant we didn't have to sign on any more and got £40 a week paid into our bank accounts. We were in showbiz, official! We played anywhere and everywhere, with many scrapes along the way. I remember a particularly scary gig in Leeds where we fell foul of the local militant lesbian-feminists. 'Try women,' they heckled. At the end of the night we had to make a run for the safety of Warren's van. We drove off at high speed. Not that *tuff* really.

Then there was the TUC Women's Conference where our swearing caused great offence. That time we got chased by tabloid photographers shouting, 'Ann, Linda, this way, this way.' Surreal. The next day there was a report on page three of the *Sun*, beside that day's 'Page Three Stunna' with the headline 'Blue Sisters Are No Joke'. We were very proud of that.

And then, significantly for us, the miners' strike happened and suddenly there were 'Coal Not Dole' yellow stickers all over Sheffield. Warren came up with the idea of the Pit Stop Tour, which gave Linda and myself the chance to perform at miners' welfare clubs throughout the Yorkshire coalfields. It was an extraordinary experience.

We would turn up on a midweek evening and take over the miners' clubs with our strange alternative bill. There was the socialist magician Ian Saville, George Faux the folk singer, comedian Mark

Hurst (or Mark Miwurdz as he was then known) and us. I really don't know what the bemused miners and their families thought of us. We were certainly not the kind of acts they were used to. I'm sure they'd have preferred the usual pub singers and bingo but they gave us the benefit of the doubt because we were supporting their strike in our own way.

Linda and Warren became very close to some of the families in the villages. I remember we all went to Cortonwood on the day the miners went back to work. All the men went up to the gates, then turned their backs, stood in silence and then walked away. They actually went back to work the next day, but it was a gesture of how they felt.

And so I think the Pit Stop Tour was a great opportunity for Linda to cut her political comedy teeth. I was lucky enough to have been around to see that first flush of Linda's huge talent and it did not surprise me that she went on to become such a brilliant stand-up and broadcaster.

It was impossible not to have fun being with Linda. She was so very kind, supportive, and clever, but above all – bloody funny.

Ann Lavelle, 2006.

TOKEN WOMEN (Linda)
Walkley and Hallam Ward Labour Parties Christmas Party,
December 1984

(Striking miners in the audience). Clive and Gulliver Guilt-merchant – his best mate – are at the vanguard of the NALGO dispute. It's been so dreadful I'm glad it was over by Christmas. I thought, bang goes our crystallised fruits this Christmas if this dispute isn't over. You can't afford it when you are engaged in the struggle with management. There's a distinct cloud over that second holiday, the cultural tour of Cuba, the rum distilleries. I've got to go now to see Clive and his friend Gulliver at the railway station, they're going to their men's remedial life skills weekend workshop. I've got a lentil chasseur on and I want to give it a stir.

TOKEN WOMEN (LINDA)
Beighton Miners' Welfare, South Yorkshire, February/March 1985
– Pit Stop Tour

Something I've noticed round here, it's great, they live in Sheffield and they come from Sheffield. Where I live in Hunters Bar, which is Hallam, no one comes from Sheffield, they all come from somewhere else. Actually, now I come to think of it, there is one family down the end of my road who are a Sheffield family. I think their house is going to be opened up to the public as a working museum – there's not that many of them. I feel really at home in Hallam, I feel more at home since the strike started because half the bloody Metropolitan Police are up in Sheffield so it's just a little home from home for me. It's terrible, the crime figures in the South have just rocketed since the miners' strike 'cos police from all over the country are coming up to the South Yorks coalfield. You may not know this but the Burglars' Union, the NUB, the National Union of Burglars – such is the state of crime in London – is putting forward this 'nick' closure plan. All round

Islington, twenty uneconomic nicks are going to be closed down, don't need them any more – all the Met are up here.

It's a terrible business, the police. I thought they'd done the worst they could till I saw this – you won't believe this. Saw this in my newsagent's window the other day – it says, 'Your Community Constable is PC Jeanette Scargill' – it's true, I swear. I thought, this is a bit below the belt. I know you've had police impersonating striking miners on the picket line but impersonating members of the Royal Family . . . (big laughs and applause) It's a very serious business really, then I thought that perhaps this Jeanette Scargill actually is a member of *the* Scargill family. You're not responsible for your family; she could be his niece, or a long-lost daughter from some little escapade early in his life – could be anyone. I thought, we've all got our skeletons in the cupboard. I know I've got mine.

As you probably gathered, I don't actually come from Sheffield. I come from South-East London, or Souf-East London as we would say. I don't think they know much about the recession. Things are pretty good down in South-East London. People don't support Margaret Thatcher – they think she should stand down for a stronger leader. And kids are all fully paid up members of the 'Thatcher Youth'. They go to schools like the Oswald Mosley Comprehensive. Their uniform is designer sportswear, gold chains, Lacoste underpants and Aramis perfume . . . furry dice on the skateboard.

As I say, I go down South and it's like another world. If people actually knew the miners' strike was going on they'd be furious. But they don't tend to watch a lot of news, which is a shame really because you can see some really good things on the news. There's this wonderful new game you can play, a new game show, it's much more popular than *The Price Is Right*. It's actually called *The Return to Work Figures Are Wrong*! It's that much more fun because you can play it every time the news comes on. They give you some absurd figure like 'The numbers returning to work at Ninnington pit are actually greater than the population of the United Kingdom.' Incredible things like this and you can write in with the real figures and you can win a night out with Chief Inspector Nesbitt⋆ (lots of laughter). Really popular game show that one.

None of this can actually compare with the big news of last year – the real biggie, which was of course the Brighton bomb. That's everyone's favourite. I'll never forget that day. I came home, switched on the telly – I wanted to watch *Brookside* – and across the screen there was this newsflash which said 'Newsflash . . . Newsflash . . . Newsflash . . . '

'Entire Tory Cabinet buried under a pile of shit'. I thought, is that news? You've interrupted *Brookside* to tell me that? Tell me something I don't know. Then I thought, no. This is a cover-up. This isn't a bomb at all. This is actually a cover-up. What it actually was, was Willie Whitelaw with one of his toy guns going (imitates gun shots), hit a gas pipe in the hotel. The funniest thing of the whole Brighton bomb was Denis Thatcher staggering out of the ruins. Didn't know what was going on, didn't know what day it was. He's probably still trying to recapture the recipe for that pink gin he was drinking at the time: 'Gosh, that packs a punch.' You can just imagine him, can't you? The frustration of it all, they didn't get *her*, they didn't get *her*. She was just two minutes from death. If only she was into the high-fibre diet, if Thatcher had had the All Bran at breakfast she'd have been on the khazi that vital two minutes and they'd have got her (much laughter and applause).

Be serious – this is just a fantasy, because if she were killed would it actually make any difference, would things get any better? 'Course they wouldn't. Don't kid yourself. They'd get worse because she would become a martyr. This monetarist martyr – a cult figure like Eva Peron. Can you imagine the televised funeral? There she'd be laid out in a glass coffin – in the blue gear, the hairdo and all the rest of it. She'd be laying there just really life-like. Just like she was in life . . . a bit warmer (laughs). It would be on the telly. You thought Winston Churchill was bad – you can imag-

---

⋆ Chief Inspector Nesbitt was a senior policeman in the South Yorkshire Constabulary during the miners' strike of 1984/85 and was a familiar figure at the picket lines of the South Yorkshire coalfield.

ine what this would be like. And then of course it wouldn't stop at that. There would be films: *The Night Brighton Rocked*; there'd be musicals. Tim Rice would be churning out the musicals about her life – *Magita*. There'd be Elaine Page belting out the big numbers: 'Don't Cry for Me, Barnet Finchley'. I couldn't handle it, I'd rather she lived, quite frankly. You can't win, can you? I know one thing. I know a lot of people who are going to win and that's the miners. Victory to the miners! Goodnight, comrades (much applause).

TOKEN WOMEN
Sheffield Trades and Labour Club, 1985

Princess Margaret – I'm sick of that woman – every time you turn on it's fag-ash Mag (gasps and wheezes like heavy smoker). It was bad enough when she actually had the operation – you know, she had that serious operation and all the news flashes about it – she had a really tiny, tiny piece of her removed – a tiny little growth – the *only* non-malignant part of Princess Margaret was removed . . . amazing!

★

Do you remember Molesworth? – you know, the siege of Molesworth – they went in – those few, the brave five thousand – they went in to take Molesworth from the peace protestors . . . peace protestors? – you've got to watch those peace protestors – perverts, freaks and child-molesters – terrible people . . . you go in there – you've got to watch it . . . if you say a wrong word to them, you're likely to get a right bit of plimsoll, you really are – and if you give another wrong word . . . you might get a cup of tea with soya milk in it or something like that.

. . . Michael Heseltine's life must have been hanging on a thread. They should give that man a medal.

TUFF LOVERS
Live at Loughborough, 1985

(Ann introduces Linda.)

ANN: Hello, Linda! This is Linda, my friend and partner, how's it been going?

LINDA: Hello, everyone. Well, it's OK actually. We are working through a few things there, I don't think those women are going to be seeing any more of those patriarchal penguins (laughs).

Heard a little male aggressive noise there. (laughs) Oorr! From the solar plexus, that hunter-gatherer noise. Oorr! (laughs).

ANN: Are you feeling all right, Linda?

LINDA: Don't get the impression that I'm some sort of mad castrating feminist, because I'm not. I think it's OK for men to have willies, but when they start thinking with them (laughs) I'm afraid they're going to get nowhere. Big round of applause for my friend Ann who's been entertaining you while I've been doing my wonderful supportive work downstairs (applause).

Good evening, freedom lovers of Loughborough. It's wonderful to be here. I've only just got here.

You will notice the programme started rather late tonight, partly my fault, I got off work pretty late tonight. I'm on an MSC scheme in Sheffield where I live. I'm a community burglar (laughs). Actually, I think it's quite important for people to be burgled by their neighbours. People they know and trust because it would be pretty traumatic otherwise. Anyway, I'm well into this community racket. Everything is community these days, community this, community that. My whole family are into it. My grandmother is a community supergrass (laughs). She's sat all day behind her lace curtains looking out, and if she sees a black person walking down the street in broad daylight, she goes down the cop shop and they give her a Goblin Teasmade. It's an extraordinary thing, this community policing idea. Start off with your friendly community policeman in the community, eventually a community replaced by 50,000 policemen (laughs), an escalating thing. Had this problem getting off work late tonight, as I said, this is actually one of the better employment schemes I have been on. I am at a tricky point in my life just now because I'm in a sort of employment menopause (laughs). You know, you are too old for the YTS scheme, but you know you can't be bothered with the Community Programme. It's a bad time of life. But actually I have been on some really bad YTS schemes, I was a tree in an environmental corridor for a year (laughs). I thought that was pretty bad, then topped it all when I was a sandbag in the Dunkirk Exhibition (laughs). Anyway, I'm through with all that.

There's another reason why I'm not really feeling much like zany cabaret this evening and that's because I had a pretty heavy scene with my own male friend, Clive, this evening. I was really upset by it. As this is a sort of front-room set-up, I feel it's a space I can trust, I'd like to talk a bit more about my problems with Clive. Main problem is communicating. We have a lot of trouble communicating. I think the main reason for that is I'm talking to him in English and he's listening to me in Bollockbrain! (laughs). I don't see a way through it actually (laughs). Now I'm coming over heavy and aggressive. As you can see, this is a spiralling effect of male violence (laughs). I didn't mean to be nasty about Clive, because actually Clive's all right. In fact he's more than all right, he's right on. Clive is pretty right on. In fact that's the problem. I've just gone right off right-on men! They're so arrogant, aren't they? What can I say, your normal sexist man is appalling as we've seen tonight (laughs) but you know where you are with them. They tell these terrible jokes, you know subconsciously they hate you. They want to fuck you, they want to kill you. They want to leave you by the side of the M1. That sort of thing (laughs). On that kind of understanding, having sussed that out, you can actually have a reasonable conversation with them (laughs). On that understanding, that that's where things are leading to. But with your non-sexist man he's got you completely snookered, you see. Because he's there before you with the right response, you cannot trust them. I mean, your average nasty sexist man really fancies himself, just thinks he's God's bollocks. Doesn't he, just fancies himself (laughs). Not the right-on man. The right-on man just knows he's God's ovaries (laughs). You can't stand it, at the end of it you just feel inadequate. You feel like a female impersonator – compared to him (laughs). He's so right-on.

So that's how it is with me and Clive at the moment. It wasn't always like this. How do relationships end up like this? They start off so well. It was a whirlwind romance. I'll never forget my first meeting with him. I'd just knocked off work, I'd had a good day's burgling. Must have been some sort of rally on because I picked up quite a lot in wealthier middle-class areas. I went to my local for a drink, I went down to the old Dog and Community Worker. It's a very nice pub, it's a theme pub, I think the theme is the Tottenham riots because there's a blazing Cortina in the middle of the lounge (laughs). You buy these little crunchy snacks called Pork Snatchings, open the bag and they leap out at you (makes knocking noise with hand). A bit of a heavy leisure concept really.

I was sat there with a half of Guinness and a packet of Wheat Eats as I often do, and suddenly I was transfixed by this vision in the doorway. The double doors of the saloon swung open (makes whooshing noise) and in walked – in a very cool, but not oppressive, sort of way, this vision in Peruvian knitwear (laughs). He had everything. He had the leg-warmers – someone over there has got them too, I'm sure they looked very nice in 1974. The little slip-perettes, he's got the leg-warmers, he had the mittens on a string, he had the little hat with flaps on it and a waistcoat. I know that Sheffield is a very hilly city but – a bloody Sherpa? (laughs). Just couldn't handle it. Anyway. He mooched over to my table, again not oppressively so, flung down his mittens like a challenge. That was his first mistake, because they were threaded through his duffel coat. He nearly garrotted himself! He would have saved me a lot of trouble anyway (laughs). So he threw down his mittens and sat down beside me, and he said, 'Hi, I'm Clive Caring Person and believe me, sister, I care.' Well, that was it, I was hooked. We drove off into the sunset in his stripped-pine Morris Minor (laughs), a quick Barley Cup back at his place (laughs), and that was it.

Mind you, I will say this for Clive, he does hold down a very good job. He's not on a scheme like me, he's got a proper job. Not many people have. But he actually has a proper job. He works for Sheffield City Council. I don't know if any of you are familiar with the policies of Sheffield City Council. Must have a few students in tonight . . . are you? Yes. One. It's a very liberal revisionist type of council and they have an equal opportunities scheme in their employment policy, which means they will even employ dickheads like Clive. He works in the alternative videos unit, a very worthwhile job. I expect you've heard of video nasties, Clive makes video nicies (laughs). He's employed to take disturbing material like Disney films which have very heavy bits in them, cut all the nasty bits out and make them suitable for the viewing of small children and nervous people – and Neil Kinnock and people like that (laughs). 'More violence! I can't stand it when Bambi's dad dies.' In Clive's film Bambi's dad doesn't die, this is the thing, you see. He moves to a higher plane, a higher plane of existence, where they have a wonderful party with incense and candles and flowers to celebrate the fullness of life cycles, and Bambi and his mum trot happily off to live in a women's house (laughs). So it's an ill wind that blows nobody any good.

Right, so that's Clive's job. What else can I tell you about Clive? That brings me on to another problem area with Clive, which is children. Because Clive is a single-parent family. I don't know who the mother is – I don't think Clive does! (laughs). On his own, completely – well, that's not true, he's not on his own completely. He has a very supportive, large child-care circuit he can call on. He's a great believer in the shared parenting concept. Sort of non-nuclear parenting, where 700 people share a child. And it works pretty well on the whole. But it has its problems. In fact Clive's little boy, little Leon, I'm afraid he's got lost on the child-care circuit (laughs). We haven't seen him for months, I don't know where he is. All I remember – my mind's a complete blur now – I remember dropping him off with some women friends . . . a steel-erecting co-op. I thought he would pick up a bit of spot welding or something. So he stayed there for a bit, then I just heard this rumour on the grapevine that he was forming a lovers' rock band in Ladbroke Grove, and I thought, this can't be right – he's only seven (laughs). And then imagine my horror, freedom lovers of Loughborough, when I received this letter with a Nicaraguan stamp on it. It said, 'Dear Linda and Clive, don't worry about me I'm having a wonderful time, I'm living with a Sandinista couple just north of Managua. I'm riding shotgun on the coffee crop convoy. PS please feed my rabbit, Engels (laughs). I did actually cheer myself up – I thought, it's nearly Christmas, I'll buy him a little present. So I went out and bought him a book. I bought him a pop-up version of Marx's *Theory of Labour* which I think he will enjoy because it's got a scratch-and-smell effect on it (laughs). Things like Capitalism (simulates smell). Oh, Jesus Christ! Don't want any of that. Very educational. So that's little Leon.

What can I say? It's very good to be here in Loughborough. A good thing about being here is not being with Clive – I'm trying to work out which I like the best. Not having sex with Clive or not socialising. I've decided it's the socialising because you can fake the sex. Socialising, it's harder to pretend you're having a good time. You're more used to it with the sex (laughs). It's driving me mad, the sex. He's into this non-penetrative sex these days. I'm sure there's a lot of women here who are familiar with this allegedly right-on concept of non-penetrative sex. He's been doing this non-penetrative thinking for quite a long time and it's sort of spread to his genitals now (laughs) and I think it's a complete and utter rip-off – it's just another form of male self-enhancement. It's like, a sort of 'I don't even need to use my prick – my whole body is a prick' (laughs). I said to him, Clive, you're literally a dickhead (laughs). Another thing he's into is sharing periods with me (laughs). I'm sorry, any squeamish boys in the audience, you'll just have to grit your teeth for this bit. He's into it. I think that's fine. So every twenty-eight days I kick him in the guts and charge him over a quid for a box of cotton wool (laughs).

So that's the sex. The socialising – the thing with Clive is that his politics are great, he's very, very left. He's very heavily involved with his union – he knows everything about struggle with management, he's a NALGO super-militant. If there are any NALGO members here tonight you might be familiar with (audience member calls out, 'Yes, there are. You're misinformed, darling. It's OK, carry on'). I'm misinformed, oh. Are you going to inform me? (No, you can have it later.) You should be so lucky, sweetheart (laughs).

I'm making free with the genre of comedy. Of course I realise there are many overworked and underpaid NALGO members but I'm only familiar with the more privileged echelons. I'm really coming across honest tonight. As I was saying, he's a NALGO super-militant and you may be familiar with some of his propaganda literature, like his badges – '£15,000 a year Not Dole' and 'Feasibility Studies Not Dole'. But the trouble with middle-class left-wingers is that they don't know how to enjoy themselves. They're great at being guilty but they're not very good at being happy. You know this is what they're very bad at (laughs and applause). Thank you. So he drags you along to this endless stream of middle-class left-wing parties. I can't imagine anything worse. But it's like the sex, you always think it is going to be better next time so you keep going along (laughs).

Last weekend I went to one. You get all dressed up, you think, well, I'm going to a party. You arrive at the door, you open the door, to pitch blackness. You can't see a yard in front of your nose. You think, have I come to a party or is this the remedial group of a social skills workshop? What's going on here? Is it some sort of co-counselling convention? Everybody's sat around in couples. Talking. You know, they're just sat in the dark, talking intensely. So you pick your way through these intense couples, make your way to the party snacks and drinks – grab a glass of home-made henna wine, quite passable . . . and a chickpea on a stick (laughs). They don't go over-mad on the entertainment. You think, I've come to a party – I'll have a dance. Then you hear the music, you go over to the lad on the disco and say, 'Look, you know and I know, that eighteenth-century work songs from Albania (laughs) are really important, but you must have noticed no one is dancing.' Then

you look around at their feet and you realise why they're not dancing because they can't possibly dance because they're all wearing
ultra right-on but really ugly Guat shoes. These may not have
spread to the Midlands but I'm sure you've seen the equivalent.
The back page of the *Guardian*, when you're looking for another
job or something, you'll see these ugly, thick, bright-coloured
heavy leather boots with straps that go right up to the top. They've
got these thick soles which are like a Weetabix on the bottom.
They're like alternative Dr Martens. They're just as clumsy, just as
ugly, just as threatening, but when you kick someone in the head
with one, you leave a rainbow print instead of a gash. So it seems
to be more acceptable (laughs).

As we have a predominantly young crowd here tonight, I think
it's time for an advertisement. For your greater edification. (Lights
dim, imitates sound effects – Linda and Ann set the scene for a
parody of a Government-inspired TV public information campaign warning about the perils of drug taking.)

LINDA: So I do heroin adverts.

ANN: I'm not getting addicted. I can control it (laughs).

LINDA: OK So I've done a few heroin adverts now (laughs). Well, I can
    'andle it. Can nearly say it: 'eroin, 'eroin.

BOTH: 'eroin, 'eroin, 'eroin.

ANN : OK. So I do 'eroin adverts. All right, I know it's not *EastEnders* but
    it's all right. It's got a good slot on a Friday night in between *The Tube*.
    A lotta kids watch 'em.

LINDA: All right, all right, so I know I'm going completely over the fuck-
    ing top with this 'eroin advert. But I can control it. I've just got a touch
    of Method acting today, that's all (laughs). I could give it up tomor-
    row, I could get up and work (laughs). Only the other day I read for a
    part in *EastEnders*.

ANN: OK. I know that as the acceptable face of 'eroin addiction I am just a pawn in a Government plot masking the inherent decadence of latent capitalism. But I've got to work, haven't I ? (laughs).

LINDA: 'eroin adverts . . . can really screw up your career.

Thank you. Goodnight, comrades. Be vigilant (applause).

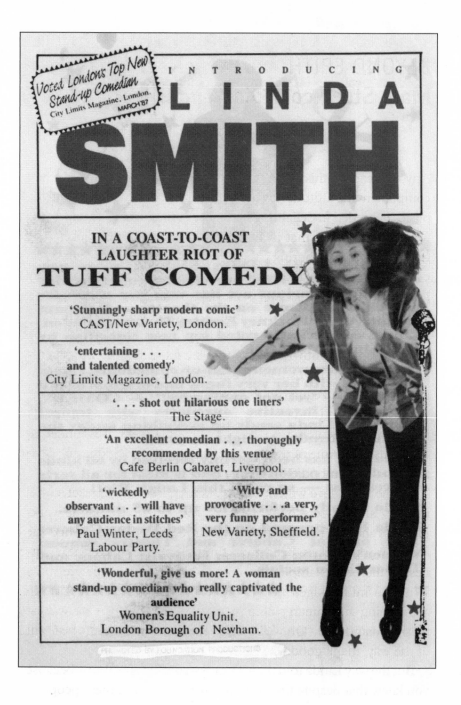

BEYOND ERITH
Mark Steel, comedian and writer

Anyone reading this book will be familiar with Linda's less than complimentary attitude towards her home town of Erith, but the place succeeded in delighting her once. In the Erith local paper, the week after an issue that included complaints about her jokes suggesting Erith was 'boring', there was an article that began, 'The competition to name the new Erith Leisure Centre has been won by the entry "The Erith Leisure Centre".'

But perhaps Erith helped Linda. Because Erith isn't so much a place as a mass of Soviet-style oblong blocks that creep by the Thames up to South-East London, a tribute to cement so complete that, in the 1970s, *Doctor Who* and other science fiction programmes would regularly film there to depict a soulless concrete futuristic world. Linda seems to have reacted against this functional environment, in the same way that Romantics responded to the industrial grime of the nineteenth century, by seeking solace in anything that embodied imagination and passion.

So she fell in love with literature, films, gardening, cricket, cooking, jazz and tea-sets, but without ever looking down on the working class she was brought up in, which was most evident when she found working-class behaviour funny. She reckoned she'd witnessed the best example of a resigned attitude towards life while visiting a middle-aged neighbour one midsummer's day. Late in the evening the woman patted the arms of the armchair she was sat in, sighed and said, 'Oh well – that's the longest day of the year out of the way, thank goodness.'

But the way Linda told these stories was especially funny because you knew that despite their odd behaviour she *liked* these people.

For example, with one tale, Linda summarised the process whereby people at work feel no connection with whatever they're producing. She was working on an assembly line, on which apple turnovers would emerge from an oven, then Linda and her colleagues would pick them up as they passed, and place them in their boxes. Every single time, she said, as the turnovers approached, one worker who'd been there twenty years would flare his nostrils, look menacingly at them and snarl, 'Here come the little fuckers.'

Maybe the trick of how to find the working class funny while remaining proudly working-class herself was helped by an episode covered in this section of the book – the miners' strike. Linda played a prominent part in the strike, particularly in South Yorkshire where she was living, arranging and performing in countless fund-raising benefits. From this position she experienced the most poignant aspect of the mining community's resistance, the way in which they became supporters of causes they'd previously been unaware of and developed a passion for books, films and ideas they would once have considered unreachable.

The miners' benefits weren't the easiest to play, and it was common to discover there was no microphone, and once I had to use the one on the DJ's turntable, so after five minutes a crowd of about twenty were still drunkenly dancing, assuming my twittering was the next record. Indeed, throughout the time covered in this section, the sort of gigs Linda performed in remained unglamorous. Perhaps to get the full sense of them, you should read them in a student union bar on half-price vodka night, missing out every fifth word as the microphone lead becomes disconnected, with a drunk heavy metal band playing in the next room, and get a neighbour to pop in half-way through and shout, 'Show us yer tits.'

One of these nights that Linda found funniest was in Lampeter, which is somewhere in Wales that you can't get to, and after an awful gig we went back to the bed and breakfast we'd been booked into. Although it was half past ten the place was utterly, utterly dark and shut, so on a freezing January night we lobbed stones at a window like a secret teenage lover, until after twenty minutes a landlady emerged in a dressing gown. And she swore we weren't booked in, until she reluctantly checked the book, then peered into our faces and snarled, 'My *husband* must have booked you in, so when I see him he's *dead meat.*' And as we shivered on the doorstep Linda found this hilarious, not just because of the situation but the wonderful use of the English language employed by this rancid woman.

One aspect of Linda's routines from this time that stands out is however much venom she poured on Thatcher, there was plenty left for Neil Kinnock's Labour Party. When many people were refusing to pay the Poll Tax, the Labour Party refused to back them, so Linda described the Labour Party campaign as being 'Pay the Poll Tax – but while you're doing so – look, you give that clerk *such* a look.'

When Linda died, some people commented that no matter how cutting her comments may appear, she bore no malice. But this is cobblers. Integral to her compassion for the majority of people was a contempt for bullies, from global leaders to local thugs, and she was proud to be their enemy.

Mark Steel, 2006.

LINDA LIVE
George IV Public House, Sheffield, 1 November 1986

(Weird heckle from audience . . .)

Right. After that little surreal episode, yes, I can cope with hecklers but not surrealism. After that I would like to entertain you tonight. My name is Linda Smith. I would like to entertain you with a bit of Comedy Against Patriarchy. I bet you can't wait. As I say, my name is Linda Smith, not my real name of course, a stage name. My real name is Wanda Starbright (laughs). I had to change it to something more glamorous before I started doing this.

I don't want any of you lads out there to get nervous, because I'm not any sort of extreme heavy feminist, because I know that you SWP boys are a bit dodgy on feminism (laughs) (heckler shouts, 'Rubbish'), so I don't want you to get worried because I'm not off the edge or anything like that, I'm not into castration or anything like that (heckler shouts, 'Why not?'), I was just going to say *only at weekends* (laughs).

Anyway, just to pause for a minute, because you are such a warm and responsive crowd, to share a little heartache with you, because before I came here tonight I did have a bit of a nasty row with my boyfriend, Clive, or manfriend, if you prefer it. He prefers manfriend . . . I prefer pillock myself (laughs).

I'm a bit nasty about Clive but he asks for it because, for example, I caught him the other night under the duvet reading this book (shows it to audience). It's called *For Men Against Sexism*, right? About as convincing as 'Turkey Farmers Against Christmas' really, isn't it? I thought, don't be reactionary, don't be narrow in your political base, Linda – read this book. Some wonderful chapters – there's one here, 'Refusing to be a man' (laughs). You wake up one morning and say, 'No, I won't be a man (laughs), I'll be something else, I'll be an antelope today.' Another one here, 'Consciousness raising for men'. I said, Clive, forget it, you don't need a book to raise your consciousness, mate, you need a fucking séance! (laughs). Another one here, 'Lovemaking with myself' he's very good at that (laughs). But the best one of all, the best chapter of all has got to be 'The socialised penis' (laughs). What can you say? What the fuck is the socialised penis? Does it go out to dinner parties on its own? (laughs). Where does the socialised penis hang out, eh? Cocktail bars, presumably. You can just see them, down the disco (being playful with her index fingers, simulating conversation between two penises): 'Hello, Dick', 'Hello, Willy, you all right?' 'I'm all right, you all right?' 'Yeah, I'm all right' 'Where's your man tonight?' 'I left him at home, he's a right wanker!' (laughs).

I'll tell you what – it's really nice being here with all you comrades because it means that I don't have to go to a party with Clive. The last party was so traumatic that we had to go on holiday to recover from it. Well, I say holiday – we tried to have a holiday in Britain which is, of course, a contradiction in terms. You can't have a holiday in Britain. Ridiculous idea. We didn't have Jeffrey Archer to restart us, so we had to go to some godforsaken spot on the coast, 'cos Clive doesn't like to go anywhere commercialised. If a place has got a Spar grocer's it's commercialised, right? So, we get to this godforsaken hole and we sort of wander into this shop. It hadn't got a Spar shop, it's got a VG grocer's – which is like Spar but less interesting. You go in and suddenly it's like you've been beamed into Poland under martial law. Because – empty shelves, mouse droppings, three things on the shelves (laughs), packets of butter beans, tins of carrots, Izal toilet paper – nothing you can buy. One of life's mysteries – tinned carrots. Who buys tinned carrots? Who goes into a shop, thinks, 'They look nice, I'll try those'? Perhaps there's three old women in carpet slippers queuing for the wheat ration or something (laughs). This is depressing. So you go to the pub – no better.

You walk in, two old locals having a needle game of doms look up, shoot you daggers: 'Go home, bastard townie, go home, bastard townie.' 'Hello.' You sit down and of course the only other occupants of the pub are a couple of old hippies who have been there since 1966 (laughs). Probably think it's still a bad acid trip (laughs). And they're sat there drinking pints of Whittakers 'Old Patchouli Oil' (laughs) – and you think, 'Oh, fuck this' and back to the bed and breakfast.

Oh God, the bed and breakfast! Why is it that British people can't cope with this idea of the paying guest? It's like you pay these people to stay there but you try and act as inconspicuous as you possibly can. It's like no financial transaction's taken place. It's as though you've just imposed yourself off the street – you've just walked into the house. And they think, 'Who the fuck are you? You've not just paid me £25, have you, to stay here?' So you get in and in fact you might as well just rip up that £25 and sleep on a park bench for all the comfort of the B&B. First you try the lounge, the TV lounge. Again, suddenly you are in Poland, martial law, because there's a curfew. You're watching a film – the telly goes off at 11.30 (laughs). A bloke stands over you (shouting), 'I've got to get up at six o'clock this morning, what time are you going to bed?' All right, yes, we're going now, we're going now. You go up to bed with a sinking heart which sinks even further when you open the door and find . . . ughh! the *mauve candlewick bedspread* (laughs). Now this is a bad sign because it is now on the cards that you are going to open up that bed and find *mauve nylon sheets* (laughs). Then the bickering starts. 'Now look, I pretended to have an allergy last time, it's your turn.' 'Now come on we've got to get these sheets changed.' 'No, no, I can't, I mean we've just paid' – 'Oh well, forget it.' You get in and sleep in them. Not only are they nylon, they are bobbly (laughs). I don't know what someone's been doing in them but it's caused a lot of friction (laughs). You get in there and it's like sleeping between two pieces of velcro.

You can't even relax going out and about in the countryside because radiation, you know, radiation, is everywhere. It was amazing during the radiation scare, wasn't it? Don't eat sheep – don't eat lambs, right? Oh, it's great the way it only affects sheep, isn't it? It's really good. Answer being 'sheep affected, eat people' obviously (laughs). Anyway, this brings me back – radiation. You turn on the television – royalty. It's either one or the other – *radiation or royalty*. And they are connected because they both induce nausea and are fatal (laughs). Fatal in large doses.

This last visit to China, Prince Philip, what a bastard, eh? What a bastard! Racist remarks about 'slitty-eyed Chinese'. Has anyone seen the Royal Family in the morning after one of Princess Margaret's cocaine parties? (laughs). They look pretty slitty-eyed, I reckon (laughs). They all have some weirdness. Like Diana. So thin. Princess Diana 'the human xylophone'. And they're all fascists. It's not just Prince Philip and Princess Michael of Kent. They're all fascists. Like the late Duchess of Windsor, what a sad day that was, when that old girl croaked, eh? That was pretty sad. And all the ghoulish pictures and everything like, coming over on the plane and then taken down to Frogmore and she's all done up for the funeral in a little black number. And then the pictures of her in the coffin. Then there's exclusive pictures of her under the ground where she's decomposing a bit now. Never mind, never mind, you can never be too rich or too thin (laughs). And of course the poor woman isn't at rest now because her arms won't stay like this (straight-arm salute), they keep going 'Sieg heil, Sieg heil'(laughs).

Turn for some crumb of comfort to the Labour Party? Forget it! Labour Party seem to be packaging themselves like a pack of toilet paper at the moment, sort of going for this pastel politics look. This sort of – Labour, little rose, a kind of tampon that uses that same logo called *'Femmes'* (laughs). Perhaps it would be even less socialist to call themselves *Labs*. Or perhaps, it's cuter . . . *Labies*. Or *Labour wabour party poos not at all like socialists* (laughs). *'Safe, strong, soft Neil Kinnock'* absorbs all kinds of shit except socialism (laughs). Expands width-wise to include everybody (laughs). I think it's time I had a drink now, I'm getting a bit sort of tired. Actually drink is a bit of a problem for Clive and me. Clive maintains that I can only bear to make love with him when I am blind drunk. I said, 'Clive, that's just very cruel and hurtful and not true. I'm sure morphine and a blindfold would be just as effective!' (laughs). On that rather bitter note I must get off to a Proust Readers Against Library Closures meeting. So goodnight, comrades, and thank you for your vigilance (cheers and applause).

LINDA LIVE
Northampton, 1988

Family presents

It was my birthday recently and someone who loves me bought these garish multicoloured stripey socks. This is how I choose to dress and this is what my mum buys me. I think I must have been swapped in the hospital – that's the only explanation I can find. I've been throwing bricks through Sock Shop windows ever since. Who the bloody hell designed them? They thought, 'Those are good colours, to go together.' Must have been a schizophrenic in the middle of a mescalin trip, I think. I look through my whole wardrobe and the only thing I could wear them with is a migraine.

Party political advertising

The Labour Party are going for these Andrex adverts image, aren't they? I don't know why they don't go the whole hog and have Neil Kinnock in the outside toilet at Labour Party headquarters, gentle music in the background, down the stairs bounds a little Labrador puppy wrapped in Clause Four of the manifesto. That would be quite popular.

For the Government it is quite hard for them to find media faces, to find people to head up campaigns, because they are all so weird-looking, aren't they? They all look like Muppets who have been left too close to a radiator. I don't like to mock the afflicted but how did anyone know that Willie Whitelaw had had a stroke? What genius spotted that? I mean, with most people it's quite a dramatic change, isn't it? But what happened? Someone thought, 'Oh, Willie's dribbled an extra pint today. What's going on? We'll run a few tests.'

Cold weather in the North . . .

The women are walking about in baby-doll nighties, it gets really cold . . . they add an extra layer of fake suntan.

LINDA LIVE
Comedy Boom, Edinburgh Festival, 1988

Thank you for that rousing welcome. Right, before we go any further I've got to lock up here (sound of door/cupboard being shut
by Linda). Perhaps I could be called a bit of a prima donna but
somehow I feel that detracts from my entrance really, that. It's not
exactly Liza Minnelli. But there are two reasons why I have to do
that. One is that if I don't do it, Shergar gets out. That's the first
one. Discover what happened to him. The other one is, as you can
see, Ian Saville attracts a pretty lively crowd and it's quite possible
that while I am stood here I could be distracted a minute and
someone could sneak past me and nick something out the back.
So it's quite important that I do that. Right, as you must know by
now, you'd have to be somewhere else not to know that I am Linda
Smith. Linda Smith. That's my name. Linda Smith. My parents'
only child . . . they called me Linda Smith. They didn't believe
in the cult of personality. It makes Arnold Brown sound like a
Dynasty character (laughs) (crowd shouting, 'Rock and roll') –
No, not rock and roll. I thought of rock and roll, but then I thought
no, only a wanker would just shout out rock and roll for no reason
(crowd cheering), I like to know where they are. There's usually
one. It's nicer down the front wearing the hat so I can spot you.
Good. And again, mate. Right (laughs and applause). If we do that
again, perhaps we are married – I don't know.

As I was saying, any visitors from Scotland in tonight? (laughs).
Yes, one or two. Well, welcome to our Edinburgh Festival.
Welcome to it. And I hope you make yourselves at home for the
next couple of weeks here (laughs). It's very nice. Actually, I did
the other festival, Glasgow Mayfest, this year, which is like Scotland's answer to the Edinburgh Festival really, but this one's nice,
it's like a party in North London with charades really, isn't it? I like
it. I think I feel more at home here. But no, it's very nice. This
venue for me is very handy because I'm staying just down the road
in Leith and I've got a nice flat there and I've got to know all the
other people up and down the stairs. It's very nice. I think they've

realised that I don't actually come from round there, not because of my accent, but because I haven't got an Alsatian, I think that's actually why – or a Dobermann the size of a young shire horse (laughs). Seems to be obligatory before you can get a flat there you've got to have one of these dogs. It's very strange. I think, actually, as I've been trying to negotiate a path round Leith, I think I've discovered the origin of Scottish dancing. It started like this, didn't it (demonstrates some footwork . . . to laughter), that's how it kicked off, isn't it? I noticed the bit of Leith I'm in is not 'Leith Sur Mer' – that bit that's got all trendified round the docklands area – I think I'm on 'Leith Sur Merde' (laughs). Where I'm staying, I had a little look round the trendified bit of the docks and it's like they are trying to revive the thirties in Leith. You know, you've got things like Rickets Wine Bars – 'You'll be seeing cockroaches under the wallpaper when you have one of our between-the-wars cocktails.' It's quite distasteful really, all that.

Anyway, I've been taking in a few shows at The Fringe. I love these people who busk the queues trying to drum up support for their show. There was a bunch today, women, young women, juggling, fire-eating, acrobatics, face-painting, and then one of them shouts out, 'And if you'd like to see more of this come and see our show about the poet Sylvia Plath' (laughs). What's that then? Perhaps this is a lost episode in Sylvia Plath's life that we don't know about. Perhaps this explains her later manic depression, you know, during her lost years as a circus acrobat she had a blow to the head or something (laughs). I thought, as I am here in Edinburgh, I'll try and catch a bit of the old local culture, so I went to see a Scottish production. I went to see the Morningside Ladies' Amateur Dramatics Guild in a very challenging stage production of *Take The High Road – This Time It's Personal* (laughs). Fascinated by those Morningside ladies in Jenners Tea Rooms – those posh ladies. They sit there like badly upholstered armchairs, tweed from head to foot, and they sit there ritually slaughtering Dundee cakes and they always have those pursed disapproving lips. It's as though they were rouged cats' bums rather than mouths. I don't know how they force the tea through them actually. Quite dodgy really – a drip to the arm would be easier (laughs). I've noticed Edinburgh is really windy, perhaps it's some sort of environmental adaptation like camels with their eyelashes in the desert as you walk along Princes Street. But no, I don't mean it, I love it here.

Well, as you probably notice I come from southern England, panto season is still in Edinburgh I see ('Boo it's behind you').Yes, I come from southern England, yes, I come from South-East London. But people get the wrong idea about London, people think that everyone is rich in London, that's ridiculous. Look where I come from, a little place on the Thames called Erith, sounds nice, doesn't it? (chorus of 'lovely' from audience). Sounds lovely, doesn't it? But it's not, is it? It's not on the Thames like Richmond's on the Thames or Henley's on the Thames. It's on the Thames like Canvey Island's on the Thames. It's on the Thames like Grangemouth is on the Forth basically (laughs). In fact it's very much like Grangemouth except less suburban really, a bit more industrial. Erith is in Kent – the 'Garden of England' – I can only assume that Erith is the outside toilet in that garden because it is a shit-house (laughs). Terrible place, terrible.

My early life was horrible for a lot of reasons. One reason was, my parents seemed to be twenty years older than everybody else's parents. Embarrassing when you're young. And another really uncool thing was I had to have a Saturday job at the Co-op. My mum got me this Saturday job at the Co-op which is like spending your youth in Poland under martial law. Except there is slightly less to buy at the Co-op, isn't there? Boring shops – they must have always been unfashionable. Like when they were built in the Victorian age they were all done out in Regency style, prob-ably, this was coming in, all this Regency stuff. I noticed in the paper the other day you have this Scot-mid Co-ops. I notice they're opening this big new branch and there's this amazing opening offer. Scot-mid in this new branch are offering you a 'two minutes' free spending spree', you can rush in for two minutes and have anything you can grab – that's a fucking mammoth prize, isn't it? (laughs).What are you going to do? They haven't even got the time to slice you a bit of bacon in that time, have they? What are you going to grab? A tin of carrots, a packet of butter beans? I think your best bet would be to mug the cashier, probably got more in his pockets than the shop's worth. Dear me (laughs).

Another thing. Yeah, I was going to give you a bit more actually, I wasn't going to go off, I've only been on ten minutes. Anyway, that's your lot, that was worth four quid, wasn't it? I appreciate the sentiment. As I was saying, went to a well rough school, really rough school, inner-city comprehensive, Bexleyheath School. Our school motto was, 'See my mate Trevor, right, he's going to kick your fucking head in' (laughs). Sounds a lot better in Latin actually (laughs). Loses quite a lot in translation, I find. It's the sort of school where you could do two 'O' levels. One of them was sitting at the front in cabarets and laughing really loud, no actually, no, that's not true. Two 'O' levels: one was Wearing a Sheepskin Jacket, the other was Stock Exchange Fraud and that was it, that was your lot. It's the sort of school where the only famous person ever in the history of the world to come from my school was the football manager Malcolm Allison. Which was a fluke really because it wasn't an academic school at all really (laughs). More of a sports school really. It was so sporty that even the really softy teachers like English teachers and Art teachers muscled round the corridors in smelly tracksuits scratching themselves and farting, hitting kids round the head. About the only teachers who didn't do that were the sports teachers, in fact – much too hard. They were dressed as Sumo wrestlers, throwing kids out of the windows. Dear me. I used to really like that Sumo wrestling, not for the sport really, but it totally changed your idea of what overweight was, didn't it really? (laughs). Totally new dimension. Like, here's Tashima, he's twenty-three and he weighs more than Central America (laughs). Pass me a Jaffa Cake (laughs). Even the music teacher wore eighteen hole steel toecap bloody Hush Puppies for Christ's sake – that's how hard it was. We had one brainy kid in the whole school and you could always tell him in the playground because he would always be trying to swap a line of cocaine for a textbook (laughs).

I could be accused of exaggerating, some could say I exaggerate, I know that most schools aren't very good, most school kids, they don't learn anything. They just doss around reading comics like *Beano* and *Jackie* – but they're not normally set books in English, are they?

That's my early life. I've left all that behind me now I don't live in London any more. I've moved right out into the commuter belt – to Sheffield! (laughs). I live in Sheffield which is nice, I like to live in northern England, but it has one drawback and that's all my mates from London coming up to see me every weekend just to drool over the property prices. It's the only reason they come. It's like a house buyer's red light district for them. It's horrible. I've never thought of the property section of the local paper as a wank mag before (laughs). Really, they get so excited, they're pawing through it, dribbling, and when you come to read it later all the pages are stuck together – ugh! (laughs). Nasty. Then they're off kerb-crawling (member of audience with a strange laugh) . . . someone shoot that seal! No, too many vegetarians in (audience hiss). Oh, gas leaks now! Knock that off the rent. As I was saying, they're off kerb-crawling round the estate agents, pressing their little snouts against the window, going 'Look, darling, look – "Castle Howard £1.99". Look, look, look, darling. If we sold that time share in that bird bath in Hackney we could buy Leeds' (laughs). 'Look, look, look, here's all the loose change I've got in my pocket, give me Barnsley (laughs). Give me Barnsley with four hotels on it' (laughs). Another thing I notice, living in the North of England, being a southerner, the further north you come on this island, the more reluctant people who live there are to recognise the idea that it is . . . *fucking cold there* (laughs). They just won't have it, they won't have it. Like you can always tell – you can always tell, the southerners and the tourists and the students because it is January, there's snow on the ground, we're wearing coats. Weirdos. Weirdos obviously. Not the locals. It's January, snow on the ground and several degrees below freezing, there's a bunch of lads coming back from the pub – they're wearing underpants. (In Sheffield accent) 'Fucking cold, pal? Somewhere near Birmingham, isn't it? Never heard of it!' And if it gets really, really cold they'll add a tattoo of a sports shirt (laughs). It's got to be really cold for that though. I don't know (sigh).

I think I'll calm down a little bit now. Have a drink. You might have noticed I'm drinking a little. I do have a little bit of a drink problem actually, I tend to drink a little bit too much, that's why I'm on the halves tonight. I've had twenty-seven halves now (laughs) so I think I'll knock that on the head. I've been doing a little bit of family duty lately, I've been visiting my old gran. Ahh! (audience goes Ahh!). I knew you'd say that, I'll tell you a bit about my gran as you're so interested because she's a lovely old lady, little, frail, smiling, grey-haired old raving fascist (laughs). That's my gran. We've all got them in our families, haven't we? We've all got that old relative (laughs), you think of yourself as a bit of a socialist but you'd like to tie them in a sack and drown 'em, because they're so 'orrible! Well, I thought, I'm going to have to see her. Now as I say, my nan she's a raving fascist and she comes from Birmingham (laughs). Wouldn't be fair to say those facts are connected in any way, but of course it would be true though, wouldn't it? I hope there's no one in who gets upset on behalf of bits of land. Because I really hate Birmingham and the Midlands of England generally. It's such a nasty place, it's like the racism capital of the universe, it's almost like a white suburb of South Africa has been beamed in by some quirk of geography and then I realised this . . . of course – the same accent! Same accent, isn't it? (laughs). That's the clue. You can't fool me.

So anyway, I think I'll go and visit my nan, knock on the door, she's in the kitchen there, bottling up little gingham-top jars of racial hatred (laughs) and exporting them to Birmingham, Alabama, with which she's personally twinned (laughs). So I think, right, I'll avoid anything that's going to provoke her because there's no point arguing with someone who, strictly speaking, isn't even alive. So I'll keep off anything controversial. But you can forget that, because you just get this monologue which is like – the line of logic is harder to follow than the plot of *Finnegans Wake* (laughs). Ah, a few intellectuals in tonight (audience member, 'That was easy'). That was easy, was it? Oh, I see, there will be a test later on. On the way out. So I want full marks from you – you are so confident, young man. Anyway, as I was saying, so you get this total, total, total obsession.

'Hello, Nan.'

(Nan in a Birmingham accent), 'Hello, our Lin, it's lovely to see you, come in, I hate blacks. Come in, sit down (laughs). I'll make you a nice cup of tea, our Lin, I hate blacks. Come on in, our Lin, would you like a nice piece of cake? I don't know if I've mentioned this before but I don't like black people.'

You think, oh Christ! Shut up! What can I do? What can I do to divert her from this monomania? Right, OK . . .

'Garden looks lovely, Nan.'

'Oh yes, Lin, I like a bit of gardening, unlike black people who I don't like at all.'

'I think it's gonna rain.'

'So do I, Linda, I also think President Botha should be running this country.'

Ah, God!

And then you realise what a mistake it was to say you would stay overnight. 'Cos you are stuck here with this person who makes Klaus Barbie look like Mother Theresa of Calcutta (laughs) and you've got to stay overnight in a house that's more depressing than *Songs of Praise*. Furthermore, you are going to be in some really poky little room, poky little spare room – they're funny those spare rooms, aren't they? Makes me laugh just thinking about them. No, actually it is quite a depressing house because everything that could conceivably have a cover has got a cover on it. You know, like there's a poodle pom-pom cover for the washing machine, there's a mock snakeskin cover for the *Radio Times*, there's a crinoline lady cover for her desk-top publishing computer, the whole works. You go into the room that you're staying in, last decorated circa 1965 – a bit of mauve, a bit of orange, and it's got that indefinable smell of every drunken old uncle that ever had a kip there after a wedding.

Right. Changing the subject a bit, I like to get out in the countryside a bit, me. Not when the weather's been like it's been today, but on a nice sunny day which is better. Driving out into a little picturesque country village, out on to the village green, to watch the rioting (laughs). There's nothing like it, is there? I like this rural violence. Perhaps you've got it in Scotland. But in England it's a big thing lately. Rural violence. Rural England – the new frontline. There's a brilliant fixture at Maidenhead this weekend – 'Skinheads versus Antique Dealers'(laughs). Should be a good one. But apart from the violence, the countryside doesn't have much going for it because it's so snooty, it's so posh and stuck up. You arrive in these little villages, you see the sign as you drive in, 'You are now entering the village of Drearily Nazi' (laughs), 'Wipe your feet.' Fine welcome! It's the sort of place where all the road signs are still swapped round from the war – you know, when they were trying to fool the Germans. I think they keep them that way in case the Labour Party come canvassing. So you head off to the village pub. Oh, this looks like a nice place, Ye Zombie Flesh Eaters Inn (laughs). Oh, have a pint here. And it's very welcoming. It's got flowerbeds outside with 'Fuck Off Townie' picked out in geraniums. Oh, there's a welcome here. Sort of pub if the barman hasn't got your voice print you're not a regular (laughs). So you stop here a bit, and if you're really, really unlucky, there's going to be some sort of folk event going on. And you are. And the place is invaded by hundreds and hundreds of weekend Morris-dancing local government officers (laughs). All dressed in chunky jumpers they knitted themselves out of old beer mats. Real beer mats of course. And they brought their own tankards with them. I don't understand that. People so insecure they can't leave their furniture at home. And they're singing the two folk songs that exist. The one folk song is 'I'm a drunken philandering old bastard with a smelly old beard (laughs) but I'll always come back to you, my lady love.' Well, that must be a comfort and a support (laughs). And of course, the other folk song is the 'Sailing Away from Liverpool' song. If everyone who ever sang a folk song about Sailing Away from Liverpool actually did it, there would be no bugger there, would there? It would just be a ghost town. I suppose it is. I suppose that's what's happened. It's not unemployment, it's keeping singing those bloody songs. They've finally done it (laughs). There would be no one there. Just Derek Hatton maybe – who no one would want to take with them. Or maybe

The Spinners to sing about 'How quiet Liverpool is these days!'
I don't know (laughs).

I'm being a bit unusually aggressive tonight. I'm aware of it. I
don't normally get this aggressive this soon (laughs). But there is,
really, there is a reason for it. And that's – before I came here
tonight, to this lovely through-lounge diner – so handy when you
have a few people round – before I came here tonight, I did actually have quite a serious row with my boyfriend Clive (audience –
Aaah!). Well, it may surprise some of you out there that I have a
boyfriend, 'cos in this soft light I probably look quite intelligent
(laughs, cheers and applause).

What gets up my nose with Clive is that he is one of these really
self-righteous political people, one of these really self-righteous
left-wingers, he really is. Like he's the sort of person, what do you
say, someone who in the event of a revolution has put their name
down to do the vegan packed lunches (laughs). What can you say?
Someone who, as we speak, is on Salisbury Plain, on manoeuvres
with the Provisional Woodcraft Folk (laughs).

Sorry, I shouldn't have done that political joke because it's a bit
unfashionable to do that sort of political joke. It's all fashion, politics – that's all it is. People like tasteful humour these days. People
like humour that matches the duvet cover and the curtains
(laughs). It's like the full set. Like today, I was talking to someone,
I referred to the miners' strike, they looked at me like I was wearing flared trousers and a kipper tie (laughs). I felt so passé. Actually, I don't like to get too self-righteous about politics myself
because we all have that nasty little sort of Thatcherite impulse
inside us – you can't pretend you haven't got it. I mean, for example, here at the Festival, there you are, you go to some late-night
radical production of *The Ragged Trousered Philanthropists*, you
stagger out and you think, yeah, get up extra early tomorrow to
start the Revolution. Meanwhile – get a taxi. Blimey, this is all
right, isn't it? Five minutes I've been waiting for this taxi! Three
o'clock in the morning . . . five minutes for a taxi! Supposed to be
unemployed people in Scotland. What's this? They don't want the
work – that's the trouble, isn't it? They don't want to do it and

they've put the prices up in the Festival. I mean, the other day I was going to a very far-flung venue – £1.60 from Princes Street to Aberdeen (laughs). Then they want a tip! So you can't pretend you're not like that.

At Clive's house, you can't see daylight out of the windows because they are covered in stickers. Isn't it terrible when someone gets up in a pub and starts shouting and everything and talking, just as if it was a show. Anyway (laughs), as I was saying, the two biggest stickers of all 'Nuclear Power, not today thank you, I'll wait and see what Neil Kinnock says' (laughter and applause), and Glenys and Neil are in tonight! They're so fair, whatever you say about them, they're so fair. And of course, the other sticker is *Neighbourhood Watch*. The one we've all got, let's face it, we all like Neighbourhood Watch. I like it. I think it's a good idea. I watched three of my neighbours get burgled last week (laughs). Teach them to grass me up to the social, won't it? Actually, when I saw their furniture coming out, I thought – is it really burglars or the Terence Conran Taste Vigilantes? (laughs). Urgh! Nasty draylon stuff.

Anyway, I'm glad I'm here because I would only be watching telly if I wasn't here. I watch a lot of crappy telly. I can never go to bed late at night. You know, you are lying there – all the crap comes up like the late-night religious slot. I love that, when you get someone talking about how they were *born again*. Normally, it's five minutes of religious contemplation with a packaging expert from Humberside called Trevor, in a nylon shirt with a really bad haircut, who explains how he got a message from God one day to redesign fig-roll boxes, perhaps God couldn't get the little buggers out of the box. I don't know. Something like that. Anyway, it's late, you nod off and you wake up in the middle of the night. You don't realise that the Job Finder Ceefax service has come up on the screen. It's like the early hours of the morning – there's Job Finder. Do you have that here? We have that in Yorkshire. It's like Ceefax that comes on in the middle of the night, with all jobs available in your region. You think, oh, fucking hell, I can't watch a French film at this time of the night. I can't concentrate on these subtitles. Then you realise what it is. And in Yorkshire it's really good because you

get this dramatic music to get you going – to get you really interested in the jobs, which goes (hums the theme tune) *Spot Welder*
(repeats the theme), *Wakefield* (repeats the theme again), *£23 a
week*. 'Cos it's not always so well paid, that's a skilled job. Twenty
years' experience.

No, I think telly's all right, but sometimes, like the other night,
I switched on by accident to see David Owen being interviewed
just as though he were a normal person (laughs). David Owen
in conversation with Esther Rantzen, all in soft focus, as though
it's shot through gauze, with Erik Satie-style romantic music.
Presumably to make him look a bit more human. I think they
would have to film him through a fucking blanket for that to work
really, wouldn't they? I really do. If he gets any further to the right
he will be back in the Labour Party (laughs). Talking of which,
Neil Kinnock has announced today the guidelines for resisting
the Poll Tax, 'Pay it' (laughs). You pay it, but when you pay it, you
give that town hall clerk such a look! (laughs). Today's Labour
Party, changing the world by going 'Dear oh lor'! Anyway, the
thing I don't like about telly is that there is never enough royal
snippets. Never enough royal news. Especially lately. Sometimes
it's only half the news, isn't it? (laughs). How do you get through
the day? I don't know. Did the Queen Mother open a biscuit
tin at Balmoral? Quite a strong likelihood, greedy old toad!
(laughs). What's the latest lunatic outpourings from the Duke of
Edinburgh? Normally described as outspoken. Now if it were
you or me, we wouldn't be described as outspoken, we'd be in a
secure hospital up to our eyeballs on Largactyl, wouldn't we?
Doing a bit of gentle basketwork.

I prefer the younger royals because you can relate better to
them, the sensitive one, Edward. The intellectual. ('The baldy
one,' audience member calls out.) Well, they're all baldy, mate. The
Queen Mother's bald. It's all a wig, the whole thing (laughs). As I
was saying, Edward, the intellectual, the one with the CSE . . . in
finger-painting (laughs). Even Edward cannot compare with the
lovely Princess Di – Princess Dianorexic – she's so thick yet so
thin (laughs). She could do an act herself round the halls, 'Diana

The Human Zither' (hums the theme from *The Third Man*). 'And for one's next trick one will slice bacon with one's jawline' (laughs).

I'd just like to end up by saying I'm a big soap opera fan myself, I love *EastEnders*, I think it's great, it's like *Take the High Road* with acting (laughs). But I really like it. But people read too much into soap operas. Some people think that Colin and Barry have been brought into *EastEnders* to show gay relationships. What nonsense, they've been brought in to make Dr Legg look like a slightly better actor (laughs). And Sue and Ali in the café – how do they make a living selling two cups of tea a week? That no one ever drinks! And Ali Osman – why can't he do joined-up talking? (laughs). Why's that? The late Lou Beale – that was never Lou Beale, that was Derek Jamieson in drag actually, for those that hadn't noticed her (laughs). And Sharon and Roly the Poodle – why have they got the same hairstyle? (laughs). Right, that's all from me. I've got to get off to a late-night production of *A La Recherche du Temps Perdu*. So thank you very much. Goodnight (laughs and applause).

SPLIT TEASE
Hattie Hayridge, comedian and writer

Linda and I first met when we were competing for the City
Limits/Hackney Empire New Act of the Year in 1987. We were
battling it out to a nail-biting finish for runner-up to a stilt-
walking-juggling double act. As the final judge gave their marks,
Linda was second and I was third. We collected our runners-up
cups on stage, polished off the sandwiches backstage, and went
our separate ways for the rest of the decade; Linda back to
Sheffield, and me off into a space sitcom.

By 1990, Henry Normal knew both of us, and would tell Linda,
still living in Sheffield, and myself that we'd get on really well
together. Probably, like me, she had a contrary reaction to that
sort of coercion. He finally took hold of the situation, and booked
us for a gig together which he compèred at The Green Room in
Manchester. As Linda would remark on the rare occasion when
two female stand-ups were on the same bill, 'Ooh, it'll turn the
milk sour!' After an open spot, Henry sauntered back onstage
with his shirt hanging out of his trousers, announcing, 'I've just
been backstage shagging those cockney slags!' Linda and I
screeched with laughter, as did the shocked politically correct
audience, and spontaneously we both hurled spare clothes over
the top of the wooden screen.

One night in London, we talked into the early hours and discovered how much we had in common; our working-class 'doff
your cap'-type backgrounds, our older parents, and both of us had
lost our mothers a year or so earlier. In these early days, Linda
would come down south to do occasional gigs, or sometimes open
spots if people hadn't heard of her. She'd often be described as just

a female Mark Steel or Jeremy Hardy, and while there may be room for a few political comics, a comic who was both political and female was a bit much to take. I think comedy is best when it puts forward a belief or a purpose, rather than for its own sake. I have never felt brave enough to make that push to be political onstage, despite actually having a degree in the subject, but I don't think my views fit into a framework as well as Linda's did. Linda's brilliance lay in her ability to focus her wide range of literary knowledge, petty annoyances, anger, political views, her idealism and enthusiasm into one laser sharp incisive comment, delivered with a wicked wit and a twinkle in her eye.

Our relationship was a daytime one. We hardly ever met up or went out together at night, probably because Linda was in a long-term relationship. We didn't talk much about boyfriends, fashion, moods, make-up, it wasn't that girlie thing. Our conversation was always our thoughts on things, conducted at a high intensive level of banter, screaming, laughing, ranting, moaning and glee. For Edinburgh 1994, we decided not to do separate stand-up shows, but something different together, about the things that 'drove us mental'! With that brief, we asked Huw Thomas, a university drama lecturer who compèred and ran his own comedy club, to direct this as yet non-existent show. Luckily he liked a challenge. We would meet up with Huw at Oakwood Tube station, at 10 a.m., five days a week during June and July, for him to drive us to the rehearsal rooms. Huw would arrive on time (I guess), I'd always be late, and then we'd wait for Linda, starting off hopefully in the car, then moving to the station café. She'd eventually arrive, completely unruffled and completely unaware of how late she was because she never wore a watch. After a journey like that, she'd need a cappuccino, after which we'd set off for the rehearsal room and quite possibly lunch. Huw encouraged us to devise a script using improvisation and drama exercises, which we did for a short while and then just took the piss. Linda and I were at the height of our mutual hysteria during this hot summer, like delinquent schoolgirls, and I felt I'd found my bestest friend in the whole wide world. Huw recently needed little prompting to recall the time with us as 'a ritual humiliation playing stooge to two sharp and waspish women continually scoring points off me'. For his own peace of mind, he devised an exercise where Linda and I had to walk around the room in silence, avoiding and deliberately ignoring each other.

In mid-July, Huw went off to Wales, and Linda and I went off into a state of panic. A month to go and still nothing written. For this fortnight, we met up at the London house where Linda and Warren were living with friends while they looked for their own place. We used their conservatory room, empty except for a long dining table and a rubber plant; a room with good light and good inspiration. We wanted to do something about this new-fangled internet lark and this tragic craze for working from home as these were top of our list of contemporary wrongs.

Linda had once had a holiday job working on an apple turnover conveyor belt, and that seemed the perfect example of a ridiculous job to satirise working from home. Huw had already set us off on the idea that we should actually play the same person; one real and one fantasy without the audience, and more importantly either of *us*, ever knowing which was which. Linda didn't have a computer, either then or ever, and laptops were not on our radar. We'd just talk the show on to my dictaphone, then I'd go home, listen to our recordings and type the muddle up into some kind of order.

What follows is an extract from a tape and an example of what might be called 'the creative process'.

HATTIE: She could still have a head movement for a while, like people who have their legs chopped off.

LINDA: Yeah. (laughter)

LINDA: A tick

HATTIE: Tock

LINDA: Tick, job done.

HATTIE: Tock, job gone.

BOTH: They think it's all over, it is now! (laughter)

★ ★ ★

LINDA: Yes, I thought of something else for the New-Agey bit. You know those awful relaxation tapes?

HATTIE: Yeah.

LINDA: They really get on my fucking tits.

HATTIE: Oh Christ, yeah, whenever I've done any of those classes and they put on the relaxation tape, it just gets me fucking irritated.

BOTH: (scream) Let's put on the relaxation tape. (both scream)

LINDA: Get it off, get it off! (both scream and laugh)

LINDA: They play a little bit and it's like dolphin noise, weeeeip weeeip. (both scream)

HATTIE: I can't bear it.

LINDA: I was in this café in Wales, in this little Welsh village, it was a really nice little café, we went in there for tea, and the only thing wrong was this fucking music that was driving me mad and I went up to the woman and said, 'What *is* this music?!' and she pointed to this little sign that said, 'Today's relaxation tape is available for £5.99 at the counter'. It made us leave.

HATTIE: Yeah, I can't bear them. (both tut)

HATTIE: Those things make me feel ill. You'd be lying on the floor and she'd be going, 'Imagine you're lying on a beach' and I'd be thinking, 'I'm going to throw up.'

LINDA: 'I'm lying on a beach', and ooh, I've eaten something dodgy! (laughter)

LINDA: Ooh, it was those prawns! (screeches of laughter)

HATTIE: We should do that.

LINDA: Yeah, ooh, let's put on the relaxation tape. This music gets on your tits, doesn't it!?

HATTIE: You are lying on the beach, you are feeling dreamy.

LINDA: Ooh aw, ooh aw. Ooh, I feel a bit queasy. (puking sounds and laughter)

LINDA: Ooh, I'll just have the English menu tomorrow. I knew I should have had the omelette! (laughter)

HATTIE: oh aw, I'm drifting away.

LINDA: I'm feeling queasy.

BOTH: Ow er, oh er. (laughter and puking sounds)

HATTIE: Yeah, turn it round! 'Sleepy, you are feeling sleepy.'

LINDA: Queasy, I'm feeling queasy. (laughter and puking sounds)

★ ★ ★

(SFX: A crash)

HATTIE: 'kin' hell, what was that?

LINDA: That was my head!

HATTIE: My God! (shrieking) What did you hit it on?

LINDA: That thing, it's pointy. (shrieking)

HATTIE: Point-*less*.

LINDA: I'm always bumping my head.

HATTIE: Are you? Why?

LINDA: We went to these people's little cottage in the country. 'Ooh, what a lovely little cottage.' Boom.

HATTIE: Yeah, Tudor beams, one after the other, boom.

BOTH: Boom, boom, boom. (laughter)

LINDA: A triple whammy. (laughter) 'Anne Boleyn slept here.' Yes, I suspect she needed a lie-down!

HATTIE: Yeah, she weren't beheaded, she just fucking whacked her head on a low beam. (laughter)

LINDA: Yeah, so we'll be trying all our New-Agey things to get over it. The redundancy.

HATTIE: Yeah.

★ ★ ★

When Huw returned, the writing and exercises all came together. *Split Tease* was the story of an urban nobody trying to fill her empty, isolated life with real and imagined distractions. The lines were rhythmical and continuous; some simultaneous, some alternate, and all our words and actions were performed without acknowledging the presence of the other 'self' until we took our bow. We'd come up with a show so complicated, we had to rehearse it at least twice a day in the Edinburgh flat we rented, to even remember it. Apart from the London preview, where we felt duty-bound afterwards to buy the audience (luckily not too numerous) all a drink each, it went pretty well most nights. We wore pink and white check nylon overalls and pink fluffy slippers, and our set comprised a computer and a pink bedspread, set off by eerie green lighting. The show started with us already on stage (there wasn't a raised stage as such) as the audience entered to the theme tune to *Match of the Day*. I would be sitting at the computer and Linda would be lying under the bedspread. We did have to put up a notice warning, 'This is not a stand-up show' after some people were left confused.

One night the performance poet John Cooper Clarke drifted in with the audience. 'Hello, Hattie, what are you up to?' 'Well, we're doing a play at the minute, John.' He looked around. 'Are you, who with?' 'With Linda' 'Linda! Where's Linda?' 'Under that bedspread.' 'Oh! What's she doing under there?' He wandered over and pulled back the bedspread. 'Hello, Linda, what you doing under there?' 'We're doing a play, John.' 'Oh, are you, when's it on?' 'Well, now, really.' 'Is it? I'll come in and watch then.' As he made his way to a seat we could hear each other squeaking as we tried to stifle the giggles.

After the month in Edinburgh we were booked to tour, but what with the props, the set, the lighting, the complicated sound cues and the lack of any crew or transport, it was suggested we just did our stand-up show. I knew Linda was totally underrated and that when she was truly discovered, she would hit with a force.

Every now and again we would try to get *Split Tease* on radio. It would get so far, helped by an enthusiastic producer, then someone on the commissioning committee wouldn't understand it, and it would be dropped. Linda and I would be approached to write something else for radio because they needed more women writers. We'd come up with an idea or two, and they'd say, 'It's not really about women.' 'No,' we'd say, 'but we are women writers,' but it didn't fit the bill.

We met with BBC TV script editor Paul Mayhew Archer, who was very keen and helpful about a sit-com idea we had, set in a motorway services station, called by Linda, *Traveller's Rest – (Strictly No Travellers)* but one appeared on the ITV in the same setting, so we had to drop it. The next idea was a sit-com called *Shelf Life*, set in a twenty-four-hour DIY superstore, casting ourselves as non-identical twins. The other shop assistants would be three men, including one called 'Wizzo' who, under the pretence of checking stock in the warehouse, would go off mini-cabbing. Linda came up with the idea that he was a Lottery instants addict, suffering from 'Scratch Card Lung', a medical condition not yet recognised, but brought about from continually breathing in the black scrapings. We found that while we could easily write the men's lines, bizarrely we found it harder to write lines for ourselves.

Our writing day ran along a familiar theme. Linda would arrange to come round mine about 10 a.m. Sometimes, around 11.30, she'd ring to say her hair was still wet or she was having trouble getting her contact lenses in and would arrive at 1 p.m. We'd go down the café for lunch, browsing round the charity shops on the way back, then get out the tape recorder, pens and paper, and pop out for cakes to go with our tea. We'd then decide it was probably too late to start writing that late in the afternoon, and we'd start again tomorrow. Warren worked at a community arts organisation nearby, and would pick her up from mine in a lovely old Jag and whisk her back to East London.

Linda was, by now, in '97/'98, starting to get better known on the radio, and there was less time for purely speculative writing for no money. Eventually and deservedly her career finally took off – hers was no overnight success, but a slow burn. Linda totally found her niche on Radio 4, even more than the stand-up. We started to go months and months at a time without seeing each other. At Edinburgh 2005, Jeremy Hardy warned me not to let time drift, and I took heed, and from then on went to see her about three times a week. The thing with Linda was, however much time you spent with her, you would always have enjoyed being with her for a great deal longer. Classic. Leave them wanting more.

Hattie Hayridge, 2006.

Split Tease
(A Day in the Life of an Urban Nobody)

by Hattie Hayridge and Linda Smith

Location: One room in a dilapidated old house
  A bedspread on the floor
  A computer on a table
  A swivel chair with arms
  Various junk
  No windows

Character: Urban nobody

**NB: Both performers play the same character at the same time,
neither performer acknowledges the existence of the other. They
never see each other or move into an area where logically one
could be seen by the other.**

Costume: Pink-and-white check nylon overall, pink fluffy slippers

Sound effects: BBC Radio shipping forecast
  'Colonel Bogey' CAR HORN
  Especially made tapes of:

Song: backing track of 'Guantanamera'
  DJ on radio game show
  Emotional workout on tape
  Company announcement
  News 'stings'
  Applause
  Relaxation tape
  Salesman
  Phone dialling tone
  Phone off the hook tone
  Old TV themes music
  Bing Crosby singing 'Don't Fence Me In'

Lighting: General lighting
  A row of green lights to represent when the
    computer is on

ACT I

FX Green lights up
FX Intro music

Linda lies under bedspread on floor.
Hattie sits at computer.

FX House lights fade
SFX Shipping forecast

Hattie turns off computer.

FX Green lights go off
SFX 'Sailing By'

Hattie reacts excitedly to forecast, miming the weather conditions. She
then gets under the blanket.

FX Silence and blackout five seconds
SFX Car horn
FX Stage lights up

LINDA   HATTIE

(sticks her head out from under bedspread)
Wakey waaaakeeeey.
Da da da da da da.
Rise and shine,
up with the lark,
Start off a new day,
can't waste it,
best part of the day,
the morning.
(head under)
                                          Better get started,
                                          can't mess about
                                          get going,

LINDA   HATTIE

                                        get on the road,
                                           hit the road.

(head out)
Hit the road, Jack
hit the road.
Hit the hut hut hut.
(head under)
                                             (head out)
                                      Can't hang around
                                          here all day,
                                       got to get going
                                          get moving.
                                          (head under)

(head out)
I'm the sort of person
who likes to make the
most of life,
start the day early,
go to work on an egg,
don't waste a second
in bringing relief.
That's the sort of person I am
(head under)
                                             (head out)
                                    If I don't get up now,
                                       I'll be late for work
                                      Then I'll be annoyed
                                     and irritated all day.
                                          (head under)

                                             (head out)
                                         Get up, get a
                                            head start
(head out)   (head under)
I won't

(head out)
Start in a minute
Ten, nine, eight, seven, six, five and
a half, five . . .

LINDA   HATTIE

BOTH
For   (head out)
                             fuck's sake get up!
BOTH
(sit up)
Yes, I like being my own boss.
(LINDA places bedspread over HATTIE as if covering a birdcage for
the night)

                              (HATTIE repeats like a
                                 parrot 'Out')

I like going out to work.
Not OUT to work, obviously.
I go out to work.
I don't go OUT to work.
I go out-to-work.
Not OUT to work,
but OUT-TO-WORK,
Out to work. Out-to-work.

(HATTIE gets up and folds up bedspread)

Have to go out to work, go mad
if I had to stay here all day. All
on my own. On my tod, all alone,
on my own. No one else to talk to.
That's why I go out to work,
the company. Get out,
get out of yourself. Get out

(FX lights computer starts)

                (LINDA and HATTIE both at front)

                                Used to go
                             to the factory

LINDA	HATTIE
All that travelling Going outside	
	All that travelling Going outside
Don't do that any more	
	No need
Miss that	
	All that travelling Going outside
Get more work done working from your home	
	Not got anybody breathing down your neck
Not got anybody	
SFX RADIO OFF	
He's a nice man	
	A very nice man
Streets were safe then	
	Have to credit them that
Credit where credit's due	
	Credit will only be given to people aged over ninety-five
If accompanied by both their parents	
	Please don't ask for credit
As a punch in the mouth often offends	

LINDA   HATTIE

	I like that one
We don't cash cheques	
	And the bank, they don't sell vegetables
Workers of the world unite, you have nothing to lose but your chains	
	Got to have a chain
Got to have a chain	
	Chain on the door
Got to have a chain on the door	
	Insurance won't touch you
Insurance won't touch you without a chain on the door	
	And a Chublock. Chain on the door and a Chublock
Insurance won't touch you without a chain on the door and a chublock	
	Chublock, deadlock, chain on the door
And a mortice lock	
	Got to have a morticelock
Insurance won't touch you without a mortice lock.	
	Chublock, deadlock, morticelock Chain on the door

LINDA   HATTIE

BOTH
Five hundred Chinese terracotta soldiers
And the insurance still won't touch you

Still it stops
them getting in

                                        No it slows them
                                        down getting out

Thank you for that report, Fiona,
Now, what's the situation as you
see it Sandy?

                                        Well Trevor, the mood
                                        here is one of fear
                                        and trepidation.
                                        Moira

Thank you Michael. Any
update on the extent of the
casualties? Zanat

                                        Well Jeremy, it's a
                                        tidal wave of human
                                        misery. On a lighter
                                        note, Martin

Cat up a tree

                                        Too little

Too late

                        ★

                                        That's what I like
                                        about this job,
                                        It's never boring

Bored! No time to be bored.

LINDA   HATTIE

                                          So much to do
Oh, days not long enough.

                                          Never two days
                                              the same
Different every day.

                                         Never know what's
                                      round the next corner.
It's a roller coaster

                          VOICE
                     Attention please.
               Company Welfare Announcement.
                We are pleased to announce that the
           Teddy Trouble Spots Mild Mustard Gas Company
            has now achieved its optimum growth challenge.
                  Your unit may now be released
                      into the Serengeti plains
                    of the wide open market.
                  So run free little module,
            out into the sunshine of opportunity,
                  happy in the knowledge
            that you leave your mother Company
                       right–sized.

          FX LIGHTS AND GREEN COMPUTER LIGHTS
                  GO OFF. SILENCE.

                            *

                                          We are having to
                                             let you go

The Company is now
right-sized without you.

                                        You are a person with
                                         employment needs

LINDA   HATTIE

You are available for work

                                           There is a skip
                                       outside. Be in it.

Your future lies in
Steptoe's backyard

                              Welcome to Dumpsville.
                                     Population you.

Somehow we're going to have to
make do without you, we're going
to have to muddle through as best
we can.

                                   To be absolutely
                                           frank

You're sacked.

                                     You're fired

BOTH
You are redundant!

It's the unthinkable

                                   Something wrong
                                     with the screen

Lucky I got talked into that
extended warranty.

                                   Not such a bad idea
                                       Huh see!

Not such a stupid bastard idea

                                   Extended warranty.

It's not to exceed......

                                   that's only parts
                                      and labour

an optimum time

                                   now that's if it's
                                      a leap year

LINDA   HATTIE

in the event of an
expanding universe...

                                              Lucky I took out that
                                                 extended warranty.
                                              Because if you pay an
                                              extra supplement, over
                                              a period of so many years,
                                              then you're covered ....
                                                 oh, for parts only

So with the premiums on that,
and I know it does seem
a lot all at once,
But once you've taken out
an extended warranty,

                            BOTH
                    You know that biro
                    is insured for life

Takes the worry out of
consumer durables

                                              I've taken out an
                                              extended warranty for
                                              everything. Everything.

I think it's worth the extra.

                                              Not to have that worry
Because once you've taken out
an extended warranty
                            BOTH
                 You know that Ronco Jumper Shaver
                    is insured for life

                                              Because it doesn't
                                              work out that much

LINDA   HATTIE

Because over the specified years when
the interest payments are spread
in a flexible repayment system,
because if you've taken out
an extended warranty

BOTH
You know that Goblin Teasmade
is insured for life

                        Well it's only ... well
                        not that much is it?

But then there's a call out charge,
I won't pretend there isn't.
There, I've said it,
there's a call out charge,
and I know it does
seem a lot all at once
But if you've taken out
an extended warranty

BOTH
You know that Disposable Lighter
is insured for life

Jaws of Disaster
Pension Scheme.
Endorsed by only
Frank Windsor! Thank you

                        Getting on in life?
                        You're never too young
                        to think about a pension

No job available?
Barry Cryergenics

LINDA   HATTIE

Why not be frozen
till there is?

So, now that you're
nearly dead, I'm sure
that you'll be thinking
of your loved ones,
and making sure they
don't get their grubby
little hands on your
hard earned cash.
Those money-grabbing
nieces and nephews
never came to see you
when you had that hip
replacement operation.

No you'll want to spend
that money on

Golf,

Caribbean cruises and ballroom
dancing on the QE2.

BOTH
Hasta la vista grandchildren

Swivel on that
because I am off to
Grey Leisure Heaven.

Golf, golf

A bit more

Golf

And the occasional game of

Bowls. Bowls,

Yes, and six months of the
year in a flat on the Costa Del Sol

LINDA   HATTIE

Yes please, Frank!

Because after all

BOTH

No-one wants to live out the
twilight of their life
in poverty and misery.
Who wants to live like that?
Living in a rat-infested slum
car alarms going off
all hours of the night,
driving you fucking mad.
Too frail to haul yourself
off your feeble little bed
with its urine-soaked threadbare blankets,
and a dangerous electric fire
just near enough to fall on and burn,
but not near enough to keep you warm,
and costing you a bleeding fortune,
with the bailiffs knock knock
knocking at the door.
Aah no!

I didn't take
that one out

I'm beside myself

BOTH

Beside the seaside
Beside myself

★

Food, that's what I need
What do I want?

What have I got?

64

Linda Smith

LINDA   HATTIE

Have I got what I want?

                                                              Do I want what
                                                                    I've got?

What do I want?

                                                              What have I got?

Haven't got what I want

                                                       Have to have what I've got

Have I got anything in?

                                                       Can I keep anything down?

Am I hungry?

                                                              How hungry am I?

Just have a small one

                                                       Don't have a small one

Got regular and large

                                                              What is regular?

Well medium really,

                                                       How big's medium?

Quite small.

                                                              Just serves one

                                    BOTH
                        Serves one right

                                                       What's the sell by date?
Hasn't got one

                                                       Must be alright then

Shelf life

                                                              Sheltered life

Life shelved

                                                              On the shelf

LINDA   HATTIE

It's got a long shelf life

                                   What's that in
                                   human years?

*

                    Shhshh. There's somebody else here

Sssshhhh

                                   Shhshh

BOTH
I'm not here on my own!
No I'm not here

                                   on my own

(Pulling back imaginary big dog)
No, I've got a dog

                               I've got a big dog

There's a big dog here
with me

                               Great big dog

He'll have your leg off

                            He's lovely though

He's vicious

                               He loves me

He'll have you

                            He's a pit rock

He's a pit rock terrier

                            He's a Pitlochry
                                   terrier

He's one of those mad dogs

                               He's a sumo

He's a Yamaha

                               He's lovely

LINDA	HATTIE

But he's vicious

> He loves me, he'll
> do anything to
> protect me

He loves me, he'll
have your leg off.

> Leave me alone

If you go away now,
no—one gets hurt

> (*petting small
> imaginary dog*)
> You're a lovely little
> dog.

Go now, and
We'll say no more about it

> You're a lovely little
> puppy dog

Down Satan, down boy,

> You're a lovely little
> fluffy puppy dog

Good boy, seen him off
Seen the last of him.

> That nasty man's
> gone away now

He won't be back in a hurry
That's for sure

> You're a lovely little
> fluffy puppy dog

You're a good boy
A good boy

> You can't be cooped
> up in here all day

LINDA   HATTIE

Not right is it? A big dog
like that cooped up in a
little flat
LINDA   HATTIE

                                                 You want to go
                                                       walkies

No wonder they go mad and
attack people

                                                 It's the owners, I
                                                       blame

I was going mad cooped up here,
I hate to think of the effect
it's had on you, Poopsy

                                            You want to be in the
                                            park running about

What was I thinking of?

                                                 It'll get me out,
                                                 the dog. Get me
                                                 out of myself

Your mummy would go mad
cooped up in here all alone
I'd be your mad mummy

                                                      Walkies!
He loves his walkies
                        BOTH
                       I like it
                   My dogs like it.

I've got a door somewhere

                                              Now where's that
                                              door?

LINDA   HATTIE

Find, boy, Find.

SFX BING CROSBY MUSIC 'Don't fence me in.'

LIGHTS VERY SLOWLY FADE

END

PART TWO

'Men are from Mars, Women are from Thorntons'

1989–1997

THE CUTTING EDGE
Mark Thomas, comedian, writer and political activist

Most people said Linda was funny, some said she was kind and generous. She was both of those things but more importantly, she remained both while drunk. Back in the days when I didn't tut at young people drinking alco-pops I once sat with Linda, alongside her partner Warren, on the steps of a dockers' pub in Leith waiting for the night shift to come off work and the bar to open. At that time Edinburgh was not yet a twenty-four hour drinking Mecca, but you could manage twenty-two if you knew where to look. As we sat on the steps a milk float rattled past, delivering for the morning. As the milkie got out, cap perched at a jaunty angle and smelling faintly of milkman musk (a mixture of roll-ups and workmen's sheds), he noticed us on the steps, and quickly lolloped over with a couple of pints of the white stuff for us.

'Here y'go.'

'Thanks,' I said. 'How much is that?'

'S'alrite, son,' he said, holding up his hand to refuse payment. 'S'alrite.'

'What a nice bloke,' exclaimed Linda.

'Yeah, that was really nice of him.'

'That was really nice of him,' she said before pausing to burst out laughing, 'Fuck me, we must look in a right state.' And she was off, riffing on how awful we must appear for a milkman to take pity on us.

'We must look atrocious. A milkman offers us milk! That's how shit we look!' So we shared the milk, wiped our chins, and ten minutes later were tucking into cheese toasties and Jamesons. Still chuckling at the state we were in.

Some people said Linda could play the boys at their own comedy game without resorting to being laddish or taking refuge in gags about her menstrual cycle, and they were right too. In 1990 myself, Kevin Day, Bob Boyton and a gaggle of other comics founded *The Cutting Edge* at The Comedy Store in London. At the time The Store was in a dodgy basement in Leicester Square. For some reason half the audience (stage right) were placed in a pit some 18 inches below ground level. Amongst Store regulars it was known as The Sheep Dip. The Sheep Dip was the place where trouble started from. After all, a bad act with decent seats was bearable, but the logic of The Sheep Dip ran: 'The show's shit! And the view's terrible!' At this point in the proceedings the punters tended to make their views known.

The Cutting Edge was all about new material and comics working together, which wasn't a concept comics naturally embraced. Being naturally self-obsessed to the point of mania and with egos the size of small urban conurbations, comics tend to grab the spotlight rather than share it. But there were a number of games designed to make us work together, one being 'gag-tag'. One comic starts talking on a topic of the week and at any moment another comic from the side of the stage can shout 'Tag' and take the mic to continue in a similar vein but with their material, until they are tagged out – normally seconds later.

In the beery haze of The Store, Linda seemed completely at ease amidst the rising tide of testosterone and bad puns. The subject of gag-tag might be the Royal Family, so the boys head for the in-breed jokes, ranting about the Windsors being German and sponging off the state. Up on to the stage amidst the smoke Linda would jump, shouting 'Tag!', flicking her long hair back, and with a disarming look of innocent confusion calmly utter, 'Princess Diana – so thick and yet so thin.'

This obviously was in the days before her death and subsequent canonisation – Diana's, that is. As for Linda, she was a performer who could beat the boys, but do it on her own ground.

All sorts of things were said about Linda when she died, but I remember her as the Queen of Incredulity. It was in her voice, in her face and in each gag. She couldn't believe that the world was quite as shit as it was, especially when it could be so brilliant, if only we sorted it out.

So she was kind, generous, funny, her own woman, but would not suffer fools gladly.

One night she and I found ourselves in the House of Commons, in one of the bars there. I had been to a political meeting and had long stopped drinking. Linda had not. She was standing in the corner by the bar.

'Linda – how nice to see you. What are you doing here?'

'Good question, what am I doing here? It is a question I've been asking myself. I was invited to some dinner with these old Labour lefties. Guest of Honour for this meal – which was very nice, but as soon as it finished they said, "Let's go to the bar," and then they just left me. That's nice, isn't it? Abandoning your Guest of Honour to get lost in this place.'

At this point several MPs entered the bar rather noisily, flushed and red-faced with fine wines by the look of it. One harrumphed towards Linda and with a drunken swirl of his vowels and consonants said, 'Ah, there you are.' He might even have added, 'M'dear.' Linda looked this pillar of the establishment squarely in the eye and before he could say another word informed him, 'You are the rudest fucking bastard I've ever fucking met!'

Mark Thomas, 2006.

LINDA LIVE
onstage at the Irish Centre, Sheffield 1990

Revolutions in Eastern Europe. That's been pretty smart, the over-throw of the Romanian regime. I was on for that because, what an evil regime that was . . . evil, corrupt, economy shot to pieces, no care for the elderly, no care for the sick, people shut up for years who hadn't even done anything – well, you can't picture it, can you? Thank your stars you don't live in a place like that!

We moan, but my goodness me . . . But I tell you what pissed me off about the coverage of the revolutions in Eastern Europe, it was that every corrupt, evil Stalinist regime was blamed by the reporter on a statue of Lenin. Every report was the same – you'd have Michael Buerk saying, 'Well, here we are in Bucharest and we look down on the scene of devastation and bloodshed as we wit-ness the downfall of this evil regime. And as we look down on the statue of Lenin – yes, you, you with the beard – you may well look sheepish – looks prettly forlorn now . . . ' Well, I don't know why . . . it's not his fault. Well, for a start he's been dead for years. It's not his fault, is it, Stalinism? But I wish we'd adopt that technique in Britain every time something goes wrong with Thatcherism – which is every day now. If we did that, every time something goes wrong we'd get out and trash a hero from the capitalist past. You'd get your Poll Tax demand and say, 'What's this? Six hundred quid? Right, that's it, I've had enough – I'm off out to trash a statue of Disraeli.'

'Look at my mortgage repayments – Duke of Wellington, you bastard!'

'Clive of India? I hold you personally responsible for the state of the National Health Service!'

But of course it doesn't work like that. And talking of the Health Service . . . I don't like this new fun-sized NHS, do you? Is it me or do we need more than three hospitals – England, Scotland, Wales? And what's this strange idea of taxi drivers becoming ambulance drivers? What a stupid idea. I don't want to go to the hospital the longest way round, some herbert in the front going, 'Cor, the Northern General Hospital – I've been there a thousand times but . . . doh, I know it – oh, I'll just drive around a bit till we find it!'

And that was a rum do, wasn't it? The Guildford Four. I don't know, but sometimes I think that Jeremy Beadle goes a bit too far. A joke's a joke but – fifteen years! They couldn't see the funny side, strangely enough but you can just see it when the Birmingham Six finally come out. He'll be there, with the wig, outside the prison . . . 'Ah, Beadle's About – you thought I was a High Court judge . . . ha! but you've been marvellous sports – thank you for playing *British Justice.*'

The whole situation in the Middle East . . . it's a funny business – sanity and madness, isn't it? There's Saddam Hussein – there he was murdering thousands of people in his own country and using chemical warfare against the Kurds . . . bit of a rough diamond! Basically OK but a bit rough round the edges. Probably wouldn't have him round to dinner, but trade with him a bit. Now he invades a fantastically wealthy, tiny little country that he owes a fuck of a lot of money to . . . *mad*! 'I just can't understand what he's doing – he must be mad, he must be completely mad!' Well, of course he's not mad. Don't you sometimes feel like going down to the NatWest, with a kalashnikov . . . and saying, 'I don't want any more of those fucking snotty letters about the overdraft, all right?' Saddam Hussein? – he's just a bloke who wants 'a different *kind* of bank account'. 'And no more bloody letters about the oil deficit, all right?'

But you do sometimes wonder when you see how many troops there are deployed out there in the Middle East – you do wonder if he isn't a mushroom short of a full English breakfast. Because there's hundreds of thousands of them, French, English, American . . . it's all shaping up like the last scene in the Blues Brothers. Saddam Hussein – sitting there saying, 'Well, I've got a full tank of nerve gas, a full packet of cigarettes, I'm 500 miles from Baghdad – no problem, hit it.'

Apparently his ploy now – quite a good move – is to get all the Palestinians – as many as possible – into Kuwait, taking over the houses of the Kuwaitis who are leaving. So he divides the Arab world. Quite a good tactic really. For the Palestinians, it must be like Butlin's! You come from the West Bank, from being shot at and God knows what – and there you are in Kuwait in these great big houses with a swimming pool – well, I suppose the house prices go down immediately – but knowing the Palestinians' luck, they'll get there and they'll be thinking 'It's a very nice chalet – lovely.' And there'll be about 300,000 Israelis – claiming to have a prior booking.

'No, I'm sorry, mate, we've booked this place before you, several thousand years before you . . . look, I've got a signature – there it is, look, A B R A H A M – see? Anyway, it's too good for you, mate – you'll only keep hostages in the cellar, go on – out!' I would be more worried about our activities in the Middle East as Britons if we weren't so *crap*. We're sending Challenger tanks. Now, Challenger tanks were actually made for the Shah of Iran and they break down all the time, so the soldiers are doing all sorts of jokes about them like, 'What's the difference between this Challenger tank and a Skoda? – about two million quid!'

Well, I get to talk about events up here – but like most people, I'm more interested in the trivia of my own life really. You concentrate on trivia, just to block out the really big threatening things in life. I'm decorating my flat at the moment, and I'm obsessed with it. My world has shrunk to the size of a Dulux colour chart. And you'll know, if you've done any decorating, that for a start paint colours have really stupid names. They don't have names like red, green or yellow . . . no – Elfin Mist, Fairy Dell, Dingly Heatherbell. When you've finally made your choice, you've got the embarrassment of going into the shop and asking for two and a half litres of Pulsating Pixie Juice . . . in a matt finish. But the worst aspect of it is that it trivialises your whole life. World events compete for your attention – I'm watching the television and I'm thinking, look at that terrible situation in the Middle East . . . is blue too cold for a bedroom? Oh . . . my God, it's getting worse, what are the United States doing? – there's mines everywhere and . . . oh look – that's the grey I wanted in the hall!

Lord Denning has come out with some corking stuff lately, hasn't he? His wonderful statement about the Guildford Four – 'If we'd hanged them all those years ago, we wouldn't have all these stupid campaigns to release them . . .' Well, I suppose the logic is irrefutable. You don't hear much about the Bring Home the Tolpuddle Six campaign, do you? or the Stop the Slaughter of the Spanish Inquisition Now campaign? If they *had* hanged them there wouldn't be much point in having a campaign really – but who would they have as their brief – fucking Doris Stokes? You'd think he'd learn really – because it was an outburst like this, about black jurors, that led to his early retirement . . . at the age of eighty-three. Well, there you are – one silly mistake and that's a young man's career down the tube! Another twenty years and he could have been at the height of his profession.

Religion. I don't hold with it myself, although like most comedians I am a Buddhist. I believe in reincarnation – in fact I tend to rely on it. But I have no truck with religion – all this intolerance goes through all religions. For example, when there was that terrible earthquake in Iran, you had religious leaders saying, 'Oh well – it's God testing our faith.' Well, I know they say the Lord our God is a jealous God – but He'd have to be insanely jealous really, wouldn't He, to do that? I'm a bit jealous, but when I'm testing someone's faith I just phone up to see if a strange woman answers the phone. I think that's enough, don't you? And when there was that terrible disaster in a tunnel going to Mecca and all those people were killed, religious leaders were saying, 'It's the will of God, they would have died anyway.' I don't think so really – do you? So they would have been sat at home in their living room and a tunnel would have fallen on their heads? No – I think that would have made the front cover of the *Sunday Sport*, wouldn't it? Even the anniversary of the Ayatollah's death led to bloodshed and people being killed and injured – I think it's what he would have wanted . . .

I think my line on religion really is . . . well, take the Bible, for example – beautiful poetry, but a pack of porky pies from start to finish. Chapter 1 – the Lord our God made the world in six days, and on the seventh day He rested. Oh yes? Well, what sort of a cowboy job's that then? No wonder it's fucked now – six days? If a job's worth doing . . . I spent longer putting shelves up! Six days? Give Him the benefit of the doubt – let's say He nipped down to MFI, got a slot-together ready-made universe – chances are He'd get home to find there's a packet of screws missing. That's a day lost, isn't it? Imagine getting a builder in now, to have a look at the world – to do a few repairs . . . 'Come in, Mr Jones . . . this is the world, er, filled with the works of God. It's in a bit of a state, I'm afraid we haven't had much done to it for millennia! What do you think?'

'Phew! What do I think? Cor blimey, just look at the place. San Andreas fault . . . look at that! Venice . . . new damp-proof course. Look at the state of it – you've got earthquakes, you've got tidal waves, you've got volcanoes . . . you've got the Jewson lot! Who put this in then? . . . oh yes? – I thought so. God! I thought so – well, you get what you pay for, don't you?'

Now the anti-Poll Tax campaign – that's been so successful – it's been brilliant. It's been so successful, no one's been paying their Poll Tax at all. Except a few Government employees who must think, 'I'd better pay it or I'll lose my job . . . no, no one will notice.' In fact, so many people are not paying their Poll Tax that to be a rebel . . . you've got to bloody pay it! I've seen people walking round in T-shirts that say I'VE PAID MY POLL TAX – BY DIRECT DEBIT ACTUALLY. 'Cos I'm a rebel, I live on the edge. But you can't get a cabinet minister on the television any more to explain what a good idea it is. They tried to get John Noakes to do it as a dare. Even he won't do it. Or Challenge Anneka Rice – to explain the Poll Tax . . . 'Tee hee! Er . . . no, I can't, ha! ha! ha!' It's turned the whole world upside down. You turn on the television and there's a Tory farmer in mid-Staffordshire saying, 'Of course I don't look like a natural Marxist-Leninist, hey! BANG! – bloody ramblers . . . but I'm not paying my ruddy Poll Tax!' But I'm exaggerating, saying that everyone is against it. Not quite everyone is against it – everyone except . . . the Labour Party, who have an interesting line on resisting the Poll Tax. Kinnock's line is 'Resist – by . . . paying it! Ah yes – you can laugh but we've been doing this for years – we know what works. You just resist – by paying. But when you pay – you give that Council clerk such a look! Take it! – but don't think I approve.' Today's Labour Party – changing the world by going, 'Tsk – dear oh Lor'!' Sometimes I get so angry, I think . . . I'm going to go out and join the Socialist Workers' Party. Then I think . . . no, fuck that – I'm too old for a paper round!

LINDA LIVE
onstage at The Gilded Balloon, Edinburgh, August 1992

You can't move on the streets of Edinburgh for all these little companies, all these people handing out show leaflets and flyers and what have you. It's awful. Your life's not your own, is it? You'll be walking along the street and a naturally trusting person like myself turns really suspicious. You're never sure whether someone's just a person or they're about to – *zip!* – spring that old leaflet on you. You think you're fairly safe – you'll be standing around somewhere and there'll be some poor old boy stamping about going, 'Aar, ye get y' fuggin . . . aye, y' basta – get fek yer shitey . . . ' and all of a sudden they go (Oxbridge accent) 'And if you'd like to see more of this . . .'

I was watching the news about Yugoslavia. Apart from the fact that it was really horrible – obviously – can anyone understand what's going on in Yugoslavia? No, I don't understand any of it. The only thing I understand is, every single leader looks well dodgy, don't they? The Bosnian, the Croatian, the Serb – the whole bunch of them. They've just got this look, the haircut and this shifty-eyed look, of a Second Division football manager who's just about to leave his wife for a bunny girl. If they just wore a sheepskin coat it would complete the look, I feel. Another thing I can draw out of the situation – the UN peacekeeping force . . . not exactly on a roll, are they? When we look around the world – they are a bit shit really.

There are civil wars all over the place now. Eastern Europe is breaking up – big changes there. In Poland, for example, you've got the situation where they're moving from a backward-looking regime of Stalinism into the white-hot post-modernism . . . of the Catholic Church. Everything's changing all over, like the ex-Soviet Union. Now Yeltsin – he went to America and met with Bush and agreed . . . well, he agreed to everything really, just agreed really, 'cos he's pissed all the time, isn't he? Standing about with his arm around Bush, saying, 'You're my bess mate – I never meant to upset you or nuffink – it wasn't me, it was the Generals – I love you . . . I fuckin' love you.'

A year back it was all hostages – everyone wanted hostages, they were all the go. And you could have a laugh with hostages, yes you could. Terry Waite – I loved him, he was a bit of a hero really. He was like the Poll Tax dodger's Poll Tax dodger, wasn't he? He gave them the fucking run-around . . .

Terry was the last British hostage to be released . . . well, I mean, it's not the winning that's important, is it? It's the taking part, isn't it? And only the other week another three hostages were released – by the West Midlands police.

And the Middle East – looks like we're shaping up for another bundle there. I hope we can get together, in the West, a better propaganda than we got for this last bundle in the Middle East. Because I didn't care for that British propaganda we had then – along the lines of . . . 'Ooh, Saddam Hussein . . . he's mad, you know, he's a mad madman. We must stop the madman – he's mad!' The Iraqis were billing the whole thing as a global conflict – the clash between light and dark, between good and evil. And they were coming out with wonderful stuff – they were describing George Bush as Beelzebub. But better than that – I actually heard, in Iraqi propaganda, *John Major* as sitting at the right hand of Beelzebub. The evil one – John Major – Satan's agent! I bet he loved that. I'll bet that did wonders for his bloody pride, didn't it? I bet he was saying to Norma, 'Come on, Norma, forget the shipping forecast – listen to this – Iraqi radio . . . Satan's agent. *That's me! Satan's agent* – early night, dear? What do you think? Satan's agent! I tell you what – I don't lose my temper very often, but when I do . . . ooh.'

Satan's agent? I don't think so. Satan's accountant – I can see that. Now then, Beelzebub, I have asked you before – keep your receipts!

I can never really picture politicians in sexual situations . . . that they haven't actually paid for, to be honest. John and Norma? Are they sexually adventurous? Do they go in for oral sex? Possibly not, I think, because there's a little design flaw with the man really, isn't there? In the lips department. It would leave old Norma with a task not dissimilar to trying to get head off Zippy from Rainbow.

I've been watching a bit of telly since I've been up here in Edinburgh and I came across a documentary about red deer culling, and I was half-way through the programme when I realised that *culling* wasn't just *killing* in a Scottish accent. Because, in fact, it's a completely different word – *culling* – meaning – *killing*. Well, that's a bit of a superfluous word, isn't it? You're not going to fool anyone with that, are you? Later on in the programme they started talking about *managing* the herd. Well, I wouldn't like to be in little Rusty the Red Deer's hooves – just before that tricky interview with the Personnel Manager. He's called in . . . 'Rusty, is it? Come in, come in. RD? I'll call you RD, shall I? Sit down, sit down, we don't want people thinking you're a hatstand, do we? Now, let's see – how long have you been here with us, at the glen? Ten years! Is it ten years? Marvellous. We've liked your work, Rusty – we've liked your work in that time, running about looking cute, eating grass, posing for photos – marvellous. Does the word *recession* ring any sleigh bells?'

Well, it probably rings a few more sleigh bells with little Rusty the Red Deer than it does with Chancellor Lamont – how did he get that job? I don't know what he knows about economics – it may be quite a lot. My objection to the man is, he's too fucking weird. People don't look like that! Oh, they don't – I've seen lots of people – they don't look like that. But be fair – all credit to the man for holding down a job like that. When you can't go out during the hours of daylight. And it *is* nice to see that little boy from the Addams family doing so well. But I love him on the telly, when he's asked a really difficult question, like 'Unemployment – a bad thing or what?' He gets a look of total puzzlement over his face. It's as if you asked Jackie Mann to give you a rundown on the plot of *Twin Peaks*. And he'll come up with, 'Well – unemployment . . . disappointing.' Disappointing? It's a little bit like the Spanish Inquisition saying, 'Well – we were only asking.'

A sex scandal that I thought was terribly unjust . . . that case in America – Pee Wee Herman. I thought he was badly stitched up for not doing anything very much. He was a wonderful actor, Pee Wee Herman, in a brilliant film – *Pee Wee's Big Adventure*. A little while back, old Pee Wee was caught, in America, in a pornographic cinema, having a wank. There's no way of dressing it up – that's where he was, that's what he was doing. In the pornographic cinema . . . relaxing. And he was caught, presumably by the police, not just by his mum or something . . . caught, big scandal, splashed all over the papers, career in ruins – just awful. No one would book him – terrible. But I thought, what was the element of shock involved here, in this situation? What was the problem exactly? Pornographic cinema – having a wank? Was he, perhaps, upsetting the other patrons, who'd come to watch the film on its artistic merits? I don't think so really – it's all context really. If he'd been sat there at a matinee performance of *A Hundred and One Dalmatians* – well I wouldn't like that really: 'Come away from the nasty man, dear, we'll go to the other cinema.' But you know – is that the worst thing a human being can do? Wanking at the pictures? It's not like *talking* at the pictures, is it? I don't like that. That spoils a film for me. As far as I'm concerned, if someone's wanking, they can't eat popcorn. Should be obligatory maybe, I don't know. But I hate that – what goes through these people's minds? 'What shall we do tonight? Well, we want something to eat and a bit of a chat – let's go to the pictures!'

HELLO CRUEL WORLD
Steve Gribbin, comedian and songwriter

Hello Cruel World was a theatre show that Linda Smith and I wrote and toured from August 1992 to May 1993. We played arts centres, theatres, community halls, hotels, leisure centres and ex-lunatic asylums. Well, that takes care of the bald facts, now for the legend . . .

Originally, the show was intended as a vehicle for myself and comedy partner Brian Mulligan, in our guise as musical comedy duo Skint Video. It was originally entitled *Exposé 92*, and we had begun writing it in the winter of 1991.

Linda and I had been friends since we first met at Sheffield University on the infamous Red Wedge comedy tour of 1986. She was performing her double act with Ann Lavelle, Tuff Lovers, and we were attempting to placate a roomful of boozed-up über-students with our usual blend of topical comedy songs with serrated edges. We hit it off immediately and had kept in touch over the years, often gigging together in far-flung corners of the UK, playing dives that made the bar from the Blues Brothers look like the Royal Ballet.

The early nineties were a strange time for political comedy, specifically the 'alternative' left-wing variety that had flourished in the eighties. The fashion in comedy was for surrealism and stupidity and cynical self-regard. British politics had taken a turn for the grey with the fall of Thatcher and the accession of the Man Who Would Be Shelving, John Major.

Certain critics were already gleefully sounding the death knell for any type of comedy that was socialist or even liberal in content, decrying the 'heart-on-sleeve' approach in favour of a studied nonchalance and a retreat into non-committal self-referential irony. Linda and I were adamant that we were going to write a defiantly unfashionable left-wing show, but with dancing and songs.

And silly costumes. The sillier the better.

We were adamant that it should be as accessible as possible, drawing on our love of films and popular culture. One of the sketches was a direct take on *Goodfellas*, dealing with Oliver Cromwell and the puritans as 'Good Zealots'.

Other film icons we plundered were the Marx Brothers. ('What are we gonna do with all the statues?' 'Statue?' 'Yeah, it's me, boss!')

We also parodied TV shows, such as *Songs of Praise*, but from a pagan Stone Age point of view. Linda did a thoroughly convincing (and strangely psychotic) Thora Hird. ('Young people today . . . they don't live long, do they? Fetch us the sacrificial knife, would you, love?') We were not above satirising those on the liberal side of the spectrum, either . . . one sketch was two completely out-to-lunch New Age travellers. (Sample dialogue: 'I said to the police . . . "Hey, man, do you have any idea of who I am?" they said, "No" . . . I said, "Oh, shit, I was hoping you could help me out!"')

We even invented a fictitious Eastern European country, Zilchistania, that had arisen from the ashes of the old Soviet Union, and still had dodgy ex-Communist apparatchiks vying for election alongside Blood and Soil Fascist candidates. They even had their own poet laureate, played as a slightly dotty Pam Ayres type by Linda, complete with execrable rhymes ('Good evening, Zilchistania/I hope I will remain 'ere/ I'll try not to detain yer/'cos you got to catch a train 'ere'). The painful break-up of the former Yugoslavia was satirised in a sketch about two countries going through a bitter divorce ('*I'm* keeping the armies, thank you very much!')

It was Linda who came up with the new title *Hello Cruel World*, and that summed the whole thing up so neatly . . . yes, the world was a cruel and nasty place, but we were going to look it unflinchingly in the eye and laugh in the face of despair. A bit like West Bromwich Albion supporters.

Linda herself described the ethos of the show as 'a mosey through History to discover the roots of the present crisis'.

We had one hell of a laugh creating the show. Linda's absurdist wit would always shine through . . . she was very adept at reproducing the sounds and phrases of a certain sort of narrow-minded Englishness to a creamed tea. We spent a large part of the time we should have been rehearsing just larking around, creased up with laughter.

We hit on the idea of two 'Statler and Waldorf' characters who would comment on the show. These two would be old retired colonel types with a nice line in surrealist leaps of consciousness. They were based on two characters that Brian and I had written called 'The Ratepayers' Association' (ah, those pre-Poll Tax days!) for a series of shows run by Ivor Dembina at The Red Lion in Soho in October 1990. Brian Mulligan in turn had based those characters on his friend's father-in-law, the most prejudiced man he'd ever met. Linda and I eventually named them 'Crapper and Hague' after a sign that we saw on our way to rehearsals, and the name seemed strangely fitting. These became some of our favourite moments of the show, and we enjoyed them so much we used to talk in their characters all night (Robert De Niro, eat your heart out), which caused some consternation down the local pub.

Mostly the show was enthusiastically received, especially at The Crucible in Sheffield, where we had to do a hastily assembled encore. (I wonder if Shakespeare had the same trouble . . . 'Oh, sod it . . . just send Hamlet on to do a song!') However, no book of anecdotes about a comic would be complete without a few instances about going down badly. The Lancaster Literature Festival was a case in point. The guy on before us was a local poet who we, rather foolishly it turns out, had fully expected to bomb. Not only did he storm the venue, it was all the audience could do to restrain themselves from physically carrying him shoulder-high round the environs of Lancaster before crowning him The Funniest Man Alive. Our show, in contrast, cleared the room quicker than James Blunt tuning up. At the end, the organiser couldn't even bring himself to come into the room . . . he just passed the cheque through the tiniest sliver in the doorway before running away. 'Christ,' said Linda, with her customary dripping sarcasm, in a voice just loud enough for the cowardly and rapidly departing promoter to hear, 'I'd hate to think what would have happened if we'd gone down *really* badly!'

The other time was when we played the Hillsborough Constituency Labour party do in Sheffield on Friday, 4 December 1992. Present was Mr Arthur Scargill, whose negative reaction to my Catholic-baiting was as ill-mannered as it was unexpected. I was essaying the Pope as a seedy nightclub comic when the doyen of the miners' strike walked past me and just sighed. All I could hear was Linda, behind the curtain, giggling uncontrollably. We were unceremoniously 'paid off' and didn't come out to do the second half. We had to pack up the van in full glare of disgusted stares and highly audible whispers of 'Well, I never . . . dirty little gets . . . never in all my born days . . .' Strangely, neither of us could stop laughing.

I have very fond memories of *Hello Cruel World*. It took up a whole year of my life, and it was a brilliant laugh and a privilege to work with Linda. What follows are samples from that show and in typing up these somewhat ancient sketches (from a Time Before Blair), I have been hearing Linda's voice leap off the page, sharp and sardonic and above all filled with that dotty English sense of the absurd, ringing out loud and clear from the printed words. I shall miss her a lot.

Steve Gribbin, 2006.

HELLO CRUEL WORLD
Sketch: The Puritans 'Good Zealots'

(Linda and Steve are both dressed in Puritan ruffs and Round-head helmets. Linda carries a pike and Steve a musket. Steve is playing Oliver Cromwell.)

LINDA: Tell us that story 'bout your vendetta with the Rump Parliament.

STEVE: Nah, they don't wanna hear it.

LINDA: Sure they do! (to audience, brandishing her pike menacingly) You wanna help us out here, or what?

STEVE: OK, OK, the Rump Parliament . . . I kicked their fucking ASS!

LINDA: You sure did, Ollie.

STEVE: So I walk in there, and I says to them assholes . . .'Listen, you're creamin' all the money off the top, you're corrupt, you don't give a shit!'

LINDA: Little pricks. No respect.

STEVE: Yeah. So I says: 'The Organisation which I represent figures you need protection. I mean . . . vessels do sink. So here *I* am, I'm like the Lord Protector, so it's the answer to your fucking prayers. . .and if you don't agree you'd better start *sayin'* 'em, you know what I mean?'

LINDA: Oh, gee, you really are not a funny guy.

STEVE: In what *way* am I not funny?

LINDA: Whaddyamean, Ollie?

STEVE: I mean, in what way am I not fucking *funny*?

LINDA: Well, you're like . . . you're Oliver Cromwell . . . you personify the Protestant Work Ethic, you're not amusing, you don't dress too good . . .

STEVE: So what you saying . . . you want me to be some kinda Royalist faggot?

LINDA: Well, no, Ollie, hey don't bust my balls . . . you've taken the reins of power into your own hands, you won't let no one else have a shot . . . it's just not *funny*.

STEVE: Listen, I built this country up . . . we got Respect. People come to me, they say, 'Hey, Ollie, got a ship full of cloth out in back . . . take a piece . . .' Huh . . . we got Respect. You got a problem with that?

LINDA: No, Ollie, I don't got no problem with that.

STEVE: Yeah . . . you sure? 'Cos you startin' to sound a little 'Irish' to me.

LINDA: Oh, Jeez, Ollie, no . . . but why did you kill all those Irish?

STEVE: You think I ain't never killed no Catholic before? I'll dig a fucking hole. Those Irish pricks, they rose up, they embarrass me in front of the Family . . . so they're gonna get whacked.

LINDA: Sure, they're gonna get whacked . . . but it's still not funny.

STEVE: I'm talkin' about the Family here . . . The Family has gotta be 100 per cent English . . . no Irish, no Welsh, no Scottish, none of that shit. Does that *depress* you?

LINDA: Sure, it depresses me. We are depressed . . . we're *Puritans* . . . we don't laugh, we don't sing, we don't dance.

STEVE: *I'll* make you fucking *dance!* I'll shoot this musket right at your foot, *then* you can fucking dance! Go on, dance!

LINDA: Hey, Ollie . . . I didn't mean nothing by it.

STEVE: (Brandishing musket) Huh? Huh? (breaks into huge grin) I had you there, didn't I, you little prick? Huh?

LINDA: You sure did, Ollie, you had me there!

STEVE: Will ya take a look at this guy? He's quaking in his boots . . . he ain't no Puritan, the guys a friggin' *Quaker!* Ha ha!

LINDA: Oh, Ollie, that was beautiful. You really are *not* a funny guy. This guy *kills* me!

STEVE: Later.

Sketch: Zilchistania à la Marx Brothers

Intro (by Linda)

But how would Hollywood deal with the current situation in Eastern Europe? We present a snuff movie version of the Marx Brothers, the world's first post-Marx Brothers film about the newest country on the Eastern bloc, Zilchistania.

(Background music: Crazy Marx Bros music)

LINDA: Boss, boss! The Berlin Wall is a-down, Eastern bloc is-a all broke up. Communism collapsed.

STEVE: Drunk again, eh?

LINDA: Everything is in a real a-state!

STEVE: Real estate? I can get into that. In which case, I hereby declare myself Lifelong President of Zilchistania! So now what are we gonna do?

LINDA: We gotta forge ahead.

STEVE: I gotta forge a head on the currency. *My* head!

LINDA: But boss . . . we gotta no food.

STEVE: Well, we'll send out for it.

LINDA: But Boss, they won't give us no credit.

STEVE: That's true. . . *I* usually take all the credit.

LINDA: What are we gonna do with all the statues?

STEVE: Statue?

LINDA: Yeah, boss. It's me.

STEVE: Listen, listen . . . what we want is some industries.

LINDA: But boss, we don't make anything.

STEVE: If you don't make anything you're working for the wrong boss.

LINDA: But boss, I work for you.

STEVE: You're fired.

LINDA: That's a-bad.

STEVE: Got you a new job. General.

LINDA: That's a-good.

STEVE: But we're at war.

LINDA: That's a-bad.

STEVE: They got no weapons.

LINDA: That's a-good.

STEVE: But neither have we.

LINDA: That's a-bad.

STEVE: But don't worry, I got just two words to say to them . . . We Surrender! What's that noise?

LINDA: Boss, the people have taken to the streets.

STEVE: Taken to the streets, eh? Well, I kinda like 'em myself.

LINDA: No, no, boss, they are appealing to you.

STEVE: I wouldn't go that far.

LINDA: Boss, boss, you better sing them the new National Anthem.

STEVE: Hold everything! Hold the front page! (to Linda)
Hold this!

(He hands her his cigar.)

Sketch: Linda as the Mythical Figure of Britannia on the British Coin

STEVE: So, Britain has come down a bit in the world of late. It's as if Britain used to have her own series on prime-time television, but has now been reduced to a walk-on, non-speaking part on some poxy daytime soap, like *Young Taxidermists*. And one of the best-known symbols of Britain's sterling values is today looking a bit tarnished herself . . .

(Music: 'Rule Britannia'. Enter Linda dressed exactly as Britannia on the British coin. She speaks with a broad Brummie accent.)

LINDA: That bloody Norman Lamont . . . he's a bad husbander of money . . . not like that Chancellor Kohl . . . *he* knows how to treat a currency, he does . . . nothing's too good for the Deutschmark. It's the Bundesbank that like to say: 'Fuck off, Norman!'

No wonder the Germans are coining it . . . they get to the stock market early, nick all the deckchairs.

Oh, I remember Black Wednesday like it was yesterday . . . I was up and down like a bride's nightie . . . one minute I was on the floor, the next I was down the toilet . . . when people found out they hit the roof . . . most people haven't even *got* a roof!

Norman said it was all decided on the toss of a coin . . . too right, 'cos he's a right tosser!

You know what, all Chancellors are only after one thing . . . and once they've got yer inflation down they lose all respect for you . . . once they've got you in the ERM they don't want to know.

I can't hold me head up in the International Market . . . I can't just nip out for a basket of currencies. I can't afford to pay for them at the check-out . . . it's highly embarrassing.

You think less and less of me . . . I'm very undervalued . . . I blame that Rod Hull and ECU, it's biting everybody really hard.

Still, that Bush household are not so high and mighty now, eh? That new space programme's had to go back to Comet. I told 'em it would.

Them Italians down the road have had to get the bailiffs in as well . . . how did they fit all that lire in one house? Millions of them there, so I heard. I said to our Franc, across the road . . . I says, 'Franc . . . you'll be next . . . just you wait!'

He won't listen.

John Major says it's all going to be all right.

Well, I tell you what, sunshine . . . if I *am* going to be made redundant, I want it all in Deutschmarks!

(Music up. Exit Linda, tripping over her flowing gown.)

Sketch: Linda as Primary School Teacher Giving a Completely Distorted Version of History

LINDA: Right, class! Pay attention, Wilson, or it'll be detention!

First there was the Stone Age. Then there was the Iron Age, where people with crumpled bearskins looked a lot smarter. Unlike you, Mellor, with that Chelsea scarf!

Then there was the Ice Age, which ended because someone left the freezer door open so the polar ice caps melted and a whole packet of peas went to waste.

Then the Romans came and built Hadrian's Wall, which was very cheap because they used YTS labour.

Then came the Dark Ages where everyone was very ugly 'cos they kept bumping into each other in the dark.

And then came the Elizabethan Age, in which Sir Walter Raleigh threw his bowls for the Queen 'cos he was a *gentleman*, and said time to finish this game of potatoes and beat the Spanish, all before tea.

And then we got Scotland and Wales and Ireland into our gang, and then after that *loads* of others wanted to be in our gang . . . Africa, India, the Falklands, the Isle of Man . . . so we let them.

And we built a lot of trains for India so they could have trainspotters, although it is a bit hot for an anorak over there. Unfortunately there was a bit of trouble with the Indian Army, leading to the Indian Mutiny, which was the result of a mix-up in the crisps sent to the Indian troops, whereby the beefy-flavoured crisps went to the Hindus and the smoky bacon-flavoured ones went to the Muslims, resulting in the Black Hole of Calcutta, which was left over from the Dark Ages (someone really should've cleaned that up), and then they all appeared on the Clive of India chat show.

Right, that's it for today, 4G, and next week's lesson is: Why Dinosaurs Are Alive and Well and Living at My House.

Sketch: Crapper and Hague

CRAPPER (LINDA): We should never have lost the Empire, you know.

HAGUE: I thought you had it.

CRAPPER: Oh, it must be in my other suit.

HAGUE: Ah, the Empire, the Empire . . . I often dream about the Empire.

CRAPPER: I thought you dreamt about a choirboy and a tin of Swarfega.

HAGUE: I thought I told you never to mention that, old boy.

CRAPPER: Sorry. Of course. Court case pending and all.

HAGUE: Talking of Empires . . . whatever happened to the Glory that was Rome?

CRAPPER: Oh, had a bad season, you know, got relegated . . . had a few injuries, Souness was manager.

HAGUE: Bad business. Of course, in Rome, Christians were eaten.

CRAPPER: Eton? What a marvellous old school. I've had my son put down.

HAGUE: What, for Eton?

CRAPPER: No, just had him put down, couldn't stand the little blighter.

HAGUE: Good show. He'll respect you for that. As I was saying, in Rome the Christians were eaten by the lions.

CRAPPER: Serves them right. Never should have taken on Millwall . . . too hard for them.

BOTH: No one likes us/no one like us/ no one likes us/we don't care.

HAGUE: They sang that at Agincourt, you know . . . marvellous little number.

CRAPPER: They do say when in Rome, do as the Romans do.

HAGUE: Oh, I did. Last time I was in Rome I hopped on a Lambretta and nicked a handbag. Marvellous. Full of traveller's cheques.

ALWAYS ON MY MIND
Richard Morton, comedian and songwriter

Anyone who has ever worked with Linda will tell you that not only was she a very gracious performer, but a very generous one too. If you were both onstage at the same time, and it was you that got a big laugh, Linda would be the first to acknowledge it – and probably helped you to set up the joke anyway. Of course, Linda would get big laughs too, and at the Edinburgh Festival in 1991 she came up with a fabulous gag in a song parody that simply stole the show from her fellow performers every night of our ten-day run, or what was left of it. Linda and I were at The Gilded Balloon doing The Comedy Store's *Cutting Edge* show along with Mark Thomas, Kevin Day and Bob Boyton. As it was a topical, satirical news-based show, it was entirely dependent on breaking news stories, so when one morning at about 10 o'clock John Connor, our producer, rang me (ridiculous, I'm sure you know, for the Edinburgh Festival) and started jabbering excitedly, I knew something big had happened. Gorbachev had been ousted in a coup, and the Soviet Union was in crisis. Perfect. John immediately set me to the task of writing comic songs for that night's show and told me that he wanted all the other comics to perform a song as well, with me accompanying them on the guitar. Linda was always brilliant at writing new material and phoned me soon after, saying she had written a version of 'Always on My Mind'. No problem, I knew the chords.

Well, as any comic will tell you, trying out new material is always a bit of a do – you tend to feel under-rehearsed and under pressure. So it seemed that it was in no time at all that we were all on stage and at that point in the show where we would do our new songs for the Soviet Union crisis. The place was rammed as Linda strode confidently up to the mic, front of stage. I moved up just behind her with my guitar. The crowd fell silent. Linda looked over to me and cued the intro. I played the opening arpeggios slowly and mournfully as Linda announced in a solemn way, 'This is Gorbachev's song to the Soviet people.' She then started to sing in a cool, clear, tuneful voice:

> *'Maybe I didn't treat you quite as good as I should have,*
> *Maybe I didn't love you quite as often as I could have,*
> *Little things I should have said and done,*
> *I just never took the time . . .'*

Then a massive laugh erupted as Linda sang: '*You were always down the mines . . .*'

Richard Morton, 2006.

EXTRACTS FROM *WINDBAGS*
BBC Radio 1 show co-hosted by Jo Brand and Donna Mcphail,
February 1993

On Thatcher

I think we've all had quite enough of the Baroness, rampaging
through the media on her 'blonde ambition' tour, looking like the
bride of Frankenstein after a few single malts, with that glazed,
crazed look on her face that you can only really accept from
women selling make-up professionally.

On Chancellor Lawson

I did take a little peek at Nigel Lawson's book, *The View from Number 11 – Memoirs of a Tory 'Radical'* – blimey, I always find that
expression as convincing as the Hannibal Lecter vegan restaurant
really . . . or Genesis 'live'. There's a review on the front of it that
describes it as 'grippingly readable' – shall I read the bit on con-
trolling public expenditure with a subsection on VAT, or shall I
save it for bedtime?

East London life

My local paper, the *Newham Murderer*, is a fine publication. It's
about twenty pages of assorted murders and the weekend TV in the
middle – which is quite handy really, 'cos you're not going out with
all that going on – and I love the small ads in it. It's got all sorts of
personal services in it, like 'kissograms' and 'granniegrams'. I don't
know what the hell 'granniegrams' do – I suppose they burst into
family parties and say, 'You're not putting me in a home!'

On Supermodels

The only Supermodels I've ever been keen on were by Airfix –
fabby 'Dogfight Doubles', Spitfires and Messerschmidts, or the

Horror Monsters range, Quasimodo with fully working guillotine. I was the kind of little girl who pulled the legs off Cindy dolls and cut their hair into nylon tufts like a bad hair transplant. Actually, also like a good hair transplant. In those days it was all fields, there were no Supermodels, only Top Models and that was Twiggy really. Before that, in the fifties no one was young and attractive, everyone looked about fifty, including models, who were just posh birds really, looked and sounded like the Queen and were basically debutantes filling in time between finishing school and the Waffen SS. New models are called 'Supermodels', for those heavier clothes – next they'll be 'Superplus' models 20 feet tall and thinner than the plot of *Baywatch*. I don't remember the intermediate 'Regular' models, but I hope that somewhere there are really crappy 'Economy' models, who trip over on the catwalk – oh no! That's 'Supermodels', isn't it?

Now, first of all, how do you recognise your Supermodels? Is it because they've got their pants over their trousers? – only if they're modelling Gaultier; Supermodels could have someone's eye out with their cheekbones, have tiny little virtual-reality noses that you'd have to get a neurosurgeon to pick for you, and skin of an impossible peachy, flawless perfection that for the rest of us looks as achievable as a Labour election victory.

Physique-wise, there are two basic types of model and now the first type is really, really . . . thin . . . thin . . . like Kate Moss who could play the Harry Lime theme on her ribcage, and whose photo if adorning a 'Help Bosnia Now' poster instead of the cover of *Vogue*, would have you reaching for a tenner with tears in your eyes, and the other sort of model is the sort that is really. . .really. . . thin . . . thin . . . thin . . . thin . . . thin . . . but with silicone breast implants, so they look like pogo sticks with waterwings. All Supermodels, regardless of what physical type, must have their names romantically linked with Prince Albert of Monaco . . . Mon-*arco*? Oh, who cares, it's no bigger than Croydon. This is a good thing, as it stops him pestering me. 'Albie, mate, it's over!'

The best thing about Supermodels is that they appear in *Hello!* magazine all the time, which is just wonderful but has one serious drawback; it sometimes contains a photo of Michael Winner, the ghastly, smirking, cigar-smoking manatee who gets off with young attractive women by means of his charming, witty, elegant and adorable money.

The other constant in *Hello!* magazine is the lovely Princess Di, but quite honestly, next to the Supermodels she looks a bit of an old tugboat. Supermodels in *Hello!* are nearly always called Claudia Schiffer. In this episode here, we follow Claudia's day.

Claudia's in a Paris hotel room. First, she wakes up in bed, in full make-up, looking gorgeous. Now, as we all know, there's only one reason why any woman wakes up in full make-up – it's because she's gone to bed in full make-up . . . because she went to sleep without cleansing – because, as we know, ladies cleanse, gentlemen wash . . . and the only reason she did this is because she was completely off her gob. There's no evidence of a drunken debauch in Claudia's room – she's managed to undress, her pillow is not a cold kebab, there's no strange night club bouncer asleep on the dressing table with his dicky bow all anyhow. If Claudia's slept in her make-up, where's the familiar, rather eerie 'Turin Shroud' effect left on the pillow, eh? Fresh as a daisy, Claudia leaps out of bed, slips into some dolphin-friendly fishnet tights, and tucks into the first meal of the day, brekkie, a hearty full English kiwi fruit.

Bizarrely, all her meals are photographed individually, but are so tiny they look like a set of commemorative postage stamps. The day is filled with photo shoots, and lots of decisions – have we got change for the Photo-Me booth? Red or blue curtain in the background? Until supper-time, when she blows the diet and pigs out on an artichoke, well, once in a while. We also learn that Elton John is a close personal friend of Claudia's, which just goes to show, no one is so gorgeous and glamorous they don't appreciate a fat mate to take to discos.

In conclusion, it's not the fact that Supermodels often starve themselves in order to do their job; jockeys do this and no one complains. I just wish they would have more sense of humour, and take the piss out of themselves a bit; I hate that look into the camera, mouth half open in a pout, eyes registering unconvincing surprise, the kind of look you used to see on the face of *Crossroads* actors when they'd been told their husband/wife had been kidnapped by international terrorists in Brazil, and unless they left three quid in a pigbin of a motorway service station outside Solihull they would never leave their key at reception again.

Now come on – lots of these girls are from South London. Naomi, Kate – so let's see a bit of South London culture, girls . . . let's see you reverting to type a bit – get pissed on Malibu and cream soda before the show – start abusing the people in the audience . . . 'Oi, Patrick Lichfield, who you lookin' at? . . . you seen enough, 'ave yer? Do you wanna fight? Outside? . . . 'Ere, you, Prince Albert of Monaco . . . my mate fancies you! Ha! . . . not really.' It would be a bit more of a laugh, wouldn't it?

But all I can say is – we're all mortal. Supermodels . . . there is always someone who is a bit more lovely than you are – now you can just see RuPaul, and weep.

DIANA – HER TRUE STORY
A review of the made-for-TV movie

An everyday tale of upper-class folk whose love lives are as unhappy and complicated as their teeth – oh, those teeth; on one level it's a splatter movie for dentists. It's wonderfully bad – slice it where you like it's a lemon, excuse the pun, Squidgy. It has the production values of a *Crimewatch* reconstruction – which basically is what it is. The impressions of the Royal Family fall into two categories – 'nothing like them' and 'really like them'.

Firmly in the 'nothing like' camp is the Duke of Edinburgh. Corking lines though: 'How long does it take to find a Protestant virgin?' A joke to which he never delivers the punchline. The Queen Mother is *ace* as she trundles in and out like Amy Turtle with as much grasp of the plot. Honest as the day is long, she could be trusted with anything except dialogue. 'That's the trouble with boys,' she says, 'they so often come up short.'

Exactly like him, however, and camp as Carmen Miranda, is David Threlfall as Prince Charles. Tight-arsed to a degree that would cause ducks to comment, lips thinner than his wife's, his teeth appear to dance about in his mouth, resulting in his apparent terror that they will escape altogether. To prevent this disaster he wraps his upper lip firmly around them, like a posh-gob Humphrey Bogart. Genetically challenged, no oil painting (unless it's a Jackson Pollock), Chuck expresses a penchant for getting to know cows by their udders (some royal milky parlour game, 'I'll name that nipple in one'). A waste of tweed but harmless.

Not so Diana – alternately screeching and simpering, twisting her neck and looking from under her eyelashes like Bambi with whiplash, she is a nightmare. Squidgy, the human pop sock, rises from riches to obscene wealth. Selina Scott Thomas who plays her, now she looks more like Joanna Lumley in *The New Avengers* and behaves like Joanna Lumley in *Absolutely Fabulous*. In fact, whenever Di sticks her head into the toilet, it's hard to tell if it's to be sick or to do something about the Purdy haircut. As for her ability to pass the Radio 4 test, even her own family agree she is a bit of a Spambrain. Poor Diana, she is so thick . . . and yet so thin. 'Is she up to the job?' people keep asking. 'Well, no she's not', but she gets it by lying at the interview. She pretends to like the brainy old crap that Chuck likes, instead of Duran Duran and novelty pencil cases. And her entertaining line, when Charles quotes Ruskin on gardens, she says, 'Oh yar, I think Ruskin said that', as her eyes clearly register, 'Who the fluffy flip-flops is Ruskin?'

But she gets her man. 'Has she got ambitions?' asks Amy Turtle. Has she? Has Imelda Marcos got a pair of slingbacks? The marriage is of course a disaster. Blimey, no wonder most of the family stayed away from Princess Anne's wedding – terrified of catching the bouquet. The girl's eating disorders start on her honeymoon, and Di goes from see-through skirt to see-through body in a trice. Soon she's chucking up like Oliver Reed at a beer festival. Everything makes this girl sick – eating, pregnancy, being with Charles, she is the All England Hurling Champion. Her sister helpfully suggests, 'You mistake throwing up for dieting.' In fact this kind of conceptual dyslexia afflicts Di quite a lot – she mistakes giggling for charm, tabloid journalists for loyal admirers, and Charles for a handsome Prince – he must have sent a mate along in his place. Well, after four hours of this brain candy I felt a bit queasy myself. At one point we see Di wearing a jumper emblazoned with the legend 'I'm a luxury few can afford' slapped across it. Mmm, a good Christmas prezzie idea for the in-laws I think, Squidgy.

LINDA LIVE
onstage at the Duchess Public House, Leeds, 3 August 1993

The artist formerly known as Prince

Well – this reminds me of last night. I went to see Prince at the Sheffield Arena and it was very much like this sort of set-up really. Twelve thousand people chanting, 'You sexy motherfucker!' I thought, blimey – I've come for a quiet night out . . . No, it was amazing because it's this huge great place and we were at the back and there was this little tiny Prince running about singing '*Ooh! You sexy motherfucker!*' – it must have been terrible if you were really at the back 'cos it looked like an erotic flea circus. There he is running all over the place . . . and he's not called Prince any more and there's this call, 'What's my name?' and everyone goes, 'PRINCE – YOU SEXY MOTHERFUCKER!' and he goes, 'No – it's not!' Well, what the fuck is your name then, if it's not Prince? Oh, he's changed his name to a squiggle now – I dunno, he's not Prince now, he's Rex – he's Rover, I dunno. He's doolally, I know that . . .

By-election

The Christchurch by-election – that was so funny. I loved it. The funniest bit about it was the Liberal Democrat winning. The look on her face! It was like – ooh er . . . no, no, er . . . no – I never win, you know, raffles . . . my brother-in-law – he always wins. He won a colour telly the other day, but no – I never win. Are you sure? Is that on a pink ticket? Oh, I've lost it now – I threw it away because I didn't think I'd win . . .

And old John Major came out with a sparkling one after that, didn't he?

'Well, what do you think – you've just been absolutely trounced here you know – they've got a 16,000 majority and you used to have a 25,000 majority, how do you feel? What do you think about it?'

' . . . er, disappointing . . .'

Disappointing? Well – a master of understatement if nothing else. Disappointing? Fucked comprehensively – disappointing? As an understatement that's on the level of the Spanish Inquisition saying, 'Well, we were only asking! We won't ask again.'

Name tags

There's going to be a review of the police, apparently – a new code of conduct for the police. I suppose that means . . . 'After you, down the stairs!' And this is under the Citizens' Charter of course – which is a *cracking* read if you get the chance – no, really, marvellous. There's a lovely bit in there about name tags for the police. They've got to have their names in their gloves and everything – so there's no arguing back at the station. No, it saves a lot of fussing and fighting, really. 'No, you share them – you share them.' They're going to have name tags, according to John Major. He's obsessed with everyone having name tags – like McDonald's . . . 'You've just been fitted up by PC McDonald.' But anyway, the Police Federation are going ape-shit about this – as they are about the productivity business as well. They should just roll up their trouser legs, I'm sorry – sleeves – and get on with it . . .

They're going ape-shit about it, saying, 'John – what a shit idea that is, it's one of your worst ideas ever, mate – this idea of name tags!'

Imagine a riot situation. An officer is wearing his name tag – a rioter could see that and use the name to taunt that officer. Well, I could see that would be upsetting really.

Just picture the scene. There's your riot – bottles, stones flying, banners, Molotov cocktails – screaming, shouting . . . there's your policeman there, riot shield, truncheon – tagged up there. Suddenly through this maelstrom he hears, 'You, you fucking fascist running pig of capitalism! – you bloody bastard! You're going to go home in a fucking ambulance . . . COLIN!'

It would be upsetting really, wouldn't it? You'd be there going, 'Huh . . . flip! It wasn't only me.' You get all the way home and you're thinking – well actually, it was Trevor's idea now I come to think of it – the whole riot . . . never hear Trevor, do you? Oh no . . .

I think it would be divisive really – I think it would.

Graham Taylor

If we get a bad result in international football, if we lose – we never just announce after the match, 'Well, we were poxy – and they weren't, really, and that's why they won.'

Take, for example, Sweden in the European Championship. When Sweden beat England – comprehensively. That great footballing nation of Sweden – I don't think they normally even play football. They normally play . . . fish . . . or something, don't they? Or kick a crispbread around – I don't know. But anyway they beat us and Graham Taylor's excuse was marvellous. He was asked, 'Well, Graham – why do you think we've lost this match?' and he said, 'Er . . . half-time!'

'Sorry, Graham, what was that?'

'Half-time! – you see, we were doing quite well up until half-time, and then after half-time we just seemed to lose it completely. And to be honest, we could have done without half-time.'

I think, well – isn't that the fucking Swedes, eh? They seemed so nice, on the surface, with their open sandwiches and their smorgasbord and their Abba music, and their soft pornography . . . they seemed so nice. And then – they revive that ancient, seldom used, half-time law. They dusted that one off, under the terms of which, half-way through the game, half-time is called.

Well, our English boys were fucked. Our brave English boys –
they left the field of play . . . thought it was the end of the match
and pigged out on oranges. Totally pigged out. Then they're horrified to find . . . they've got to play another half!

They're bloated. They come running back on – and then they've
got to play the other way round. So they're dizzy – disoriented . . .

And then – we're not used to those big scary goalposts . . . we
normally have two cardigans on the grass!

To a heckler

. . . who stands up amidst the tables and enunciates clearly and loud-
ly, after Linda's reference to the small railway station at Kirk Sandall:
'I bought tickets to go there!'
You bought tickets to go there ? Well, you'll miss it if you're not
careful – don't let us keep you, please.

He starts speaking loudly again . . .
Oh no! – that wasn't an invitation – just sit down. Show-and-tell
time is finished now – sit down. Has someone got some keys or
something he could play with for a bit? But you can tell he's an
anally retentive sort of heckler because he was going, 'Miss, miss –
oh miss . . . *me!*'

Go on – just play nicely and you'll get an extra milk at break. Sit
down now – you should have gone at playtime.

LINDA LIVE
onstage at the Lescar Hotel, Sheffield, 26 July 1993

Well, thank you for choosing this evening above all the other rival
attractions in Sheffield on a Monday night. It's very nice of you
to have turned out tonight. I only wish I could think of something
to say . . . I feel such a fraud. The only problem with so many of
you in this room is, of course, passive smoking. It's a terrible
thing, it's a terrible problem these days, passive smoking –
as you've probably found. How many of you out there reckon

you're passive smokers? (cheers). Well, that wasn't all that passive, was it?

'Yes, we're passive smokers – and we're bloody annoyed about it! Probably going to kill us in thirty years' time, you bastards.'

Yes, well, I'd just like to say to the passive smokers out there – would you mind, start buying your own! 'Cos smokers are fucked off about it, to be totally honest . . . some of you scroungers are smoking 150 fags a day! You've never shelled out for a box in your life – how's that right? – never right . . .

Now then, what have I been up to lately? Well, I've been to see Jurassic Park and what a beautiful sports arena it is. We spent our money well on that, didn't we? Really! What is going on in Sheffield – what is going on? One good thing, I suppose, about the whole debacle – the whole World Student Games lark – , is, you can pick up some right bargains in the Sheffield Closing Down Sale. Bargains! I tell you what, I bought thousands of 'It's our year!' T-shirts – and I tell you what, they're shifting like wildfire in Bosnia . . . they're the biggest sellers this season, they really are, and those attractive little World Student Games tracksuits – in those lovely, sort of bed-jacket colours – very fetching. Make you look like a student from the Christian Union . . . they're selling rather well. I think we've got to cheer ourselves up, through the recession in Sheffield. There is something intrinsically and wonderfully Sheffield about the 'Under 25' column in the *Star*. I do love that actually – such bizarre things for sale. Crossbow parts, I saw the other day . . . *Crossbow parts, suit enthusiast – no time-wasters.*

I bet there are people who turn up and say, 'Nah! I wanted a blue one really . . . it wouldn't go with our curtains, would it, that?' Bizarre things . . . *the ability to see into the future – ten quid. Unwanted gift.*

Anyway, while some things in Sheffield – like the transport – are a bit on the skids, there are other things that are opening out really. Like you can now go, once again, overland to Afghanistan, that route's re-opened – overland to Afghanistan. But the 52 from Broomhill to the railway station . . . I have been down roads on that bus I never knew existed. In fact, I don't think they do exist. I think, I'll hop on the bus down to the railway station – now I've walked three or four hours, something like that . . . and you know where it's diverted to now, don't you? Down Mardy Street . . . 'Mardy Street? Mardy Street? There ain't been no Mardy Street in Sheffield these past thirty years, my dear.'

And as if the bus wasn't bad enough before . . . the fucking Eager Beaver – no . . . the Stupid Bastard, it ought to be. For a start, there's no room for any luggage. If you're going to the railway station on the Eager Beaver, you can't have any luggage that's more than . . . your ticket really. Oh Lord, and then you get to the station and then you're faced with those lovely little local train services – the Sprinter! The Sprinter? . . . well, it's not Ben Johnson, is it? If it is, it's taken the wrong fucking drugs and it's on Mogadon! Great train journeys of our time – Sheffield to Leeds! Who, what or where . . . is Kirk Sandall? What kind of a name is that for a town? How can you have a bit of civic pride in a place called Kirk Sandall? Colin Slipper! Ben Hush Puppy! 'Cos whenever I travel on those services I think, I think . . . I can't help feeling what a pity it is, that all these evil explorers like Christopher Columbus didn't have to start their journeys with the Sprinter between Sheffield and Leeds. 'Cos they'd get as far as Kirk Sandall – it would take all day . . . and they'd get really fucked off and get a taxi home, wouldn't they? Save the indigenous people of the world a lot of trouble.

I do like living in Sheffield. I've lived here for quite some time now. One thing I do find a bit of a drawback with Sheffield is, I like the sea myself and it's not at the seaside, Sheffield, is it? Of course, with global warming, Lincoln will go. So that'll be all right. It wouldn't be missed really, would it? I should think the sea would rather be here than at Skegness at the moment – like Siberia, isn't it? No, that is a problem – but not such a problem if you live in Broomhill really. 'Cos you always have that wonderful stirring sight, that stirring sight of a fleet of wheelie bins in full flight, in full sail, billowing their way down Lydgate Lane. A noble sight for a seafaring nation, I feel. But enough parochial stuff really – I won't use that one in Edinburgh . . . how am I going to crowbar that in then? 'You may have visited Sheffield – ah well, if you do . . .' Hardly likely, is it really? American tourist sitting there thinking, 'Well, what shall we do? We've come over to Britain – shall we go to the Edin-boro Festival or She-field? Hey, let's go on an Eager Beaver!'

Well, let's move to more international matters, shall we?. . . serious and important matters of state. He's gonna have to go really, isn't he? It's been a bad week for your man at the top, hasn't it? He's gonna have to go – Ted Dexter!

I really have enjoyed watching the cricket – I really have enjoyed it so much, largely 'cos of Geoffrey Boycott and Fred Trueman. Now – who's going to take over from Ted Dexter? Well, it can't be Fred Trueman, because I've worked out over the past few days that old Fred is suffering from the early onset of Alzheimer's disease – this is true. Because he's sitting up there in the commentary box, looking down at the devastation below and saying, 'What is going on out there?' And I'm thinking, well, Fred – it's what happened yesterday, isn't it? An England collapse. It happened yesterday, and the day before . . . he gets confused, with it being the bowling collapse yesterday and the batting collapse today. You'd think he'd never seen it before. 'What is going on?' For fuck's sake, you should be able to follow it by now, Fred. And Geoffrey Boycott – well, yes, he . . . well I'm in two minds about Geoffrey Boycott, really. 'Cos on the one hand I'm almost sure he's not a fictional character, because I remember him batting for England and all that and now he's on the telly all the time doing commentary, but you're almost convinced that he's a Harry Enfield character. He's like the northern version of 'Oh, you don't wanna do that!' He's a fucking know-it-all. All the time – 'You don't want to bat like that, you don't play *crikkit* like that – on that sort of *wikkit!*' He thinks he knows everything and he's not exactly pushing himself forward for that job of England manager, is he? Ooh no – 'I think what you need here is really . . . you need someone who knows a bit about *crikkit*, you know – who's batted on a sticky *wikkit*, who's not impressed by what's happening for batting

these days – up at t'younger end . . . and someone who hasn't
booked their winter holiday yet.' I think it could be yours, that job,
Geoff . . .

I must admit, I am a bit of a cricket fan, I do enjoy cricket.
Largely, I think I enjoy it because it's the most civilised sport really.
I really think it is. Because I love the idea of a sport played, internationally, for high stakes – a lot riding on it, a lot of national pride
. . . in which people stop for tea. There's such a thing in this sport
as tea-time. I love that.

You know, there's a serious game going on . . . 'And now, in this
Fifth Test against Pakistan, Wasim Akram is coming on to bowl –
and there's a lot to play for here, everything depends on . . . oh –
tea!' And they're off straight away. No moaning, no whining, is
there? There's no 'Time for tea, Wasim.' 'Oh no, I want to bowl this
over, 'snot fair. It's still light!' Never any messing about – straight in
for tea. Very gentlemanly, in for tea. I like that. And another thing I
like about cricket is, because most of the commentators apart from
Boycott and Trueman – who are old tykes – are very old-worldly,
they have an innocence and naiveté about them that makes them
sometimes say, in the course of their commentary, inadvertently
rude things. They sometimes do little double-entendres – you know,
little innuendos – without realising it. It's quite charming really:
'Now we're at the start of play . . . and we're coming in to play –
and the bowler's Holding, the batsman's Willey.'

Quite rude . . . and, 'Here we are and we're about to commence
play. And there's Simpson, in his usual position – standing with his
legs wide open, at first slip . . . waiting for a tickle.' Ooh, quite
rude.

Still, an ungentlemanly element is creeping into cricket, I'm sad
to say. Well, we can't bear to lose, can we? Because we had an
empire once, we think we should never lose at games, and if we do
we're going home and we're taking our bat and that's it – we're not
playing.

It's ludicrous because the idea of the British Empire is such an
outmoded idea. The British Empire now, if it were a being, would
be living out its days in some sunshine home on the South Coast,

wouldn't it? Boring the tits off everyone, shuffling around in oversize slippers, boring everyone with their press cuttings of when they were famous.

'Ooh look, ooh yes! I was very popular in the world once – ooh yes! I went all over the world. Look, you see here – they loved me here . . . Sri Lanka – Sri Lanka. Of course we used to call that Ceylon. In my younger days it was Ceylon. Now let me see, what have we got here? Oh yes! they loved us there – Zimbabwe. Zimbabwe! Of course we didn't call it Zimbabwe then, it was Rhodesia. Rhodesia, you see? And this, oh, this marvellous tour I had here – now what was it? India! India – what did we used to call that? Oh yes! . . . Ours!'

It's nonsense now of course, but we still think we should win at everything. And so, like I say, we are playing cricket with Pakistan and the Pakistanis are winning by the expedient of being quite good at cricket . . . and so the English fans – I was there at the time – started taunting the Pakistani fans, shouting,

'One Salman Rushdie – there's only one Salman Rushdie . . .
you can't beat the boy from Penguin, the boy from Penguin he's
our boy!'

And I thought, well, I can see what you're getting at there, lads, really. They're trying to find an upside to everything – they're trying to see a little good in everyone. And I think . . . well, at least it's an educated heckle – at least it's a literary heckle – I quite like that. You know, the Pakistanis should have responded in kind. They should have started chanting,

'William Shakespeare – William Shakespeare, you're not writing any more,
you only write when you're alive – write when you're ali-ive
you sonnet-writing slaphead.'

That would get the lads.
How would you taunt a French sporting team? How would you

go about that? You'd have to get a bit philosophical – a bit deep, wouldn't you? You'd have to sit there chanting,

'One Jean-Paul Sartre, there's only one Jean-Paul Sartre . . .
being and nothingness
being and nothingness
Simone de Beauvoir
Simone de Beauvoir
get your tits out for the lads!'

I don't like rugby. The only good thing that happened in rugby was when the tiny little, weenie island of Western Samoa beat the great rugby-playing nation of Wales. I think that's brilliant. I love giant-killing in sport – I think that's great. Western Samoa beat Wales . . . not even the *whole* of Samoa, is it? When you think about it – they didn't even pick a team from the whole island. It's like Germany being beaten by North Kent.

That's enough about sport. Sex. I think we'll talk about that, shall we? Sex and politics – sex and politicians. I never understand how *any* politician gets a shag really – can you? A classic example – the David Mellor sex scandal. This stands as a classic example because, frankly, shagging David Mellor really isn't a job for the voluntary sector. I don't think so. I think that should be a proper job, with a pension and things like that, you know. It has to be done – I think they would be even loopier without sex, but let's pay people handsomely to do it. Because that case was extraordinary and I bet you're the same as me – we're not shocked by these scandals involving politicians. I bet when that happened, when you opened the paper, your response was not, 'Good God, that's outrageous. A man in his job – he should be running the country, not messing about like this – no wonder we're in a state – terrible.' No, that wasn't the response. You open the paper, you read about that and you go . . . 'Ha ha ha ha – I don't think so, Dave!' I don't think so . . . in your dreams, perhaps. You can't believe it. The interesting person in that relationship is not him, it's her, Antonia. She's an interesting woman, I think. A woman of mystery . . . a mystery woman.

Antonia de Sancha – always described as 'unemployed actress'. Unemployed actress? That's never right, is it? How's she an unemployed actress? God – if you can feign sexual interest in David Mellor . . . I should think Chekhov's a piece of piss. Oh, she'd always work, wouldn't she – a woman of her talents? She'd always work . . . so she thinks – I'm an actress, it's a role – I'll prepare. She gets to the bedroom situation. He's in a kit-off situation and there's Antonia giving it 'Red lorry, yellow lorry – Peter Piper picked a peck of pickled pepper'. Because he does come into that category of chap who you dress with your eyes really. He's a man for mentally dressing – even if he's wearing a suit at the time. One suit, David? – not enough – another, please, on top. And a balaclava – on backwards. But the hair – that's the main unattractive thing. What barber told him that suited him? Someone winding him up there . . . 'Yes, David – that'll suit you, mate . . . a greasy, oily flap of dirty-looking patent leather wafting about down one side of your mush – that'll drive those unemployed actresses mental!' You look at that hair and you think . . . the last woman who ran her fingers through it was the fucking nit-nurse.

I watched a bit of that programme about Kinnock last night – until I was sick . . . the Prime Minister we never had! Well, thank fuck for that, really! Don't you just hate him – he's useless, he's terrible . . . and he bloody *lost!* That's another reason to hate him – he lost. How could he have done it? You look at him there and he's looking all ill and you think – good! Good! – glad you're ill – good! Because how could you do it? They were three points ahead beforehand and they thought that was good? The Hezbollah would have been twenty points ahead! It's incredible. And there's all this about how it would have been different. Well, of course he wouldn't have been different from John Major because they're exactly the same bloke. They're blokes who were not up to the job – lied at the interview – got the job . . . panic. You know yourself how it is, probably. You talk yourself up at the interview – you say you're good at computing and stuff you can't do. Then, oh no – you've got the job – you panic, you're frozen sat at the desk. It's the same with John – he'd be sat there all day, staring into space . . . as you do – hiding all his work in his desk. Hiding it all in there. Sat staring out of the window – until someone comes past. He's just spent the whole day photocopying his bum, really. Flicking paper clips and making long-distance phone calls – like you do. Until you get tumbled – that's all you're going to do.

It's a mysterious business, sex, isn't it? They try to make laws about it – like for the sado-masochists. Blokes who were sent to prison for a bit of sado-masochism . . . bit of a flawed logic, that one, isn't it? How do you punish a sado-masochist? How does that work? 'Oh! You're a sado-masochist. We find that so unacceptable, we're going to bang you up in jail. Horrible hard bed to sleep on, nasty food, all the warders being horrible to you – all the other prisoners will hate you because you're a sex offender.' And they think, 'Oh – result! My romantic life is sorted for the next seven years.' Ridiculous idea. If you're serious about punishing them, I suppose you should sentence them to three years of aromatherapy . . . but it's mysterious – sex. Sexual allure – what creates sexual allure? In pursuit of that aim, I've been watching *Diana, Her True Story*. I don't know if you've watched that – *Diana, Her True Story*? Interesting – interesting bit of film. It's like a filmic version of a not properly defrosted, really nasty Bejam Black Forest gâteau. It's like – you're really pissed and you come in, and you think, oh, that's horrible . . . I'll have a bit. It's really horrible – it's crap, it's rubbish. Half an hour later you find yourself saying, oh, I can't believe I finished all that!. I've realised the whole thing of her allure, of her being one of the most beautiful women in the world, is based on her posing like this all the time . . . well, come on, you should all be under my spell by now – come on. But she just looks like Bambi with whiplash. Dozy woman.

But I do feel sorry for these royal women, on the whole, because they have these miserable marriages. I do have a theory about this, actually. I think what it is really is that these upper-class women spend their adolescence in the company of horses . . . well, they do, don't they? Romping around at the gymkhana and what have you. And then they reach puberty – marriage arranged – and there's the husband. Immediately disappointed, aren't they?

Because they spend all their time with horses and they expect their husband to be equally . . . as well read! Oh, do keep up, please! There's a lot to get through there – you can be too subtle sometimes, can't you? People like a good knob-joke, really. But there you are – it's not all beer and skittles, is it? But yes – royalty. The Queen Mother. She's going to die soon, isn't she? Well, you can see it because little things keep going wrong with her. And you think – any minute now, she's gonna die. And it shows how things have changed, because I used to dread the Queen Mother dying. I used to dread it because I used to think, well, that would be the telly fucked for two weeks, wouldn't it? Two weeks of solemn music and Scottish Highland scenes. But now no one cares about royalty. Now it would just be the last item on the news, wouldn't it? There would be Martin Lewis saying . . . 'And on a lighter note . . .' 'Cos now no one cares.

I thought it was really funny when she got that thing stuck in her throat and there was a big announcement on the news: 'The Queen Mother has got something stuck in her throat and has been seen by a specialist.' And I couldn't help thinking . . . that's rather a narrow field of specialisation. Can't be a living, surely, can it – retrieving gear out of the Queen Mother's throat? I thought, you lazy bastard, you've only worked twice in ten years!

Someone should tell that old girl – you can't eat a whole salmon sideways. Showing off down the pub, I suppose, with her mates: 'Yeah! I can eat a yard of salmon – any way you like.'

The international scene isn't too encouraging really. You look around at the international scene and it's a bit grim, really. Eastern Europe – what used to be the Soviet Union – there's anarchy and just a terrible mess. And you think, well, it's good that the Soviet Union broke down, Stalinism was terrible and all that. That leaves some good things that are happening. Like they're no longer producing nuclear weapons – in fact I believe some of the old nuclear weapon factories are being turned over to civilian use, and some of them are being used to make microwaves. Microwave ovens – in old nuclear component factories . . . you'd want to be careful of one of those, wouldn't you? And I bet I know where'd they'd stock them . . .

the Co-op! Next to the tinned carrots. No, but I can't imagine there's much of a home market for them – microwave ovens, in Moscow. Can you imagine? Kids coming home from school –

'What's for tea, Mum?'

'Nothing – but it'll be ready in a trice!'

All the states are breaking up and there's all this stuff about ethnic division. Yeah, there is that . . . but basically it's about money. When countries split up, it's just the same as when couples split up. What you're really arguing about is, who gets what. OK – so there's a bit of emotion involved. But who gets the video, who gets the settee – I bought that, I bought that. And it's the same with these countries in the old Eastern bloc. They've got Georgia and what have you – they're all arguing like couples. They've lived together miserably for twenty years – they've decided to split up, and now they're arguing about who gets what.

'Go on then, go – just leave. Just go back to your Mother Russia, go on.'

'You leave my mother out of it – at least my family aren't mad.'

'Well, who certified my family mad then – put them all in psychiatric hospitals, just because they wouldn't come every year to your bloody May Day party? To watch you playing with your tanks. To listen to your favourite records – *Now That's What I Call Martial Music!* – over and over again. And while you're at it – take your stack of *What Submarine* magazines, all right? 'Cos I'm sick of dusting them. And Chernobyl – I think you'll find that's yours.'

'No, that's yours.'

'No, no, that's definitely yours.'

'Oh you never want to do what I want to do, do you?'

'Oh yes? Aren't you forgetting something? What about our lovely little holiday in Afghanistan, eh? What about that? That was your idea. It cost us a bloody fortune. The hotels were demolished before we even bloody got there – you lied about the beaches . . .'

'All right then, if you're gonna be like that – I'm having the army!'

'Oh, are you? Having custody of the army, are you? Are you sure it's yours?'

'You can't hurt me any more . . .'

'Oh, can't I? Can't I? – well, every treaty I ever signed with you – I faked!'

That's how they'll split up – just like people.

And what can you say about Bosnia – well, we're fed up with it now, aren't we? I think the UN with Bosnia, now, are pretty much like your dad with last year's Christmas tree lights – fascinated for half an hour. 'I'm going to get this to work . . . fuck it, we'll get another lot.'

Fed up now, aren't we? The UN peacekeeping force – that's inspired a bit of confidence, hasn't it? The UN peacekeeping force – not exactly on a roll are they, when we look around the world. Not exactly on a roll.

'Well, we tried – we sent our best people. I mean . . . what do you want – Sam Fox? All the top diplomats – they all went . . .'

But again, the main problem – well, yes, there is the ethnic divide, but the main problem is – they're tooled up. Loads of people hate each other when they live next door . . .

Brighton and Hove! Can't stand each other. And they're next to each other – and they hate each other. But it's no problem 'cos they're not tooled up. If they were, we'd have that here – we'd have conflict here. They're tooled up. And who tools them up? The arms trade. I always think that's a bit of a misnomer – a bit of a weird use of language. Arms trade. Not a trade really, is it? You can't get City and Guilds in arms dealing at a tertiary college – no. Arms trade – it sounds so innocuous. Arms fair – let's go to the arms fair, down the village green! Perhaps we could win a goldfish – in a body bag. Arms fair . . . if there was a legitimate trade, they'd sell those things, guns and bombs, in a supermarket. Or big chain stores. You'd have a chain of outlets – like Deadenhams . . . Unsafeways . . .

You'd have demonstrations and free offers. In fact you'd have demonstrations by those bloody awful Cole Brothers women and the women who shanghai you in the perfumery bit. You're stunned by the perfume and suddenly there's this woman with baked bean-coloured make-up coming towards you . . . and that's what the arms trade demonstration would be like. It would be like a cosmetics demonstration and you'd have a little bit of shopping music in the backgrounds – *Eine Kleine Shopping Muzak*.

Oh, it's just like Meadowhall, isn't it? Or Tinsley shopping precinct . . . and so, here's our arms trade demonstrator – 'Hello – and welcome to our new "Twilight of the World" range, our stunning new collection for nuclear winter. Now, for those persistent racial problems, why not try our new Ethnic Cleanser, "Pogrom" – apply vigorously to the affected area and then wipe off the face of the earth. For persistent outbreaks, to eliminate those last spots of resistance, why not try our new "I Can't Believe It's Not a Kalashnikov" – go on, leaders, treat yourself. Treat yourself to a bit of territory. Tell yourself, I want it, I need it, I'll have it. Now, for those particularly sensitive areas, why not use our new range -- UN. It's entirely cosmetic, it does nothing. Apply half-heartedly with our new hand-wringing cream. Now, people often come up to me and say, "Can you save my face?" Well, I can. So for those secret little deals, those secret little Iraqi liaisons – those little rendezvous you would like nobody to know about . . . why not try "Embargo", the mark of the middle man? Now, for a touch of mystery, that adventurous touch, that Latin touch – why not visit the "Missing Body Shop"? Collect your free nail remover and watch your problems disappear. Now you're probably sitting there thinking, "Oh, I'm such a hideous old, blood-soaked dictator of a thing – nobody will deal with me." How wrong you are! We are sole suppliers to the United States government of "Turn a Blind Eye Liner" – use always in conjunction with "Oil of Kuwaiti", a touch of "Massacre" and blusher – oh, you won't need that . . . I'm Marlene from the House of Charnel – thank you for your time and patience. And for that finishing touch, for those romantic evenings when you really want to take the enemy out, why not try our stunning new nerve gas . . . "Paralyse", by Calvin Klein. They'll know you're using it.'

Oh dear me, that was a bit grim, wasn't it? It was a bit miserable but there you are – as you get older you get preoccupied with these things. When you're young and carefree you don't worry about these things. When you're a teenager you don't think of that, the world. You think about yourself. You are the world – totally.

We are the world – I am the adolescents. Yes. You just think totally of yourself – you're obsessed with yourself. You're morbidly, morbidly sensitive, aren't you? Also, in your teens, you put on an awful lot of weight . . . on that bottom lip. It all goes there, doesn't it? Three stone. You could walk around with a window box on there, just sulking and moaning the whole time. Moaning – obsessed with your personal appearance. My particular hang-up when I was a teenager – my nose. Obsessed with the size of my nose. I kept staring in the mirror, trying to reduce it by hypnosis – I should have come here of a Wednesday – I think you've got hypnosis then – but of course you get older and wiser and you don't worry about crap like that any more, do you? When you get older you just tend to drink more – well, you do. But just when you're at your most sensitive – your family are at their most insensitive. They think you're invisible, don't they? It's like you are this invisible teenager – they think they can talk about every detail of your private life – while you're there. You're the invisible teenager but you forgot to put those bandages on. And you're sitting there – and you're just this big pair of trainers and a lip, in the chair. And they're going, 'Oh, she doesn't go out with boys yet – she's a bit shy – I SAY YOU'RE A BIT SHY!'

That brings you out of your shell a bit, doesn't it . . . ? And you realise – no matter how old you get – your family never know you, do they? And I tell you what makes you realise this – the cards they send you on your birthday. Always, if you're a lad, it's a picture of a vintage car or fly fishing. If you're a girl, pony trekking or ballerinas . . . all very popular activities in South London, I can tell you. You open it with a sinking heart to read this mawkish verse, because you know your auntie or grandad has spent hours choosing a *nice verse*. And it'll be something like –

> *On your birthday*
> *Be happy for ever*
> *A chain of love*

That time will not sever
Have a lovely time
My darling Trevor

And they've spent fucking hours looking for that. And if they really knew you and they really understood your lifestyle, instead of the fly fishing and labradors and the rest of it, on the front of that card there'd be a few empty cans with some fags stubbed out in them. And an unpaid Council Tax bill. That's what would be there, and the verse inside would be something like –

Dear grandchild
On your birthday enjoy a few jokes
Have shitloads to drink and a few lines of coke
My dear, on your vomit, please try not to choke.

That would be more it, really, wouldn't it?

But you get older and you do notice your attitudes changing. I find myself changing quite a lot – especially with children, really. I do get a bit hacked off with kids. Especially at shows. Now this is unusual, well, it's unusual for Sheffield – in that it's a show and not a benefit for something, isn't it? And the main advantage of it not being a benefit is – no raffle. The scourge of entertainment land – raffles. I hate a raffle. And when you do them for political organisations, like the SWP – I did one in London for the SWP, really nice do – there was this raffle. Massive mega-raffle which was like Live Aid or something. It just went on and on and on and on. There was a speaker *for* the raffle and a speaker *against* the raffle. And what gets me at these do's is the raffle prizes are not like a commercial raffle, where the goods are ordered in terms of how big a consumer item they are . . . like, first prize – mountain bike, fifth prize – nothing. That would be logical. In these do's the raffle prizes are organised in a triumph of optimism over what we know of human nature.

First prize – a pamphlet version of Trotsky's *Theory of Continuing Revolution* . . . in the cyrillic alphabet.

Fifth prize – a new car! And a trip to Brazil at carnival time!

The main thing about getting older is, I find myself irresistibly drawn to the Body Shop these days. Come out of it with a load of old tut, which brings you out in a rash 'cos it's not tested on animals!

I'm sorry – I'm fond of animals . . .

I've got sensitive skin – get that in a bunny's eyes please!

I'm not a bunny – there's only one me. You know what I'm saying.

The worst thing I ever bought from there – Cucumber Cleansing Milk. Makes the salad taste like shit.

Everything's rubbish these days. I watched *Stars in Their Eyes* the other night – have you ever watched that? *Stars in Their Eyes* . . . Matthew Kelly – he's nothing like Leslie Crowther, is he? How did he get on there? I'm more like Leslie Crowther than him!

Thank you and goodnight.

THE TREATMENT
Stuart Maconie, writer and broadcaster

Funny thing, 'this crazy business we call show', as Linda would have called it with a twinkle of irony. You can do the big high-profile telly shows or share a stage with superstars, or wangle some glamorous gig in an exotic locale, and yet the memory evaporates like Lew Grade's cigar smoke. Huge amounts of people may see or hear these moments but no one remembers them, nothing lingers, no one carries a torch for them down the years.

Then on the other hand you can do another show, one that wins no awards, tops no ratings and is, at best, tolerated by the network. And yet some people love it enough to organise their lives around it. Maybe not enough people to stop it getting cancelled, mind you, but enough to win it a real place in people's hearts. As I go about my business these days, people regularly stop me and ask about a show I used to host once. They tell me it was their favourite radio programme ever, recite choice moments they still remember, and ask whether there's any chance it might be coming back. I feel almost heartless telling them that as it was cancelled six years ago, I'm not holding my breath, to be honest.

That show was Radio 5 Live's *The Treatment*; the show on which I first met Linda Smith in 1996. I hosted *The Treatment* for most of its life, taking over from original host Simon Hoggart as the programme changed from being a fairly straight op-ed review of the week's news into something pretty unique, a decidedly comedic entertainment show (it even had sketches) that nevertheless had real journalistic substance.

In any given week, the show might feature comics like Steve Punt, Mark Steel, Jo Caulfield or political commentators, now media colossi, like Matthew Parris, Peter Oborne, Kevin Maguire or Steve Richards or columnists like Zoë Williams or Victoria Coren. It gave a chance for funny people to be serious and for the serious to loosen their corsets a little. The then unknown Rob Brydon performed the sketches, to give you some idea of the stellar array of new talent we encouraged on the show. And no one shone brighter than Linda.

The Treatment's format included both authored pieces and quickfire, knockabout discussion, and thus it suited her beautifully. She had one of the fastest minds I've ever encountered, dazzlingly quick and witty. But she was also an elegant craftswoman with words: she understood the music of scripted speech; she could lull you with gently rolling verbal landscapes but knew just where to lay the comic mine that would explode and bring the house down.

She appeared forty times between 1996 and the show's demise in 2000, delivering beautiful, mischievous, hilarious pieces about, among other things, the Millennium Dome, Mobile Phones, Digital TV and Frank Sinatra's funeral. No one was ever left unsure of Linda's politics, but even when she was skewering her favourite bêtes noires – Jeffrey Archer, the Royals or Tony Blair – it was always with a finesse that meant you didn't notice the blade till it was right between the ribs. She had a lightness of touch and a kind of charm that made most comics look boorish by comparison. Glancing at some of those subjects she wrote about now, no bells ring whatsoever. David Evans MP, anyone? All that remains of him is the echo of laughter that Linda inspired.

I also appeared several times with Linda on a Radio 4 programme called *Booked*. You will find examples of Linda's contributions later in this book. It was the kind of show that no focus group would ever approve of, no advertiser would ever court, and that only the BBC at its most endearingly high-minded would ever make. Essentially, it was a comedy panel game on the subject of literature, but that gives no idea of the level of erudition and preparation required. As well as being able to crack wise at a moment's notice about the works of, say, Walt Whitman or

Graham Greene, you'd also be expected to prepare elaborate skits and parodies and perform them, after scant rehearsal, with the rest of the panel. Backstage at *Booked* every week was like a common room on finals day: people chain-smoking, clutching sheets of notes, swearing and muttering partly remembered doggerel about Emily Brontë or Tolstoy, partly terrified, partly eager to show off.

To succeed properly on *Booked* – I'm not sure I ever did – you needed to be both bloody clever and pretty damn funny; Linda was both of these and always stood out, even in company that included David Stafford, Mark Thomas, Richard Coles, Mark Steel and others. Even when it infuriated you, which it did often, *Booked* made you feel glad that there was still room for this somewhere in a media world where 'lifestyle', 'makeover' and 'reality' were becoming the Holy Grail. It was also nice that it was recorded in little theatres in front of live audiences and you could have a pint with them afterwards in the little bar. In situations like these Linda was always charming and personable to fans and well-wishers. I think they could tell that Linda was at heart just like them: an ordinary person but one with an extraordinary mind.

Going back to *The Treatment*, we went on location quite a lot and so I got quite spectacularly drunk with her in, to name a few, Belfast, Edinburgh, Manchester, Birmingham, Newcastle – where a defeated hotel barman just gave us the key to the bar and let us get on with it – and once in Television Centre when she threw her shoe at me over some argument about Northern soul. Then she fell asleep on Rob Brydon. We've lost someone very special. But we have these flashes of imperishable brilliance to remember her by.

Stuart Maconie, 2006.

CLEAN UP TV

On Tuesday, Heritage Secretary Virginia Bottomley announced plans to curb gratuitous scenes on television and help to educate parents on the programmes they should make efforts to stop their children viewing. Linda Smith has been considering this vexed issue.

My old mum, as more famously did Jeanette Winterson's dad, liked to watch wrestling. And if he got as worked up about it as my mum, there can't have been much peace round their house of a Saturday afternoon. 'Pull his legs off! Break his neck! Jackie Pallo, you dirty sod!' I don't think I ever saw her happier. She also liked police dramas and would watch car smashes, stabbings and shootings with complete serenity. Then a cop or robber would say 'Piss off' and with her catchphrase 'nice talk' she'd hit that switch and start channel paddling (there weren't enough to surf in those days).

And now Virginia Bottomley (nice talk) wants to get her hands on the remote. She wants to protect children from sex and violence (always together these two, like Richard and Judy), perhaps with a 'V chip', which of course only kids will know how to work, whereby a password, say *IRANU*, would programme the TV's level of Richard and Judy.

Now, the fact that there is a lot of sleazy exploitative rubbish on TV should hardly surprise Mrs B., as it was her own Government that introduced the legislation that caused it. Shocking, isn't it? You give people a licence to print money and they only use it to, er, print money. How disappointing it must be when Carlton TV, instead of producing a season of Chekhov plays featuring Vanessa Redgrave, come up with the 'How much blue fluff is there in your man's belly button?' game show with Vanessa Feltz.

However, you are on dodgy ground claiming that entertainment is getting more violent and brutal when it's not that long ago that public hangings were real ratings busters. The Crusades, the 100 Years War, the Crimea War, all managed to get going without the benefit of *EastEnders*.

Therefore, I find it hard to believe that cheese and biscuits are the inevitable consequence of watching *Cracker*. No, my mum might have been Upton Park (a couple of stops short of Barking) but I'd rather trust her with the ostrich egg-sized hot potato of censorship than the cynical electioneering Virginia Bottomley. Nice talk.

FOOD TRENDS

Sixty-five per cent of women take just half an hour to prepare, cook and serve the family dinner, a survey revealed this week. Here's Linda Smith.

I'm the girl for this subject, Stuart, because I cook a bit, I know a rocket salad from an accident on the MIR space station, but I also get through a lot of takeaways, and the odd ready meal from the 'Lazy Bastard' range. Over the years, though, our eating habits have changed so much.

We've more convenience foods now: instant Instant Whip and of course Instant Tea – so much quicker. Just pour boiling water on Instant Tea. At last! An end to 'pouring boiling water on to a tea bag' misery. I must try and let go of my anger about the wasted years of tea bag drudgery behind me – oh, the time I could have saved! I could have learned languages, pottery . . . oh, leave it, Linda, it's gone, it's gone. I believe Marks and Spencer now market a cup of tea that's already been drunk for you – just a brown ring in a mug.

But what I really want to know is – where do they get those precocious little freaks who go on *Junior Master Chef*? Who is breeding these weirdos? With their warm salad of smoked venison and their seared red mullet with a top note of lemon grass, bass line of coriander all nestling on a duvet of swiss chard! Give them some fish fingers, half a pound of sherbet pips and send them out to play in the sunshine, for God's sake! And why, when we form a relationship and move in with someone else, do we buy a sandwich toaster? Deluding ourselves that it will be brilliant, we'll really use it a lot and have 'toasties' all the time, with all different fillings, what a tasty change from raw sandwiches . . . knowing full well even as we buy it, that by the end of the week it will be gathering dust in the gadget graveyard that is the cupboard under the sink. I don't know, but I'll leave you with a bit of advice: in a restaurant, never order the 'fan of melon' – it's just a waiter singing, 'Ooh aah, cantaloupe, I said ooh aah, cantaloupe!'

DAVID EVANS MP

A bloke called Evans was in trouble for mouthing off this week, but for once, not the one with the ginger hair. David Evans, the Conservative MP for Welwyn and Hatfield, landed himself, not to say his party, in a spot of bother after an unguarded interview with some schoolchildren. Linda Smith has been following the story.

Who'd be John Major, eh? In the opinion polls he's now slightly less popular than the Hezbollah, he's got Douglas Hogg apparently thinking that slaughter-house safety reports should be saved up as a surprise for a special occasion, he's got Tony Blair pestering him all the time: 'Are you leaving those carpets and curtains, John? How does the central heating work?' And now, what rough beast is this? It's a David Evans beast, wreathed in chins, mouthing off with the blissful un-self- consciousness that comes as a twin pack with pig ignorance. You think, blimey, if he says this to school kids what could Jeremy Paxman get out of him? Plans for a 1,000-year Reich. So now, of course, Mr Major has to go into his version of the despairing Dr Frankenstein 'Damn you, Igor, I told you to keep that creature in the laboratory!' routine, which with him comes out as 'Oh dear, someone's tired aren't they, eh! . . . showing off . . . now, have a little lie-down and one of these blue tablets.' He is cross, but you will notice he's not surprised. In the same way that I'm not surprised to see my feet at the end of my legs – I know they're there because they are mine. And Mr Evans belongs to Mr Major. Oh yes, one or two MPs have expressed horror, like Tory MP Elizabeth Peacock who says he's an outrage. Oh, is he really? Well, if you're surprised by that, missus, here's a shock – you know when Santa brings you presents at Christmas? It's your mum and dad really!

How can a party for whose membership the ultimate sexual fantasy is Miguel Portillo in a leather thong and jackboots singing 'Tomorrow Belongs to Me' not be full of weirdos? I know it's unfashionable to say so, but these people are not like us; they have an alien culture – they are aliens, at least one is a Vulcan. Oh – I'm afraid I have to raise the 'C'-word here. Class! Just as Sybil Fawlty would explain Manuel's shortcomings with the phrase 'He's from Barcelona', Evans's apologists say, 'He's working class', expecting us to decode this as 'so naturally he's a fat ignorant bigoted nutter bastard. Salt of the earth.' Well, Sir Oswald Mosley, Lady Birdwood, Alan Clark, are they all working class? As far as I know none of them ever started a sentence with the words ''Ere, guess who I had in the back of the cab the other day . . .'

No, the 'least said soonest mended' tendency in the Tory Party, who prefer not to think about the logical ends of the policies they espouse and the type of people their policies attract, need the now legendary Danny Baker-patented slap around the head. And in the interests of trade descriptions, the repulsive Mr Evans should be cloned, and stand as Tory candidate in every constituency under the banner:

ASK NOT WHAT YOUR COUNTRY CAN DO FOR YOU
OR YOU'LL GET A SMACK IN THE MOUTH
ALL RIGHT

TELEVISION AT SIXTY

Today sees the sixtieth anniversary of the spy in the corner – television. On 2 November 1936, Leslie Mitchell introduced the first official day of BBC broadcasting – the world's first public high-definition service. Linda Smith has been glued to the box.

Television, my childhood friend, companion of my youth and delayer of my adulthood, is sixty years old. Many Happy Repeats. But is telly nice or horrible? It's nice, definitely, I mean, do you know anyone who chooses not to have a TV? Of course you don't, because people like that are too weird to know – they don't have friends, they *hate* humanity, they're smug and anti-social – they think they're clever but they're not, they're stupid. They're psychopaths who should be registered with the police along with firearms enthusiasts and corporal punishment fans – these categories will overlap considerably, you'll find.

Far from destroying conversation, TV inspires it. When I was at school one episode of Monty Python would keep us going all week – *apart*, that is, from the homework-doing, non-smoking, middle-class saddies whose mum and dad wouldn't have TV in the house (see above). If television hadn't caught on, we'd be in a right state, people would have even more stupid hobbies than they've got now – more DIY, more putting up shelves, shelves would have shelves, nests of shelves, furniture smashed and turned into shelves. The Horror, the Horror. Children can learn so much from the telly – I don't mean from things like *Blue Peter* (*I* used to prefer the groovier, slacker-generation *Magpie, Blue Peter* was for *Look and Learn* readers), but from the strong emotions TV provokes. For me the word 'betrayal' was defined by the discovery that Johnny Morris was not a real zoo keeper. From watching Belle and Sebastian I learnt that French boys are pouty and sulky and that Pyrenean mountain dogs need a lot of exercise and thus are unsuitable pets for flat-dwellers.

I know some people think that watching telly leads to attention-whatsit thing, where you can't concentrate: oh, I'm bored, let's talk about something else – radio.

Yes – also nice. Like television, only the pictures are better, they say. But this is only true if you're on heavy medication.

APRIL FOOLS

Tuesday was on April 1st. Time-honoured folk tradition or incredibly irritating blot on the early spring landscape? Linda Smith . . .

It's a little-known fact that the feast of April Fools originates in medieval Transylvania. On the night of St Anorakus of the Internet, Vlad Beadlecula, the evil count, lured a hapless village wench, April, to his ancestral home, Castle Bouncy. Then, for a laugh, he mashed her up with custard and served her to his mates for pudding. Thus the wretched girl (played by Ingrid Pitt in the Hammer biopic, wasn't she a good sport?) became the first April Fool, and to this day we eat strawberry fromage frais in her memory – and once a year let nasty bastards with no sense of humour play tricks that aren't clever, or grown-up, or big in any way.

Oh, but what about that really clever and famous *Panorama* April Fools, you say, the report on spaghetti being harvested from pasta trees? And I say, yeah, what about it? That was in the sixties when all we ate in Britain was Spam.

Naturally people thought spaghetti grew on trees; they probably thought avocados were made from bathroom suites. Isn't it a bit suspicious that April Fools Day is popular in the same countries that Mr Bean is? In France, par exemple, they love an April Fools prank, that's after they've finished laughing at Marcel Marceau trying to escape from an imaginary box. Like weekends, weather and Bank Holidays, April Fools Day exists to give brain-dead DJs something to talk about: like the radio station that announced a 15-mile per hour speed limit in Blackpool and brought the town to a standstill – nothing funnier than sitting in traffic, is there?

As for the newspaper stories: a chimpanzee taking an award-winning photograph, yeah, Swampy to stand for Parliament, yeah, Lady Thatcher to be Prime Minister Blair's ambassador to Washington – you'd have to be really thick to believe any of those, wouldn't you?

HYGIENE

A recent survey showed that two-thirds of Americans say that they are more conscious of germs today than only a few years ago. Nearly 40 per cent are so anxious to dodge infection that they avoid touching surfaces in public places. Do we Brits have the same concerns or is this more American neuroticism? Here's Linda Smith.

What a break this is for Oprah Winfrey – just as she's thinking, 'Christ, I can't do *Hookers who love to crochet* a third time', along comes this survey. 'Well, Oprah, I realised I had a problem around hygiene when I forced my own mother to drink TCP before I would air-kiss her.' 'I know that pain, honey, I've been there myself, I too had a dysfunctional relationship with cleaning – I was once so abusive I used to napalm my toilet. We'll be back with hygiene abuse therapist 'Mr Muscle' and more of those *Women who love to kill the germs they hate too much* . . . after the break.'

I say women, because the received wisdom is that along with pot-pourri and salad, bleach is woman's gift to man – use it regularly, grasshopper. This isn't my experience, though, perhaps because I live with a Jewish man. Judaism's dietary laws make you more aware of hygiene, I suppose. In his parents' case, obsessed with it. The countryside is a place of fear and loathing for them due to its lack of wipe-clean surfaces, and a snack at their house is a rehearsal for senile dementia: 'I thought I left a cup of tea down there, oh . . . did I eat that sandwich? I must have done, the plate's gone, I don't remember though. Nurse, nurse, I'm frightened.'

My own mother had a firm but bizarre idea about hygiene and imbued the state of neighbours' washing lines with a moral dimension – a medieval code of justice, trial by washing. If she'd lived next to the Wests she'd have said, 'They must be innocent, their whites are lovely – you could go snow-blind looking at them sheets.' But she'd also say, 'You have to eat a bit of dirt before you die,' and never really believed that germs are invisible. If I talked about microbes and bacteria she'd say, 'Oh, are they really?' with the same placid disbelief with which years before she'd greet my stories about my invisible friend. But the old sayings are the best, I think, so here are my tips for health and hygiene;

> *Don't swallow chewing gum, it will wind round your heart*
> *Shed not a clout till May is out*
> *Red sky at night, excellent acid*
> *Never eat blackberries after November because the devil*
>   *spits on them then.*

Typical bloody man.

FOOTBALL WIDOWS

Manchester United claimed another scalp this week – Emma Morgan of Leamington Spa. She's divorcing her husband Kevin on the grounds that he loves his beloved Manchester United more than her – and what other team would he support, living in Leamington Spa? Linda Smith has been considering the matter.

Kevin is a Manchester United fan, an unusual Manchester United fan, in that he lives in Leamington Spa – a mere 80 miles from Manchester; not nearly far enough away, a typical Reds fan being a Cornish lighthouse keeper. What puzzles me about this case is why did Emma marry him? *When* did she marry him? – not a Saturday afternoon, obviously. I mean, didn't she notice this mania of his? She must have noticed he had rather more red T-shirts than most people have? Was her first inkling of the horror to come when the vicar said, 'Do you, Kevin, take this woman Emma. . . ?' and he answered, 'I do, ah Cantona, I said I do ah

Cantona.' But let's not be too quick to mock him because there's class prejudice at work here, for example, middle-class Arsenal fanatic – best-selling author. Unemployed Man U fanatic – nutter.

There's snobbery within football, and then football itself is looked down on compared to other more legitimate and admired obsessions. I mean, we wouldn't sympathise with Mrs Stephen Hawking if she'd moaned about his interests. If she'd nagged, 'Oh, Time, Time, Time, that's all you ever think about – well, never mind your quasars and quarks, when are you going to decorate that back bedroom?' She'd be bang out of order. And at least Kevin is mad about a proper sport, proper sport being football and cricket and nothing else. Everything else is a game or pastime. Except golf. Which is an abomination, encouraging bloated publicans and estate agents to waddle around a twee and unnatural landscape in lurid tight-fitting pastel jumpers like pregnant Teletubbies.

I have my own enthusiasms of course, such as *The Simpsons*, but I keep a sense of proportion. Possibly, if I had a child, I'd call them 'Bart, Lisa, Maggie, Homer, Marge, Patty, Selma, Flanders, Mo, Barney, Apu, Smithers, Mr Burns, Milhouse, Martin, Otto, Krusty, Sideshow Bob, Sideshow Mel, and Sideshow Raheem Smith'. But that's just a bit of fun. I do sympathise with Emma though, because I once went out with a bloke who collected old comic books and it used to bore the tits off me. So, Brian, if you're listening, whenever I showed an interest in your stupid *Marvel* comics, I was faking it every time.

DIANA

Now then – to start the programme Linda Smith has something that has been bothering her . . .

Can we talk? I mean, is it all right? Please don't take this the wrong way but you see the thing is – I didn't know Princess Diana. And that's not even the worst of it – I'm not part of a tidal wave of grief and I resent being told that I am every time I turn on the TV or radio. To add to my thought crimes, I don't think there is a tidal wave of grief, because those weeping crowds and daytime telly presenters may feel something but it's not grief. It's New Grief, Virtual Grief, grief with most of the pain taken out. It's the feeling you get from a sad film, you can switch it on and off, you can encourage each other in it and it's pleasurable – you feel better for it.

Regular grief has none of these perks, it's a heartcrushingly solitary sentence without remission – sorry to be 'downsy' but there it is. Diana's children are grief-stricken – I'm sure shoving them in front of cameras to be snogged by strange wailing mad women did them the world of good and was definitely not a desperate attempt by House of Windsor Plc to appease a mutinous mob.

I would guess that Prince Charles's feelings are more complex. From repression comes great art, thought Sigmund Freud; Thomas Hardy, guilt-stricken upon the death of his unloved wife, channelled his remorse into great poetry. Similarly placed, Prince Charles just looks even more like a bewildered haddock than usual. The Queen, in response to pressure from tabloids and Government alike, went on air to express her 'grief' at the passing of a woman whose name she never wanted to hear again (I think you've had *that* one, Your Majesty).

The media described her performance as 'relaxed' and 'heart-felt'. What! She looked like a battered hostage paraded in front of the cameras to explain how well she was being treated. I imagined Tony Blair off camera with a balaclava and kalishnikov saying, 'That's right, ma'am, keep talking, that way nobody gets hurt.' But that's nothing compared to the makeover done on Dodi Fayed. Pre-accident the columnists' attitude could be summed up as, 'Blimey, Di, don't fancy yours much – you could do better than that, girl!' Post-accident he became a prince of love, the only man to make her happy and definitely not a playboy, all right?

Well, I've had enough of this hypocrisy and I'm out of the closet:

1. People who leave bottles of champagne in memory of someone who died in a car driven by a drunken driver are really, really stupid.
2. People who photograph coffins are quite disturbing.
3. I couldn't stand the music-type stuff produced by Elton John before, I still can't stand it, and my only consolation in the harrowing weeks to come is that at least it isn't Chris De Burgh.

COMRADE IN ARMS
Henry Normal, TV comedy producer and poet

In the late eighties I toured with Linda. At the time we would play almost anywhere (both ends of the food chain), often for very little money. Comedy clubs were very scarce in the North so we'd do jazz clubs, folk clubs, theatre bars, upstairs in pubs, hospitals, prisons, works canteens, working men's clubs. At one gig in Sheffield the stage was an old mattress and the act on first was some chap reading *Winnie the Pooh*. College gigs were hard work, especially when the rugby club was in. Linda always had great courage and I remember her going on at some London college and looking the rugby lads in the eye and saying, 'Rugby, what a great game for people with no fear of head injuries . . . and no need to fear them.'

Linda always had some brilliant lines, although she would have her notes half scrawled on dog-eared bits of paper. I once gave her a clean sheet of paper to transfer them, but she never did.

Her references were often so diverse she'd say when a joke fell flat, 'There is a reading list for this act on the way out.'

It's Linda's fight and her passion for comedy I shall remember most, though.

I remember we did a working men's club in Sheffield once where they'd never had 'alternative' acts before. We couldn't swear and neither we nor the audience (mostly being non-members coming just for the show) were allowed to drink alcohol. It took on the air of a children's show as the first act was a magician. On another occasion there was a hen night and a stag night from different weddings on the front row. A week later we might be playing to a nice WI-type audience or a music gig where everyone just wants to talk between bands.

You are supposed to deal with each audience that is thrown at you. It's at such times you really need someone with you who is more than a friend. To say Linda was family would not do it justice. It's more of a 'comrade in arms' thing.

When you're starting out, often the only person you know in the city you're playing is your fellow act. You can travel for hours, wait around to go on, and it all comes down to minutes on stage alone fighting to win over mostly people who've never heard of you. I'm tempted to say it must be even harder for women, but I know Linda would hate that. Linda never played the 'female card'.

Linda and I did thirty-odd dates at the Edinburgh Festival together at a place called Marco's Sports and Leisure Centre. Every day we did a gig to the smell of chlorine, testosterone and stale sweat. Such is the glamour of showbiz.

I got given a TV series in the mid-eighties by Channel 4. It was eventually called *Packet of Three*. Originally it was to be called *Normal Services* and I very much led the development.

I tried really hard to get Linda in as one of the three main stars but the producers, Jon Blair Film Company, wouldn't go with her. I even got them to come and see her perform in Manchester, but to no avail. She was in good company, though, as they also said no to Caroline Aherne as a guest. What really impressed me about Linda was how pleased she still was for me and that she even agreed to guest.

In time the show came and went as all TV does. Linda, though, remained true to herself. I saw her gig in Brighton about a year before she died. She seemed to have the same passion for comedy as she did twenty years ago.

Henry Normal, 2006.

WOMAN'S HOUR
BBC Radio 4, Summer 1997

Men and masculinity course

In Literature, Art, Science, History, there are hardly *any* men to study – luckily this shocking injustice is about to be put right – a degree in Men's Studies is now available from, oh! . . . an American university . . . well, knock me down with a great big lorry.

Men's Studies? Which men do they study exactly? Arnold Bennett? Alan Bennett? Lenny Bennett? And what are the textbooks? *Men Are from Mars, Women Are from Thorntons? Men Who Pub Too Much? Iron, John . . . and when you've done that, come and help me change this duvet cover?*

Apparently, lots of women enrol on these courses – for the same reason they watch male strippers, I suspect – to have a laugh.

Will this trend spread to Britain? If it does, there will be a few differences to the American classes:

'Hi there! I'm your tutor, Swamp Everglade! How the heck are you doing?'

Yeaaah! Whoopee . . . Right, sister! . . . All right! Yeah! Hoo-wee!!

'Hello, I'm Clive. Get here all right?'

'Mustn't grumble.'

'Before we start, the caretaker has asked me to ask you not to hang wet kagoules in the cloakroom. Especially when it's not raining. Later on we'll be discussing sexual harassment and the objectivication of women in pop music.'

'Yes, Keith, it is sickening. First it's time for our lad-ism workshop. I'll start. . .'

'Did you knock my pint over?'

'What if I did?'

'Oi, you – outside!'

'Any time, my son.'

'Come on, come on – fancy a portion?'

And Ladies . . .

'Leave it, Darren, it's not worth it. You'll kill him.'

Excellent . . . and – rest.

Never mind New Men or New Lads, a campaign for Real Blokes is what we need. The proper study of man is DIY.

'This is a man's world . . .this is a man's world . . .'

And it could do with a lick of paint actually, James. Never mind your inner child, find your inner Barry Bucknell and make yourself useful. If you want to express yourself, lads, say it with tiles – be the Gaudi of grouting, make the bathroom your Barcelona. No need for existential angst; when you ask, who am I?, you can answer confidently, 'I'm the bloke who put those shelves up, and a tidy job it is too.'

Of course, the kind of useless wallies that do Men's Studies had better be careful if they swap to DIY. . .

'Welcome to amateur electronics, I'm Dave and . . . oh no, Keith, keep away from that socket . . .'

ZAP! Yeeee – ow! Aaaargh!

. . . in that wet kagoule. Oh dear!

Children are to be entertained at Downing Street this week . . .

'Entertained'? 'Downing Street'? – words that sit together as easily as 'Brian Sewell' and 'jellied eels'.

Oh, Tone, Cher, have you really thought about this ?

It's one thing to have Gordon Brown turning up to banquets in a shell suit, and calling your ministers by their first names with the queasy chumminess of a headmaster at a school disco – but children's parties ? Entertaining the modern child isn't just a case of bunging them a few sausages on sticks to nibble and an elderly conjuror to eat alive; kids' parties these days have to be planned like a U2 tour, but with more punters expected. If there's no laser show, simulated earthquake, and Gladiator Wolf handing out the trifles, they're not interested. This is especially true, as I've got a sneaking suspicion that a spot of 'education, education, education' is going to be slipped in with the fun, in the way that an eagerly awaited school theatre trip would turn out to be a bunch of drama students dramatising the World of Chemical Elements. 'Look, children, it's hydrogen, and he's juggling with oxygen, what does that make?' Kids bored actually. Still, the Blairs are a trendy pair, they've got a teenage son, they're not Old Labour preaching to the converted – they're New Labour preaching to the loft-converted.

So let's go, live and direct to Westminster – where PM Toni and Rapper Queen Cherie will lead you through the Downing Street Experience. . .

Check it out, take it, Cherie. . .

'Youth, I'd just like to say Yo! Welcome to our yard. . . now give it up for my husband's posse – first, respect goes out to our Home Boy, Home Secretary Boy, that is, Jack Straw . . . no, it's cool, Jack, they're invited . . . no, they haven't nicked anything and it's hours till curfew, chill out a bit, Jack, know what I mean? Next, Heritage Secretary, so that makes him our Stately Home Boy, Chris Smith. Meet the Chancellor of the Exchequer, or as we call him, 'Economy Spice' – Gordon Brown.

Yo! It's Harriet Harman, Social Security Spice, wot you want, babe?'

(Fx Spice Girls sing)

I tell you what I want, what I really really want – I wanna, I wanna, I wanna . . .

(Fx Audio clip Harriet Harman) . . . 'Network of afterschool clubs.'

'Safe!, Harriet, safe!'

'Check out – Ann Taylor, Leader of the House . . . what do you mean, bored?'

'Yeah, right, OK, crew, PM Toni and I are not complacent, we're taking nothing for granted, but I think the food's arrived . . . oh blimey! Humphrey – get off those trifles, you flea-bag! From now on, that cat goes out during meetings. No wonder the Majors wanted to keep him.'

LINDA ON STAGE
recorded at The Pleasance, London, for BBC Radio 2 *Stand-Up,*
10 April 1997

I can't believe it's April – I'm still paying for Christmas. I'm still taking my Christmas presents back to Marks and Spencer's. Which is
a result really, 'cos they were all bought from PoundStretcher. But
I don't want to talk about girlie things – I'm not much of a girlie. I
quite like a bit of sport, but I don't like what's happening to English
football. I don't like the new manager. I'm not keen on Glen Hoddle
really – I'm sure he knows a lot about football, I'm sure he's a very
good football manager – but he's just too dull. He's Mr Average, Mr
Normal, Mr Nice Guy – probably lives in a house called 'Dun-
rovin'. I preferred Terry Venables – he's a lad. He's a bit leery – like
a cheery but slightly criminal brother-in-law – that's what I quite
liked. You got the impression with Tel that if you needed a video a
bit cheap, Tel could get you one. I always like to think, that while he
was England manager, Tel was signing on at the same time. Now,
Tel – he would live in a house called 'Dunbrilliant'.

Violence in sport – people go on about violence in sport. They
say, 'Oh, sport is so violent these days' – I don't think that's true.
It's just that the violence that there is in sport is not fairly spread
out amongst all the sports. Say, for example, at one end of the
scale, we've got some sports that are undoubtedly quite violent.
Boxing is quite violent – rugby can be violent. I don't like rugby
actually, I'm not a fan of rugby – I don't know what it is – there's
something about the players. Call me old-fashioned but I think
people should have necks. The way their heads nestle in their
shoulders like that, it's a little bit spooky, isn't it? And rugby lads –
they're always so leery, aren't they? And they're always dressed for
a game of rugby, day or night – just in case you don't realise. They
have to wear rugby kit – they've probably got a whole wardrobe of
them at home, a little silky one for nightclubs and one with a tie for
weddings. And they always have to shout at women, don't they?
Because they are really worried that you might think they're gay –
because they spend every Saturday afternoon cuddling other

men. They always wear their rugby kit – they don't feel secure unless they wear their IQ on their backs. So that's rugby – it's a reasonable game for men with no fear of head injuries – and no reason to fear them. And at the other end of the scale you have twee little sports that have no violence at all – like bowls. There's no violence in Crown Green Bowling, is there? Which is a pity, I think – because violence would give it the edge of excitement which it lacks as a sport. You have the elderly, immaculately clad, white-clad participants with their little hats and their woods, turning up for the game, being frisked by the old bill on their way in . . . looking for bottles of sweet sherry and packets of dry biscuits. And they'll be winding each other up across the perfect green, saying, 'You what, you what? You what?? YOU WHAT?? WHAT WAS THAT?? YOU WHAT?'

I think that would be sweet actually.

PART THREE

'I Was an Avon Lady in Kabul'

Linda on the Radio

1998–2005

A RADIO COMEDY STAR
Chris Neill, comedian and producer

Linda Smith's place in the pantheon of radio comedy stars is assured. She joins the ranks of those people whose clever wit and verbal sophistication shine on radio in a way never quite matched elsewhere. Her performances on *Just a Minute, I'm Sorry I Haven't a Clue* and *News Quiz* made her loved by listeners and in demand from producers. But her own eponymous sit-com is possibly the show which most provided the scope and time to let us have an uninhibited view of Linda's astonishing, humane and deeply funny universe.

There can't be many comedies covering such wide-ranging and seemingly disparate references as are contained in *Linda Smith's A Brief History of Time-Wasting*. We are treated to a tremendous selection of topics, filtered through the prism of Linda's amazingly swift and fertile mind. Subjects might include the philosophy of patriotism, poet Robert Frost, or curtain-making. She might give consideration to the constituent parts of a modern art installation, urban gentrification, the ludicrous results of public utility privatisation, the sham of television makeover shows, East Londoners' capacity for self-myth-making and the ubiquity of certain Radio 4 personalities. The etiquette of viewing paintings in galleries, daytime TV ads and the nasty-sounding dish of Pop Tarts Mornay (the haddock had been stolen by the cat) would not be overlooked, either.

The show ran for two series on Radio 4 in 2001 and 2002. Her ferociously enthusiastic audience on radio helped make it a hit, and had illness not got in the way the series would have continued. Linda wrote beautifully for the medium: the scenes she created were so varied, vivid and colourful that the audience is playfully tempted into envisaging her anarchic world for themselves. Linda played a version of herself living in her East London home surrounded by an array of regular characters and other occasional participants. The writing of these characters was never monochrome, and despite often being infuriating and aggravating in their way, there was nevertheless sympathy and warmth in their expression, too. Similarly, Linda's innate beneficence meant her supporting cast were always given good and funny lines, not just the feeds for them. They were never simply sit-com fodder.

There were three main characters besides Linda: Betty, played with a quiet comic brilliance by Margaret John, the mordant and death-obsessed next-door neighbour ('not so much young, gifted and black but rather old, soppy and Welsh') ever requiring Linda to do favours for her, based on a neighbour Linda had endured whilst living in Stratford; Wara, the Nigerian cabbie who drove faster than the speed of sound, a performance of enormous brio given by Femi Elufuwoju Junior; and Chris the Builder played by me, a tradesman so inept at his work that he kept himself in constant employment by the unsuccessful remedying of his previous disasters. Apparently he was based – to some degree at least – on a builder Linda and Warren had had the misfortune to encounter and I can only assume the fact that he was rather camp and called Chris was to enable me to get some grip on the characterisation. The show's producers, Lucy Armitage and Jon Rolph, also secured the talents of Jeremy Hardy and Martin Hyder to provide an array of voices and there were also parts for many other great performers including Mark Steel, Dillie Keane and Rob Newman. Linda even found space for a number of cameos for Radio 4 luminaries including Jenni Murray and Rabbi Lionel Blue.

The plots in *Time-Wasting* revolved around the minutiae of life: Linda's dealings with her dreaded neighbour Betty and the chaos caused by Chris. She employed what is surely the most idiosyncratic ever running joke in a sit-com, which concerned itself with the frequent updating of the Franklin Mint Limited Edition Songbird Collection of Great Britain. Usually this meant smashing certain examples as their numbers declined, but it also occasionally involved sticking them back together when some particular bird had started breeding again due to the establishment of new wetlands somewhere or other. Despite all this domestic activity, we didn't just stay in the house. There was a memorable episode where we went to visit Derek Jarman's garden in Kent, a place of bleak and fragile beauty entirely lost on Chris and Betty who simply wanted to redo it with serried rows of begonias and busy lizzies. Another edition revolved around a terrifying trip to Argos ('the form of shopping which brought down the Eastern bloc') where Linda conjured up a brilliant sequence melding together the banality of the attempted purchase of a carpet sweeper (thwarted at every step by Argos's arcane system of shopping) and the imagined ravings of someone imprisoned, and exhausted by terrible heat, all in the style of a World War Two escape-from-Colditz-type film.

I had met Linda initially in 1998, producing as I was a frankly quite forgettable comedy game show for Channel 5 which we recorded on cold November evenings in Norwich. A good work / life balance is an extremely ugly phrase describing an extremely desirable state of affairs. Although I'm sure Linda would have expressed it more elegantly, one of her great qualities was that she had this very much sorted. When she took her solo shows on tour – and their schedules enabled them – Linda and Warren would often stay around to see the place she'd been gigging in, maybe even make a weekend of it.

Likewise, instead of trekking back to London with all the other comics after our filming, Linda opted to stay for dinner and a chance to look round Norwich's antique shops the next morning. It makes me extremely happy to recall that something obviously clicked between us that evening (initially a great part of it was the mutual dislike of another comedian) and from that point on we became firm friends. To be honest, I can't remember how it came about that I would have a part in her sit-com. But I do remember long phone conversations where she talked about the development of the idea and what I could do in it. What *I* could do in it? I had only taken part in one or two radio shows, had never acted, wasn't a comedian at the time, and yet here was one of the funniest people in Britain, with her own series to cast, offering me a major role in it. I remain astonished at quite how warm-hearted, if not reckless, this act of trust was – Linda's casting of me in this show was the single most generous thing anyone has ever done for me in my professional life.

The episode you are about to read revolves around Linda's attempts to hold everything together while the *Newsnight Review* team (with particular reference to Tom Paulin, memorably played by Jeremy Hardy) become the presenters of *Ground Force* for the job of Betty's garden's makeover (don't ask). Meanwhile, Chris reminds Linda that they are expecting a visit from an upholstery expert from *How's It Hanging?*, a new shop on the high street – Curtain Woman was played with acidic aplomb by the wonderful Hattie Hayridge. 'Who's Curtain Woman?' Linda asks. 'One of Batman's frumpier villains?' Unfortunately, this is one of the few episodes where the mini-cabbing talents of the Panglossian Wara are not required. I think Linda wrote some of her best lines for this character. He combined an astonishing bright-eyed excitement about the world with moments of great hilarity. Here's just a quick example: 'What? You don't like Carol Vorderman? I don't believe it! When she can count so high, and explain margarines so well! And always a smile for everyone, even though her hairdresser is clearly a certifiable lunatic! OK, now as Bette Davis says, fasten your seat belts, we're in for a bumpy night.' I hope you have as much fun reading the script as we had recording it.

Listening to some episodes of *Linda Smith's A Brief History of Time-Wasting* again recently, I was reminded what a huge treat it was to be involved, but needless to say there was a strain of sadness and even melancholy, too. Linda was a brilliant writer and comedian but also, I'm proud to say, an utterly wonderful, lovely friend.

Chris Neill, 2006.

LINDA SMITH'S
A BRIEF HISTORY OF TIMEWASTING

Written by
LINDA SMITH

Episode 3

****

With
Jeremy Hardy
Hattie Hayridge
Martin Hyder
Margaret John
Chris Neill

Produced by Lucy Armitage

****

REH/RECORD:	THURSDAY 12 JULY 2001, 1500-2100
STUDIO:	RADIO THEATRE, BROADCASTING HOUSE, PORTLAND PLACE, LONDON W1A 1AA
SM'S:	ROGER DANES & CHARLOTTE HUME
BA:	ANN OSBORNE, 5354 BHXX EXT: 54672
TAPE:	SLN128/01LM0086 PROG NO: 01LM0086LH0
TX:	THURSDAY 26 JULY 2001, 1830, RADIO 4

FX   Birdsong. Radio 4 very faintly in background

LINDA: Ah! Another day amongst the familiar sights of old East London. The traditional cheap phone-call shops offering such bargain rates on long-distance calls you curse your luck for not knowing anyone in Lagos or Accra. The exotic cockney food stuffs from stir-fried saveloys to Halal Dixieland Chicken. And above it all, the light atop Canary Wharf winking like a raffish uncle at Christmas.

FX   Radio 4 fades up quickly

RADIO 4 ANNOUNCER: And next on Radio 4, *All in the Mind* with Dr Raj Persaud, followed by the News and Shipping Forecast read by Dr Raj Persaud. Later, in our classic serial *War and Peace*, the part of Natasha is played by Dr Raj Persaud, as are all other parts. After that, *Front Row*, presented by . . . actually, no one's been confirmed but has anyone got a phone number for Dr . . . oh, there you are, Raj!

LINDA: Well, if you want something done, just ask a busy man.

FX   Digging, garden-type machinery, etc.

LINDA: Ah! I wonder how my live-in builder is getting on in the garden?

FX   Opening sash window

LINDA: Morning, Chris. How are you getting on with my Italian sunken garden?

FX   Digging stops

CHRIS: Morning, Linda love. Ooh, marvellous. In a couple more hours I'll have your garden lower than the share price of Railtrack.

LINDA: Steady on, Chris. I want a sunken garden, not a journey to the centre of the earth! Fancy a cuppa?

CHRIS: Yes I do, but you've run out of sugar yet again!

LINDA (sighs): I'm afraid the combined efforts of the sugar-producing nations, Tate and Lyle, and Eddie Stobart's, cannot keep pace with the monkey on your back. You could have some cereal, I've got Sugar Puffs.

CHRIS: Sugar? Cut with puffs? Are you trying to kill me? Addicts like me need a pure supply. Anyway, I must get on.

FX   Pneumatic drill – sound of pipe shearing off. Followed by hiss of gas

CHRIS: Oh, wouldn't you just know it?

LINDA: Oh, not the gas main?

CHRIS: Yes. Maddening, isn't it? Of course, I bet if I were looking for the gas main, I wouldn't find it! Luckily I've got a bit of masking tape here, that should hold it for the time being. You better call the Gas Board.

FX   Unrolling of masking tape and winding it round

LINDA: Oh yes, I'll call the Gas Board. And when I've done that, I'll send the kitchen boy to Swan and Edgar's for some antimacassars and a bottle of laudanum. Gas Board! The last time they supplied my gas, Roy Hattersley was right-wing.

CHRIS: Ooh, of course, deregulation. Well, who supplies it now then?

LINDA: I'm not entirely sure, I've lost track. There's been so many of them at the door with their tempting offers and dishonest sales techniques. I can't remember the last one I said yes to, or even the last one I said, 'I'll think about it' to, which apparently these days is a legally-binding contract. And if they manage to leave a brochure in your house, that's a Faustian pact.

CHRIS: 'Ere, I know. I can recover that memory for you, I can do past services suppliers' regression.

LINDA: You can put me in a trance?

CHRIS: No, you're always in a trance. I can bring you out of it briefly so that you can remember things.

LINDA: Go on then.

CHRIS: Now, just watch the plumb line. Swinging to and fro, you are feeling less sleepy, less sleepy, less sleepy. You are increasingly alert, not your usual dozy self.

LINDA: Yes, thank you, that will do. I remember now. First of all it was Eastern Energy, then Southern Electricity, then, oh yes, SEEBOARD . . .

(fades out in a time-passing sort of way)

CHRIS: . . . and after Matrix Churchill?

LINDA: There was Gloria Hunniford. Oh, she can sell anything from adjustable beds to loan sharks. Then next was the Ilfracombe Tourist Information Centre, followed by a brief heady period when all my essential services were supplied by Matthew Corbett and Sooty. Oh, if you phoned them with a billing inquiry, what a palaver! You'd either get total silence at the end of the line from Sooty or 'They are naughty, aren't they, Sooty, they've not paid their bill!' from Matthew. If you got Sweep, it was 'What's that, Sweep, you want my account number?'

FX   Squeak

LINDA: (cont.) Is that a squeak for yes or a squeak for no? And worst of all, there was Sue, with her simpering voice, like talking to a glove puppet of Felicity Kendal. Bizarre really, as all inquiries were answered at a call centre in Northern Ireland.

CHRIS: So can you remember who it is now?

LINDA: Yes! It all comes back to me now. My gas supplier is currently the English National Opera.

CHRIS: Oh, that's right. I remember them coming to the door. They said if we didn't let them supply our gas, they'd show their lighter side by releasing a CD of contemporary popular music all ruined by being sung in stupid operatic voices.

FX　Phone rings. Answerphone clicks on

LINDA AND CHRIS: Ssh, ssh, giggles (phone clicks on).

BETTY: Hello, hello. Hello, hello.

LINDA: Oh, it's Betty. I'm her neighbour on one side, and death's her neighbour on the other.

BETTY: Is there anybody there?

CHRIS (as a medium): Yes, it's Chris and Linda, your guides in the spirit world.

LINDA: I better pick it up. Hello, Betty.

BETTY: Oh, that's right, leave me hanging on here with my bones crumbling like my sister Marjorie's dried-out fruit cake. You'll have to come round.

LINDA: Well, it's a bit tricky at this end . . .

BETTY: It's a bit tricky at this end actually. I got that television programme coming round, see. You know, where they do up your garden and it's a surprise. Ooh, what's it called? That gardener's in it. The one with no bra.

LINDA: Alan Titchmarsh?

BETTY: That's the one. *Ground Force*, that's it.

LINDA: Well, you're not supposed to know about it, are you?

BETTY: 'Course not. Your family's supposed to do it. But since I'm an only child, apart from my sister Marjorie, I had to do it myself. I pretended to be my granddaughter, Linda.

LINDA: Oh yes.

BETTY: Which means you'll have . . .

LINDA: I think I know what it means, Betty. I'll be round in a minute.

BETTY: Thanking you. Goodbye. Goodbye.

LINDA: Oh, brilliant. Now I've got to hang around at Betty's all day while Alan Titchmarsh and his mates turn her perfectly nice garden into a gravel pit. Chris, you'll have to listen out for the English National Opera.

CHRIS: Oh no, sorry. I've got to go out.

LINDA: What!

CHRIS: Oh yeah. I've got group therapy. It's a special workshop for builders, it's called 'Closure'. It examines the builder's pathological fear of ever finishing a job. It should be very challenging. It's run by Dr Raj Persaud.

LINDA: Raj Persaud! How can one man be in so many different places? I think he must have little helpers dressed as him, like Father Christmas. However, unlike the good doctor, I cannot be in several places at once. How am I supposed to supervise Alan Titchmarsh's sham panic about the time round at Betty's and be at home to answer the door to the English National Opera's Corgi-registered gas fitter?

CHRIS: You could always use this little gizmo that I got from the Innovations catalogue – Travel Bat's Ears . . . no more 'hearing not as good as a bat's' misery with our new Travel Bat's Ears . . . comfortable, fully washable, they fit discreetly behind your lesser human ears.

LINDA: You haven't got any Travel Bat's Ears, have you?

CHRIS: No. But you could run a piece of string between the door knockers. So a caller to our house also knocks at Betty's. Oh, by the way – you haven't forgotten the Curtain Woman, have you?

LINDA: Curtain Woman? I've never heard of Curtain Woman. Is she one of the frumpier Batman villains?

CHRIS: Yeah. 'Suffering pelmets, Batman. It's Curtain Woman.'

CHRIS AND LINDA (sing to the tune of 'Devil Woman'):
'She's just a Curtain Woman,
with curtains on her mind.
Beware the Curtain Woman,
she's gonna make you some blinds.'

CHRIS: Actually no. She's much scarier than that. She's the lady from How's It Hanging?, the new soft furnishings shop, she's coming to measure up for curtains. You arranged an appointment, remember?

LINDA: Oh yeah, I find those people so intimidating with their arcane knowledge of fabric and fittings. They ask you so many questions. There's so many decisions to make. It's probably easier to adopt a child. Especially one of those older, not so cute ones.

FX   Exterior

LINDA: Oh, here we go. Flipping *Ground Force*. I hate these makeover programmes. What's this mania people have these days for endlessly remodelling their homes? It's only recent – after the Second World War, people's idea of a makeover was to take down the blackout curtains and elect a Labour Government. No wonder kids can't concentrate. They leave their house in the morning and while they're out, their parents get that big ponce round from *Changing Rooms*, the one that looks like Margaret Lockwood in *The Wicked Lady*, and by the time the kids get back from school, their perfectly normal semi has been transformed in to a Moorish palace. Must be very unsettling.

FX   Betty's funeral doorbell.

BETTY: Come in. Ooh, you took your time. They'll be here in a minute. I better make myself scarce. I'm off cruising on the Rascal to Epping Forest but you better tell 'em I'm on a team-building weekend in the Lea Valley.

LINDA: It's funny that your motorised mobility cart is called a Rascal, 'cos somehow I can't picture Errol Flynn or Leslie Phillips on one.

BETTY: I'll be at my sister Marjorie's tonight. I'll phone up from hers pretending I'm getting home a half hour early, but I won't really. It's just to create dramatic tension and the possibility that Tommy the Builder will punch Titchmarsh's lights out. It's great television when that happens. Right, I'm off.

LINDA: All right, but rewind that surgical bandage, Betty, I don't want you doing an Isadora Duncan.

FX   Betty revving up Rascal and then driving off to
'Get Your Motor Running' from *Born to Be Wild*.

LINDA: Well, I suppose I better . . .

FX   The double door knock.

LINDA: No, one at Betty's door, so I better nip home.

FX   Running on gravel path.

LINDA: No, don't go. Are you the gas fitter?

CALLER: No. Household insulation, madam. I'm here to sign you up for your special discount, available for a limited time only.

LINDA: Household insulation? Would that be double-glazing?

CALLER: Er, some call it by that name, yes.

LINDA: Is it double-glazing?

CALLER: Er, yes. Yes, it is. But it is specially discounted for a limited time only.

LINDA: How limited?

CALLER: It's strictly limited to . . . well, eternity really.

LINDA: I see. It's an attractive offer but I'm afraid I don't like double-glazing.

CALLER: I'm sorry, for a minute there I thought you said that you don't like double-glazing.

LINDA: I did. I don't.

CALLER: Don't like double-glazing? Are you sure about that? Everybody likes double-glazing. I mean, you might not want it because you've got it already or you can't afford it – but not to like it!

LINDA: I'm sorry.

CALLER: I've never met anyone who didn't like double-glazing. What's not to like? A house without double-glazing, well, it's like The Beatles without Yoko. Isn't your house really draughty?

LINDA: A bit. I don't mind.

CALLER: (sorrowfully leaving) Well I've heard it all now . . . good day, madam . . . (shouts as leaving) You'll catch your death, you will!

FX   Walking fast on gravel path.

LINDA: Ooh, just in time, they're here.

FX   *Ground force* theme.

TOM P: Hello. This is *Ground Force* with Tom Paulin.

LINDA: Eh, Tom Paulin?

TOM P: And I'm here in East London with my chums, Tony Parsons, the working-class one, and of course, the wild-haired bra-less one herself, Germaine Greer. And we've got just one weekend to deconstruct Betty's garden. I've drawn up a plan, taking as my inspiration the work of the Delft School, with particular reference to Vermeer. Germaine will be constructing a water feature . . .

GERMAINE: No I won't.

TOM P: . . . based on Vermeer's extraordinarily moving painting of a housemaid with water jug.

GERMAINE: I absolutely disagree with everyone.

TOM P: So wish us luck, everyone. Oh God.

LINDA: Tom Paulin – why the long face?

TOM P: This is awful, I hate it. This is terrible. I can't stand *Ground Force*. I'm a poet and a critic.

LINDA: Why are you doing this?

TOM P: Have you ever compared the viewing figures for *Ground Force* and *The Late Review*?

LINDA: I think you know I haven't.

TOM P: Well, Greg Dyke has – now Alan, Tommy and Charlie are doing *The Late Review* to boost the audience and we're doing this to enhance our profile (sighs). You're the granddaughter? You sound different.

LINDA: Yes, on the phone I sound older. And Welsher.

TOM P: I better get on with it. It's Day One and only forty-eight hours to the deadline . . . the final reckoning. When in spite of cormorant-devouring time we'll have to have this patio laid.

FX   Brass band music.

TOM P: Oh Jesus, that music. It's awful I hate it. I . . .

FX   Phone rings.

LINDA: Just a minute, Tom . . . hello!

CHRIS: It's me.

LINDA: Chris, how's your workshop going?

CHRIS: Oh, marvellous. All kinds of theories have popped up to explain the classic builder's half-finished job, everything from reluctance to end the relationship with the client, to alien abduction. Anyway, Raj

Persaud's just nipped out to write a newspaper article, so I thought I'd just phone for a chat.

FX   Double door knock.

LINDA: Ooh, door, I'll call you back.

FX   Walking back to house.

LINDA: This better be the English National . . . Oh no.

CALLER: Look, I just need to understand this. Have I got this right? You. Don't. Like. Double. Glazing.

LINDA: Yes. That's pretty much the situation. I'm sorry. I'm sorry.

CALLER: (sighs heavily). OK. OK. I knew it really. I suppose I just didn't want to believe it.

LINDA: You need to move on from this now.

CALLER: I know. I know.

LINDA: Look, you're a good salesman. It's not you. It's me. I've got to go now, OK?

CALLER: Yeah, yeah, go, go, I'll be fine.

LINDA: Oh dear. While I'm home, I'll just check on that gas pipe, masking tape should hold it but . . .

FX   Double door knock. Door opens.

LINDA: Yes?

CON MAN: Hello, madam, I'm a con man.

LINDA: I beg your pardon?

CON MAN: I'm a con artist, a trickster, a scam merchant, call it what you will, but the gist of it is, I call at your door, get you talking, con my way in, then steal cash and valuables. Here's my I D – registered con man, number 6399.

LINDA: Oh. You better come in then. So, what were you thinking of stealing? I've got an increasingly valuable limited edition Franklin Mint set of porcelain songbirds. Here, hold on a minute – what's that in your hand?

CON MAN: Nothing! What?

LINDA: Give me that!

FX   Snatches documents.

LINDA: I thought as much . . . contracts to supply gas! What a dirty trick – sneaking into people's houses, pretending to be a thief, when really you want them to sign up to your company for their essential services! You're not a con man, you're a gas man! Police! Stop that gas man!

CON MAN: Lawks, that's torn it. I'm off!

FX   Running off down gravel path.

LINDA: You've got to be so careful these days. Right, I'm going to see how Tom Paulin and his chums are getting on. I'll leave a note on the door for the English National Opera – ooh, note, opera, ha ha. And also for the Curtain Woman. Dear Curtain Woman, pull yourself together and call next door. Pull yourself together, ha, ha. Must remember to tell Chris that one.

FX   Walking on gravel path. Double door knock. Door opens quickly.

TOM P: For pity's sake, who's that? . . . Oh, it's you. I keep hearing a knock at the door, then there's no bastard there! It's a Kafkaesque nightmare, or rather it's like Edgar Allan Poe's 'Tell-tale Heart'.

LINDA: No, it's more like a bit of string. Calm down. I meant to say, duck under it if you're going out or you'll bisect yourself. How's thegarden coming on?

TOM P: Terrible – Germaine's flouncing about in a wet T-shirt, flicking her hair like an Afghan hound in a car wash. Tony Parsons keeps going on about tongue and groove, young people's music I suppose – how's he going to build a pergola with that? I'm supposed to be planting out roses.

LINDA: And?

TOM P: I can't plant these, just look at their names! They're awful, absolutely dreadful! 'Peek-a-Boo', 'Whisky Mac', 'Southampton'.

LINDA: Mmm. See what you mean . . . 'Disco Dancer', 'Champagne Cocktail', 'Drummer Boy' . . . sound like racing greyhounds. I'll have a pound each way on 'Drummer Boy' , ha, ha. Tell you what, Tom, why don't you think up some better, more poetic names for them, and I'll . . .

FX   Phone.

LINDA: Hello . . . Oh, I don't know why . . . I suppose I just prefer sash windows . . . I wish I had answers for you. It's not as if I ever led you on. Oh, what's the point of going over and over this? I'm hanging up now, goodbye. No, it's definitely goodbye.

FX   Hangs up phone.

LINDA: Gordon Jackson.

FX   Phone rings.

LINDA: (answers) Look, I've got nothing more to say, it's finished!

CHRIS: What's going on? Are you seeing another builder? He'll never match my quotes.

LINDA: No. Oh, Chris, I'm still waiting for the ENO to fix that gas pipe.

CHRIS: Well, you will be, you soppy date. You haven't called them yet. You said, 'I must call them' and then you didn't.

LINDA: Of course. I've got a mind like a sieve.

CHRIS: Actually, you've got a mind like a hoop. Anyway, Raj has just nipped off to host a phone-in with Richard and Judy, so I just called to tell you about this exciting new theory of unfinished job syndrome. Apparently the latest thinking is that the builder believes they have finished, but this is an hallucination brought about by their vast intake of sugar throughout the day . . .

LINDA: Fascinating. But I can't chat now, Chris, bye.

FX   Hangs up phone. Redials. Recorded message.

FX   'Thank you for calling the English National Opera emergency helpline. You are being held in a queue.'

FX   Music. Some Lloyd Webber crap.

LINDA: Oh, I hope I'm not waiting too long. This music is torture. I can't stand Andrew Lloyd Webber. Webber – that's almost Weber, isn't it? I bet he nicked that name off another composer and just changed it ever so slightly to cover himself.

OPERA SINGER: (sings) How can I help you? My name is Maria . . . Maria, Maria, Maria . . . and suddenly that name . . .

LINDA: Shut up! Coor, there's no standing charges with this lot but you pay in other ways. My gas main's been severed. Send a fitter round please, Maria. My account number? 1739 Figaro, Figaro, Figaro, Figaro, – oh, you people never give up, do you?

FX   Double door knock. Opens door.

CURTAIN WOMAN: Hello. I'm the Curtain Woman.

LINDA: Oh, that was quick.

CURTAIN WOMAN: Yes. I would have been round even quicker if it wasn't for your hilarious joke. Pull yourself together – side-splitting. I may have to form a pressure group, 'Save Our Sides'.

LINDA: Just trying to break the ice.

CURTAIN WOMAN: You wouldn't be the first. But believe me, you'd need a blow-torch.

FX   Walking next door. Door opens and closes.

CURTAIN WOMAN: Right, there's a saying in soft furnishings – you can't make curtains without measuring up.

FX   Sonic measure, going blip, blip, blip.

LINDA: A sonic measure, give us a go!

FX   Blip, blip, blip.

LINDA: Brilliant! 'So you want to be a Jedi?'

CURTAIN WOMAN: Give me that.

LINDA: Hmm, the Force is strong in this one.

CURTAIN WOMAN: Now pick a fabric, any fabric.

FX   Rapid flipping through sample book. As in deck of cards.

CURTAIN WOMAN: Do you want chintz, draylon, linen, velvet, damask, silk, brocade or waffleweave?

LINDA: Er . . .

CURTAIN WOMAN: If silk, I've got raw, shot, watered, or jacquered.

LINDA: Er . . .

CURTAIN WOMAN: Plain, patterned, self-patterned or devoré.

LINDA: I don't know really. I just want something to go with the furniture.

CURTAIN WOMAN: Ha! May I suggest a migraine? Do you want these curtains thermal-lined?

LINDA: I don't know. Do curtains feel the cold? I suppose they are in a draught.

CURTAIN WOMAN: Do you want them weighted at the bottom?

LINDA: Weighted at the bottom? I'm not using them to wrap up a body I'm dumping in the Thames. No thanks.

FX   Door opens.

CHRIS: Oh, hello. Cooee, I'm home.

LINDA: Oh, Chris, thank goodness. This is the Curtain Woman.

CHRIS: What's she like?

LINDA: Terrifying. Like Anne Robinson with toothache.

CURTAIN WOMAN: Right. Choose your curtain rails. Pine, oak, brass, brass-rich aluminium, steel, brushed-steel, gilt, bistro, gothic, gilded, rustic or neo-classical.

CHRIS: I'd say more like Anne Robinson with piles. But I won't let her rain on my parade. That workshop was fantastic. I've signed up for another one – 'Builder's Bum Cleavage – A Cry for Help?' I'm so invigorated. I have conquered my fear of finishing. I've slain the dragon of incompetence, and to prove it, I'm going straight outside and I'm gonna make you the best damned Italianate sunken garden since Percy Thrower did that one for *Blue Peter* that was so cruelly vandalised.

CURTAIN WOMAN: Finials.

LINDA: What?

CURTAIN WOMAN: You need finials.

LINDA: Do I?

CURTAIN WOMAN: Yes. Otherwise, every time you open the curtains, they shoot off the end of the rail and go flying about the room like ectoplasm at a seance.

LINDA: Oh well, I . . .

CURTAIN WOMAN: Knobs, fleur-de-lys, ellipses, chevrons, tridents . . .

FX	Door bell

LINDA: It's Tom and the gang.

TOM P: Excuse me. Aren't you supposed to be helping me with this *Ground Force* farrago? Making anxious phone calls to the lucky recipient of our garish creations? Pretending to help with the donkey work? Bringing us tea and bickies?

LINDA: Sorry. I've got a lot on my plate.

TOM P: Lucky you. I'm starving. Alan, Tommy and Charlie's victims never stopped feeding them. Sandwiches, cakes, it's a non-stop buffet. No wonder Tommy's so corpulent, and I've been working so hard on my poetic rose names. I don't suppose . . .

LINDA: Yes, of course, I'd love to hear them.

FX   Rustle of paper.

TOM P: (clears throat) 'Mutabilis', 'Beauty of Glazenwood', 'Climbing Lady Hillingdon', 'Great Maiden's Blush', 'Hannah Gordon', 'Felicia', 'The Empereur du Maroc', repeat flowering. FLOWERING.

LINDA: That's beautiful, Tom, but all those roses already exist.

TOM P: Bollocks. My muse has deserted me.

GERMAINE GREER: It's a stupid idea anyway – why labels? So the flowers can wear their little name tags like salesmen at a conference? It's so anal, so male.

TONY PARSONS: At the risk of sounding anal and male, my concrete's going off.

TOM P: Just kill me. Kill me now.

CURTAIN WOMAN: Pleats?

LINDA: What?

CURTAIN WOMAN: Pleats. Do you want box pleats, pencil pleats, pinch pleats, tabs, goblet or islet?

TOM P: Hmm. Box pencil pinch, box pencil pinch. I like that. Nice rhythm.

FX   Double door knock. Door opens.

BETTY: Oh, hello, Linda . . . can I stay here tonight?

LINDA: I thought you were staying at your sister's.

BETTY: We've fallen out. So touchy, she is. All I said was, if she was going to use the same J-cloth for the draining board and the worktops, she might as well keep pigs in the kitchen and wallow about in their filth. I can't go home, see, 'cos of *Ground Force.*

LINDA: Ssh, Betty. The *Ground Force* team, they're here.

BETTY: What, this lot? No! I've never seen this lot before in my life.

TOM P: Maybe Greg Dyke has a point.

BETTY: Here, are you the Irish gardener from *Planet Patio?* Tut. The camera really does add ten pounds.

TOM P: No, I'm not. And you're not your granddaughter either

LINDA: And I'm not her granddaughter either. It's a scam. Betty wanted to be on *Ground Force.* Her sister was meant to phone in. But they had a row, about how long you should boil cabbage for. Betty said nine years, her sister said seven, and it all kicked off.

BETTY: Vegetables are not properly cooked unless they can safely be eaten by someone in a deep coma.

TOM P: I love it, a fake guest for a fake show with a false premise. The artifice is irresistible.

CURTAIN WOMAN: Nets or blinds?

LINDA: Sorry?

CURTAIN WOMAN: Under the curtains, nets or blinds? If nets, jardinière, draped . . .

LINDA: Blinds, blinds.

CURTAIN WOMAN: Venetian, Roman or Austrian?

LINDA: Anything but Austrian. They're horrible. All ruched and criss-crossed like Jeffrey Archer's forehead.

FX   Brochure through letterbox. Footsteps running away. Maniacal laughter fading into distance.

LINDA: What's this through the letterbox? There's something scrawled across it. By hand, I think. Unless there's a Ransom Note font. 'Here's what you're missing, bitch, you're laughing at me now, but in the winter I will be the one who is laughing. I am strong like aluminium.' It's a double-glazing brochure.

TOM P: I love double-glazing. There's something about the way it contains the space around the window that reminds me of Rachel Whiteread's work.

LINDA: You're cheerful all of a sudden.

GERMAINE GREER: (whispers) We sprinkle Prozac on his cornflakes every morning – it takes longer and longer to wear on.

CURTAIN WOMAN: Pelmets? Hardboard, flounced, swags or frills?

TOM P: This imagery, it's laden with eroticism (growls).

CURTAIN WOMAN: (giggles) I have a passion for soft furnishings. Do you want these curtains remote-controlled? It's a marvellous effect. The curtains glide regally apart to reveal the outside world, like it's your personal cinema screen.

LINDA: Yeah, with a really boring film showing – a never-ending season of Andy Warhol.

FX   Double door knock.

ENO: (sung) Good evening, madam. I'm a gas fitter.

LINDA: You must be the English National Opera?

ENO: Yes. The English National Opera, the fourth emergency service.

LINDA: I thought that was Pet Rescue. I'm afraid my builders hacked through the gas main.

ENO: What's that you say, he's sawn through the pipe?

WOMEN: He's sawn through the pipe, he's sawn through the pipe, oh what can we do, he's sawn through the pipe.

ENO: Oh, it's a disaster. We're all going to die. I will have my revenge on the clumsy builder.

LINDA: Don't get hysterical.

ENO: I'm sorry, madam. It's company policy. We always make a drama out of a crisis. Also I must warn you, at some point in the proceedings, I will put on a big hat. When I have my big hat on, nobody recognises me. Even though I am the same bloke that they have just been talking to for the last half hour.

ff Lovers – Linda and
n Lavelle on stage
Sheffield, 1985

With the manual for
right-on men

Good companions - Linda and Test Match Special

On stage, 1989

With Mark Thomas, 1990

With Steve Gribbin before 'The Hello Cruel World Tour', 1992

Backstage at the Route 52 cabaret club, Sheffield, 1992

With Cutting Edge team mate, Phill Jupitus, backstage at London's Comedy Store, 1992

Hattie Hayridge and Linda in costume for the show 'Split Tease', Edinburgh, 1994

Rabin's Nosh Bar, Soho, London, 1994
L – R: Jeremy Hardy, Jo Brand, Ivor Dembina, Linda, Arnold Brown

Linda's first appearance on *Just A Minute* at the Lyceum Theatre,
Sheffield, November 1998. Back L-R : Tony Hawks, Linda, Graham Norton,
Derek Nimmo. Foreground: Nicholas Parsons

Live at the *Sunday Times* Hay Literature Festival, 2001

Paul Merton, travellers' reading aid and Linda on the set of *Room 101*, August 2003

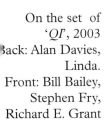

On the set of '*QI*', 2003
Back: Alan Davies, Linda.
Front: Bill Bailey, Stephen Fry, Richard E. Grant

Linda and Paul Merton during the recording of *Have I Got News For You*, December 2004

At the recording of 'I'm Sorry I Haven't a Clue's Christmas Carol', December 2003
L – R: Stephen Fry, Jeremy Hardy, Graeme Garden, Andy Hamilton, Tim Brooke-
Taylor, Linda, Barry Cryer. In foreground: Ian Pattinson

Panelists on the 25th
anniversary of
The News Quiz, Radio 4,
September 2002 at the
Playhouse Theatre, London
Back: Alan Coren, Francis
Wheen, Simon Hoggart.
Front: Jeremy Hardy, Linda,
Andy Hamilton.

Linda before the
show at the Kings
Lynn Arts Centre,
May 2004

LINDA: I hate that in opera. A hat isn't an effective disguise. If it was, the witness protection scheme would consist of a selection of headgear.

ENO: I'm sorry, madam, I don't make the rules. Righty ho, where is the problem?

WOMEN: He wants to see the pipe, take him to the pipe. We must really beseech you, take him to the pipe.

LINDA: It's out the back.

ENO: What did she say?

WOMEN: She said it's out the back. It's out the back, it's out the back.

ENO: That's what I thought she said, it's usually out the back.

ALL OPERA SINGERS: We're going out the back now, we're going out the back. To see the clumsy builder and the severed pipe.

LINDA: Gordon Jackson. I need to relax for a minute. I know, I'll update my porcelain songbird collection, where's that masking tape? I'll mend this Skylark.

FX   Pieces of broken china, masking tape pulled off roll.

BETTY: I thought you smashed that Skylark because of its dwindling numbers.

LINDA: Yes, I did. But due to closed footpaths and lack of grazing animals, they're breeding again on sites where they haven't been seen for years. It's a full-time job keeping this collection up to date.

FX   Radio switched on.

NEWS READER: Here is the news. The popular media psychiatrist Dr Raj Persaud has gone raving mad under the pressure of his inhuman workload. The responsibility for the mental health of an entire nation has proved finally too much. 'It's a terrible blow, Raj is irreplaceable,' said fellow psychiatrist Dr Oliver Sachs, who will be replacing him.

LINDA: Oh, Chris will be . . .

FX   Sudden commotion. Chris and ENO dive into the house shouting and screaming , 'Help, get down' etc. Huge noise of house sinking into ground, creaking and finally settling. General coughing and spluttering.

LINDA: Chris, are you all right? What's going on?

CHRIS: Well, I think I may have overdone it a bit with the sunken garden. I was so fired up, I was digging and digging. I must have dug through the foundations.

LINDA: So what you're saying is, I haven't got a sunken garden, I've got a sunken house. And judging by the top soil half-way up the windows, the garden is in fact slightly raised.

CHRIS: Yes. And the other thing is . . .

ENO: Look, we're standing in three inches of water.

CHORUS: Our feet are getting wet.

CHRIS: Yes. That's because . . .

CURTAIN WOMAN: This might be a good time to raise the subject of fabric care. What does this label say?

LINDA: Dry-clean only.

CURTAIN WOMAN: And again, please.

LINDA: Dry-clean only.

CURTAIN WOMAN: Precisely. Because you would be surprised how many people see the words 'Dry-clean only' and read them as, 'Shove these items in a washing machine whenever the fancy strikes you.' And then start complaining when they're left with curtains so badly shrunken they wouldn't cover a window in your diary.

CHRIS: As I was about to say, the sudden and dramatic sinking of the house has severed the main water pipe.

ENO: Oh no, we're all going to drown.

BETTY: Don't worry, I got something in my bag that will soak up some of this water. My sister Marjorie's fruit cake. It's the driest thing in the world. I'll just drop it in.

FX   Cake plopping into water.

BETTY: It's down half an inch already.

CURTAIN WOMAN: I'll measure the depth with my sonic measure.

FX   Blip, blip, blip, of sonic measure. But at same intervals you get in a submarine.

ENO: It's so eerie down here.

WOMEN: And claustrophobic too.

ENO: We can only guess what's going on up above. We are all crammed together in this subterranean hell.

LINDA: Stop it, you lot. I feel like I'm trapped in a musical version of *Das Boot*.

ENO: What a fantastic idea! *Das Boot The Musical.* That's what we'll do if we ever get out of here.

TOM P: If I get outta here, I'm going to be the poet in residence at the 'How's It Hanging?' soft furnishing shop. In the Curtain Woman, I have found my Maud Gonne.

CHRIS: Well, no one is going to get out of here until we call the Water Board.

LINDA: I'll call the Water Board. Then I'll send the between-stairs maid out for a penn'orth of oysters. The Water Board haven't supplied my water since . . .

CHRIS: Well, who does then? (pause, sigh) Watch the plumb line, you are feeling less sleepy, less sleepy . . .

LINDA: First it was Yorkshire Water, then The United Arab Emirates, then The Gobi Desert District Council, etc., etc.

ENDS . . .

PERFECTLY LINDA
Michael Rosen, poet, writer and broadcaster

Linda was voted Britain's Wittiest Person by listeners to a programme I present on Radio 4, *Word of Mouth*. As the votes came in, we could see that her main competitor was Stephen Fry. This may or may not explain why most of Linda's obituaries said that it was Stephen who awarded Linda this particular gong. Not so. The occasion of the awarding was while she was recording an episode from her wonderful *Time-Wasting* series. I headed down to the Drill Hall in the West End and watched from the wings the extraordinary ballet that is radio drama and comedy. You know the sort of thing – people stepping forward towards microphones and saying, 'I can't come down right now, I'm in the toilet.'

Anyway, I rudely interrupted the show, barged in and announced that Linda was now officially the wittiest person that anyone anywhere was ever likely to come across. Linda blinked, then one of her wicked twinkles appeared in her eyes, and she said that she had heard that the previous recipient of a great-user-of-language award from *Word of Mouth* was Enoch Powell, so she wasn't really sure that she was the right person to be bracketed with him . . . but, yes, even so, she was delighted.

Perfectly Linda. Someone loved to bits by the people who knew her and by her many audiences and neatly able to drop the little depth charge to undermine anything puffed-up, anything hung about with the stench of prejudice.

Michael Rosen, 2006.

BOOKED
BBC Radio 4

Dear Diary – entries from famous literary characters
The Scarlet Pimpernel (who rescued aristocrats from the tumbrels
in the French Revolution)

Dear Diary

Faith but I've been elusive today. In my mission to rescue the suffering aristos, hounded by the baying mob just because of their noble blood, I today assume the guise of a squeegee merchant. However, damn it, I arouse suspicion by washing windscreens with a bucket of champagne. Alas, I was too late. At Westminster the poor aristocrats had already been evicted from the House of Lords. They wandered College Green dazed and confused, crying out piteously, 'What's going on? Are we going on an outing? Matron, I'm frightened. You're not my grandson.'

All the while, Citizen Blair – 'The Incorruptible' – looked on, mad eyes ablaze with power. Curse him. Oh well, perhaps I should find another cause to support, something a bit easier. These GM foods seem very popular.

Goodnight, Diary.

Dear Diary – entries from famous literary characters
Charlotte Brontë

Dear Diary

I awoke this morning to a drear, dark prospect, the driving rain lashing against the casement, our little vicarage shrouded in freezing fog. So, it's brightened up a bit. I dressed hastily, and knocked gently on the bedroom doors of my dear siblings – to check that none of them have died in the night – happily, all are spared – there's another bit of luck. I feel good about today. I descend to the breakfast room, to glimpse Father disappearing back upstairs with some tea and toast. It is six months since I saw him leave his study – goodness, he's quite the social butterfly these days. Later, I descend to the village to purchase a catering pack of laudanum for my brother Branwell. His cough's no better apparently. Mr Arkwright, the apothecary, stamps my loyalty card – it's full so I get a free black veil – you can't have too many of those. 'Your Branwell's cough's no better then?' says Mr Arkwright, rather unpleasantly I thought, as he fork-lifts the laudanum into the cart. 'You'll find this generic stuff, "My Mum's Laudanum", works out a bit cheaper.'

Luncheon, and the entire family still alive, I really ought to buy a lottery ticket today. Afternoon, and the weather turns sunny and bright. Only joking, it's still raining, but I spend the afternoon in the garden, scrubbing gravestones, before trudging to the village again to visit the tubercular poor amongst the smoke-belching factories. Oh, I know, but you've got to relax once in a while. Hurry home before my clothes shrink. After leaving a 500-page note for the milkman, signed Currer Bell (I like to keep him guessing) I repair to bed, lulled by the crash of hailstones on the window pane, and Branwell's maniacal screaming. If only every day could be like this.

Goodnight, Diary.

Dear Diary – entries from famous literary characters
A Day in the Life of Gregor Samsa, from Franz Kafka's
Metamorphosis

Oh, oh dear, oh dear, what a night . . . I feel rough as old boots . . . never again. I'm really dehydrated, I can hear my skin rattling, need a drink of water . . . blimey! I'm seeing eight arms! I must have had a right skinful . . . this Czech beer is lovely but lethal . . .

here, hold on, it's not just my arms . . . it's my whole body . . . oh what! I'll kill those lads. A laugh's a laugh but this is ridiculous, I mean the gorilla suit on my birthday, but this . . . oh, where is the zip . . . oh no . . . it's not fancy dress. I've only turned into a giant insect.

Typical. I've just bought new trainers. I'll have to get another six pairs now – I can't afford that on my wages. That's another thing – how can I go to work like this? I'm a travelling salesman – easier to hail a cab, I suppose, but I'll look stupid tearing down the M1 in my Mondeo with my right arm on the window, all four of them. I can't stay in hotels, I'd close the place down just by going down to breakfast. Oh no, it's my mum at the door . . . 'Don't come in, Mum. Well actually, yes, on this occasion I have got something you haven't seen before . . . no, I've not had a tattoo; no, not body piercing, it's not that disgusting, I've just turned into a giant insect, I can't get out of bed. Of course, I'm sure, well either that, or I need to exfoliate on a more regular basis. Look, you better phone in sick for me.'

Oh well, I suppose there might be advantages as a beetle with special needs. I'll probably be able to get into Sparta Prague football matches for nothing. There's probably a support group for Franz Kafka characters – KAFKAID – I'll probably be invited to lots of stag beetle parties, then there's my insect eyes! With their myriad surfaces, it will be like watching all the digital channels at once. Wicked! I'm spending the rest of my life as a bed bug.

Noel Coward reviewing Laurence Llewelyn-Bowen's Fantasy Rooms

Judging by the delightful title, *Laurence Llwelyn-Bowen's Fantasy Rooms*, I fully expected this programme to involve an artistic young friend of Princess Margaret's and a suite at the Savoy. I was terribly, terribly wrong. This Bowen fellow turns out to be some sort of shabby genteel workman, inexplicably dressed as Margaret Lockwood in *The Wicked Lady*. Apparently, the boy is an expert at doing it himself. Ha! By the look of him, one doesn't doubt it for a moment. Basically, he transforms a drab but perfectly acceptable room into an utter fright. Firstly, he paints the room a lurid puce emulsion matt – awfully flat, matt. He then attempts a faux baroque with tin foil and raffia, one can only assume he has been overcome by glue fumes – strange how potent cheap Bostik can be. All in all, a *Design for Living Death*. Next week I'll be reviewing a show called *The Royle Family*. How lovely. I love the Royals. Sounds much more up my street.

P.G. Wodehouse reviews Damien Hirst

Famous literary figures criticise aspects of modern culture. The creator of the immortal Jeeves and Wooster reviews a Damien Hirst exhibition.

There was this fellow by the name of Georges Braque, believe he was some sort of Froggy paintbrush wallah. Anyway, this cove Braque once said, 'Art is meant to disturb' – though I rather fancy he said it in French, being, you know, French. What's more, I daresay he said all sorts of other things too, bound to have done really, when you think about it. But I suppose nobody thought those other things were worth jotting down – or perhaps there was no one handy with a pencil. Makes a fellow wonder, don't it? I mean to say, who chooses the winners from the also rans amongst a chap's mutterin's and mumblin's?

I mean to say, did 'Art is meant to disturb' win by a length, or did it just pip 'Cocktails, anyone?' to the post? Getting back on the A road, if the aforesaid Gallic canvasbotherer, Msr Braque, is spot on and art is meant to disturb, well then this fellow Hirst must be the bally cat's pyjamas, because he gives a chap the screaming heebeegeebees. Rum. Dashed rum. Anyway, next week I'll be reviewing the daubs of Tracey Emin, a plucky gal and by all accounts, a bit of a flapper. So until then, art lovers, toodle pip.

Oscar Wilde reviews lunch at The River Café, London, that bastion of New Labour style

Yearning to drown my senses in the voluptuousness of Italy, I took lunch at The River Café, that shimmering oasis on the Thames, as redolent of luxury and intrigue as a Medici palazzo. Indeed, is not the pontiff himself, Tony Blair, seated but a table away? It seems at this, the court of Mr Blair, the soul of man under socialism has been replaced by the seared blue fin tuna of man under New Labour. How amusing it would be to scandalise him with my own particular New Deal scheme for the young unemployed. But I must order. I have the beef carpaccio scented with the finest Amalfi lemon. My companion has some rather incriminating letters of mine. Tiresome. How tiresome. But ah! there is Robin Cook. Dear Robin, one always feels there is a portrait in his attic in which he looks fine. Ah! and there's John Prescott, one wonders what cathedral he fell off. Oh dear, he's not happy with his food, in fact I never saw a man who looked with such a wistful eye upon that little tent of rocket salad and wishes it was a steak and kidney pie. What a bore these New Labour types are – on the whole, one prefers feasting with panthers. After all, we are all in the gutter but some of us are pissed and eating kebabs.

Hotel du Lac

Create a new Beginning and Ending for Anita Brookner's novel or indeed any Anita Brookner novel of your choice really, they're pretty interchangeable, I find.

Beginning: When a thing is forgotten it can never again be remembered for remembering is the opposite of forgetting. A forgotten thing is lost, a remembered thing is found. When we forget we are hiding, when we remember we are seeking, and I fear I am too old now for games of hide and seek. Besides, there is no one to find me. If I hide, I would end up suffocating in a wardrobe full of cardigans, and if I sought I would be at it all day for I live alone since Mother died. I cared for her, I cared for her, a querulous difficult invalid for thirty years. It was no trouble. I wasn't doing anything else. The mention of wardrobes reminds me, I must buy a cardigan, I'm down to my last fifty. What made me think of all this I can't remember. I forget.

My name is Agnes Winslow – Miss Winslow to my close friends, of whom I have none. I'm a librarian at the Central Medical Library where I catalogue works on skeletal nomenclature. I have two colleagues at the library: Julie, a laughing, vibrant young woman who is basically in the book to contrast with my own drabness, and Neville, a man as shy, quiet and civilised as myself, with whom I could find happiness if we weren't both so clinically mousey. Perhaps, perhaps in time, after all we've only been colleagues for twenty years.

Ending: Now, with Mother dead, the library have insisted that I take a little break from work as I have apparently accrued some two years' paid holiday. Therefore, I packed a small suitcase of lightweight twinsets and set off for two weeks all in at the Hotel du Lakeside, Thurrock. The train pulled in to Thurrock and I entered another world, a world of glamour, the high-spending shoppers, the powerful businessmen barking into mobile phones. I felt dizzy. I sat down in the piazza and ordered a tall, semi-skinny mochachino. As if that were not excitement enough for one lifetime, a brash but not unattractive man approached me. 'Coconut cake?' he offered. 'Yes,' I stammered. 'Desiccated?', 'I suppose I am a bit, but I do get a lot of comfort from knitwear.' We talked, and it looked for a while as if I might get maried, but I panicked and backed out of it.

On my return home I determined to be bolder. I would invite Neville to share my sandwiches in the park or even ask him to the flat for a sherry and a dry biscuit, but it was too late. He had eloped with Julie, never to return. No matter, once a thing is lost, it is forgotten, and can only be remembered if it is found, which it can never be because it is lost. I wish, I wish, I wish, I wish I'd bought that lovely polo neck in Jigsaw.

Henrik Ibsen, the father of modern naturalism in the theatre,
reviewing Mamma Mia – The Abba Show

Scandinavian drama has sadly declined in recent times – I am personally sick and tired of telling people that *Hedda Gabler* is one of my plays – and not the name of a coffee table from IKEA and certainly not a practice popular with White House interns.

It's very refreshing then to see the tradition of intense Nordic Theatre examining realistic problems of personal and public morality revived so brilliantly in this Swedish masterwork, *My Mother* by Abba. *My Mother* is in many ways a homage to my own work – in fact they nicked a load of my ideas.

In Abba, as in my plays, the women are the more attractive characters, and the men are a bit funny-looking – in fact, Benny and Bjorn really should be living under a bridge. Many of my central themes are revisited: the corruption, greed and rottenness of society depicted by me in *The Pillars of the Community* are explored in the trenchant, Brechtian number 'Money, Money, Money, must be funny. It's a rich man's world'. The destruction of a marriage depicted in my *Doll's House* is here reworked as 'Knowing Me, Knowing You, *aha, there is nothing we can do*'. The success of *My Mother* has encouraged me to rework some of my own plays, so do look out for *Ghosts* with Whoopi Goldberg and Patrick Swayzee, *The Wild Duck* with Keith Harris and Orville, and on a lighter note, keep 'em peeled for *Confessions of a Master Builder* with Robin Asquith.

Cider With Rosie

To create a new Beginning and Ending for Laurie Lee's famous novel. This is a very charming book about an idyllic country childhood but, of course, the countryside has changed a bit.

My earliest recollection is the heady familiar harvest-time scent, the 'all is safely gathered in' smell of choking black smoke as the farmer burns off his fields of stubble, singing merrily as he flings petrol about, 'I'm a firestarter, twisted firestarter . . . oy yes . . .' No other grown-ups are in sight, the women are in the local pub 20 miles away planning the harvest festival karaoke night. The men are off shooting badgers. I feel sorry for the Badgers – an unpopular family from the council estate who get blamed for everything, from joy-riding to giving cows TB. However, Mum said that if our little village of Much Monsanto in the Marsh has any chance of winning Britain's nastiest village award, 'Them Badgers have to go.'

I find myself alone with Rosie – we hide behind a mountain of old tractor tyres. 'Bob Flowerdew's wet dream innit,' says Rosie. She shyly offers me some Ventolin – I've got my own inhaler of course – who hasn't? but it's more sophisticated to share. I offer her some cider but she refuses . . . 'Nah, cider's old-fashioned, have some of this pooch – it's alcopops.'

'What's alcopops, Rosie?' 'S'brilliant, it's alcohol, but for little children.' We sip pooch until the E numbers drive us barmy. 'I know, let's vandalise the bus shelter!' I cry. 'Nah', says Rosie. 'Ain't a bus due till next April. Don't hardly seem worth it.'

Rosie brightens 'I know . . . let's pick mushrooms in the woods.' 'Yes! let's pick mushrooms in the dappled shade of oak trees amongst the shy little rabbits and Badgers hiding from justice . . . and then we can sell them at the grand country fayre where folk gather from far and wide . . . Glastonbury!' 'Yeah,' says Rosie. 'They don't know them ain't magic mushrooms. They'll buy anything – bloody townies!'

Don't Give Up the Day Job
The second Mrs de Winter gives a business presentation

Preamble . . . you may remember Mrs de Winter from the novel Rebecca, *which famously begins, 'Last night I dreamt I went to Manderley again.' Well, now Manderley is a carpet warehouse and she is addressing the staff.*

Last night I dreamt I was in Underlay again – a humble trainee, before Maxim – as you know, Maxim is our West Country area manager – promoted me to the dizzy heights of Persian rugs, a position formerly held by Rebecca de Winter. It was difficult at first . . . I had no confidence, I didn't want to change any of the window displays . . . Rebecca had such exquisite taste . . . I couldn't compete. Maxim was so cold and aloof and my assistant Mrs Danvers was a *bitch on wheels* – incidentally I've had to let her go. For future reference, encouraging your boss to jump out of the window and kill herself is now a sacking offence.

It's silly really, it was all a misunderstanding. There was I, thinking that Maxim wanted Rebecca back and wished he'd never promoted me; all the time it was that he was worried that people would find out that he'd murdered Rebecca! Talk about making a mountain out of a molehill! This brings me to my first rule of business – *communication* – talk to each other. I can't stress this enough, people. Well, I helped him to conceal that crime and now we're a great team, and sales of Persian rugs are through the roof.

This is my second point. The importance of co-operation. Partnership with Management. Never be afraid of new ideas. As Maxim always says, 'Shoot her dead, put a hole in her planking, shove her out to sea and see if anyone finds her.' A couple more points I'd like to make: firstly, in the light of recent events, could staff please take fire drills a little more seriously – insurance companies aren't complete idiots, you know.

Secondly, there has been a very disappointing response to our Outward Bound weekend, 'Sailing with Maxim'– come on, team, you know how important these bonding sessions are – so let's all pull together and I know we can make this place the best darned fire-damaged carpet warehouse in Cornwall. Thank you.

Don't Give Up Your Day Job
Puff Daddy writes Alastair Cooke's Letter from America

Yeah, Puffy Daddy here to represent the word on the street to all of my homies Radio Fourside – that's 92.4 – 94.5 FM KILLER HERTZ – this one goes out to my brother rappers Brian Ice T

Perkins, MC Peter Donaldson, not forgetting Queen Charlotte Green.

> *Now I'm sure you all know from way back in the*
>   *day 'bout*
> *Snoop Cooky Cooke's letter from the USA*
> *Now I ain't disrespectin my homie AC*
> *But he's been banging out these letters since*
>   *1903 – 1903*

> *I don't say the letter's boring*
> *But I couldn't tune to that*
> *If a mother friggin gangsta*
> *had an uzi in my back*

(Yeah, and I listened to *The Archers* that way once – hey, this one goes out to the Ambridge posse – come on, Ambridge, big up yourself . . . big up! ooo ooo . . . yeah, you know what ? I'm gonna go to the garden centre in Borchester and I'm gonna get me a ho', yeah, a real fine hoe and do some serious weeding.)

> *Yeah! That letter from America is so long I gotta say*
> *with huge sections in parenthesis that seem to last all day*
> *it seems to last much longer than ten rounds with*
>   *Sugar Ray*

(Yeah, that a long time, bro. Hey, sending out a special request to *Poetry Please*. Hey, anyway, why ain't none of my rhymes on *Poetry Please*? Let's hear from the *Poetry Please* posse, big up! Come on, Frank Delaney, you're my main man. The homie sent me to see *Shakespeare in Love,* told me it was full of doublet and hose, well, I see the doublet but I didn't see no hose, disappointing movie.)

> *So I'm gonna keep it real rapping 'bout the USA*
> *it don't take very long to see what's going down today*

'cos it's all about the Benjamins ain't nothin' more to say
yeah, it's all about the Benjamins
don't listen to no jive
'cos you'd be better off listening to Money Box Live.

(Respect to the *Money Box Live* posse, help you hang on to your Benjamins – Louise Botting big up Louise Botting, told me a real cheap place to buy the game of subbuteo. Guy in the shop said, is this subbuteo bought as a gift? I said yeah, gonna wrap my pitch up!)

Old AC puts out the word from departed presidential
    bros,
Dead Kennedy, Nixon, LBJ and Wilson – Woodrow
But I represent what's happening now
It's all you need to know
I keep my letter brief, I know what's goin' on
Now it's time for the Morning Story *–*
Just William *– straight outta Richmal Crompton*
That's all the word I'm giving you with my big beat box
so you folks get back to wondering,
whatever happened to Slightly Foxed?
So goodbye, UK posse, goodnight and sleep tight
My final words to you are Fisher, Dogger, not
    forgetting German Bight.

Chekhov Meets The Sopranos – A Litcom (a literature-based sitcom)

Linda reworks the entire output of Chekhov as The Sopranos – Channel 4 TV's hit Mafia drama series set in New Jersey.

(Cue: Theme music 'Woke Up This Morning' by The Alabama Three)
(Scene: A heavy-set, menacing man enters a psychiatrist's consulting room)

DR MELFI: Mr Supranovitch, do come in, take a seat.

TONY: Thanks, Doc.

DR MELFI: So, how are you feeling?

TONY: Ehh, what can I tell you? If you want to test Prozac to destruction, just give it to a Chekhov character.

DR MELFI: So are you still depressed?

TONY: Are you kidding me? Am I still depressed? Is Jimmy Hoffa still missing? Yeah, I'm still depressed.

DR MELFI: I'd like to try and find the roots of this depression – last week you talked a little about your family – do you find them difficult?

TONY: Again, are you kiddin' me? Do I find them difficult? Do I find pasta a good source of complex carbohydrate? Forget difficult, try unfuckin' believable. Take my Uncle Vanya . . . please. Guy's a schmuck on wheels. Sits around all day, whining and belly-aching about the futility of human existence with his deadbeat pals. What a loser.

DR MELFI: What do you mean?

TONY: Take the other day as a 'for instance', I'm round at his place. 'Hi, Uncle Vanya. How ya doin?' You know what he says?

UNCLE VANYA: I have wasted my life! I have not lived! Yet, if I could annihilate the future I would do it! Unbearable!

TONY: And then, the crazy old borsch-eater starts waving a piece about.

DR MELFI: Piece?

TONY: Yeah, a piece, a gun – then the son of a bitch tries to whack me – and misses! Twice! Can you fuckin' believe that? Uncle Vanya is a made guy . . . I don't know what to be more depressed about, that he tries to whack me, or that he misses.

DR MELFI: Oh my goodness – what did you do?

TONY: Look, forget about it – you don't need to know, it was a Chekhov character thing – it was among the blini eaters – there was a problem and I took care of it.

DR MELFI: But don't you have any happier family relationships? What about your three sisters, aren't they more congenial?

TONY: What, the three sisters? Congenial? Lady, for your information, the three sisters are called Olga, Masha and Irena, not Curly, Larry and Mo. Congenial! That's a good one! Those broads drive me nuts! Always breaking my balls about going to Moscow. 'When are we going to Moscow? Take me to Moscow. I want to go to Moscow, nee nee nee nee.' I keep tellin' em, I don't control the Moscow territory – it's run by the Tolstoy family and I don't want a problem with that crazy fuck Leo – he's the Counto de Tutti Countos. Believe me, I've had War and Peace with Tolstoy and I know which I prefer.

DR MELFI: Apart from this conflict over Moscow – what is your relationship with your sisters like?

TONY: Terrible! I'd rather spend the evening with an FBI snitch with a wire tap.

DR MELFI: What about your friend Ivanov?

TONY: What! That nutjob! Talk about a fruit cake – the guy had raisins for eyes! One minute he's getting married, the next minute he whips out a piece and bang! Turns himself into street pizza. So naturally I'm upset, right?

DR MELFI: Of course.

TONY: Yeah, so I turn to my girlfriend Masha for consolation.

DR MELFI: That's Masha from *The Seagull?*

TONY: Yeah, that's it – I go to see her, there she is, sitting there with a face like a frozen yoghurt – hey, babe I say, how comes you're always wearing black? You know what she tells me? 'I'm in mourning for my life. I'm unhappy.' 'Oh,' I says, trying to lighten her up a bit, 'I thought it was to make you fat but look smaller.' She went nuts. Starts mouthing about her tormented Russian soul. Jeez, I gotta get out of this nuthouse, Doc.

DR MELFI: Well, why don't you get out – change your life?

TONY: Lady, have you actually read any Chekhov? Chekhov is like New Jersey – there are just two ways out – a bullet in the head or the New Jersey Turnpike. Except in Chekhov, there ain't no New Jersey Turnpike. No, I'm stuck here with all the freaking suicides and nihilists, the damn birch trees and samovars.

DR MELFI: Samovars?

TONY: Yeah, samovars, everyone's always swilling this goddamn faggotty Russian tea – hey, doesn't anyone ever think to offer a person a cappuccino or an espresso now and then? . . . God forbid they should keep biscotti or canolli in the house . . .

DR MELFI: Mr Supranovitch, I think I might be able to help you. I'm increasing your medication. I'm giving you 500 gallons of Prozac.

TONY: What! Are you kidding me?

DR MELFI: Take it, Mr Supranovitch, and the next time you're at a tea party, just slip a couple of pints into the Samovar – I think your situation will improve.

TONY: Doc, you're a genius . . . a fuckin' genius.

★

Women in Love *in the style of* Are You Being Served?

The D. H. Lawrence classic reworked in the style of this equally classic British TV sitcom. Women in Love *is a story of passion and relationships and great theorising about life and philosophy and* Are You Being Served? *isn't really.*

Scene: Grace Brothers Department Store

Miss Brahms: played by Linda Smith
Mr Lucas: played by Stuart Maconie
Mr Humphries: played by David Stafford
Mrs Slocombe: played by Dillie Keane

(Junior assistant Mr Lucas stands by the lift)

MR LUCAS: First floor, lingerie, silk stockings, negligees, going up! Up, thrusting up, burgeoning up, the sheer hydraulic vigour of the lift. The inexorable lift force, the elemental lift force bursting like a flood tide through soft furnishings and customer care.

MR HUMPHRIES: Er, Mr Lucas . . .

MR LUCAS: And then down, down, crashing down through the mezzanine level, hosiery and umbrellas to the dank primeval basement, the very bowels, the viscera, the fecund nether parts, the sacred brutal womb savage and real, the deep dark eternal pit that leads us to the very core of our authentic animal self, and of course, to china and glass.

MR HUMPHRIES: Mr Lucas, are you free?

MR LUCAS: Free, does it sound like it? Never free. No. Trapped in the sickly death-loving maw of consumerism. How can I be free? Or you, Mr Humphries, or Miss Brahms, or you, Mrs Slocombe.

MRS SLOCOMBE: Just a minute, Mr Lucas, my pussy is stuck in the cat flap.

MR LUCAS: Oh, Mrs Slocombe, if we are to have a true understanding as God's beings you must say what you really mean.

MRS SLOCOMBE: I mean my pussy is all of a doodah.

MR LUCAS: No, please stop hiding behind these double entendres.

MRS SLOCOMBE: But my pussy is suffering from exposure.

MR LUCAS: You can say that again. Miss Brahms, you're in bondage.

MISS BRAHMS: No I'm not, I'm in haberdashery.

MR LUCAS: I mean you're in chains.

MISS BRAHMS: Not on a first date I'm not, saucebox.

MR LUCAS: Throw off the shackles of convention, Miss Brahms. Join me in a true blood marriage, the eternal . . .

MISS BRAHMS: Marriage. Ooah, are you proposing?

MR LUCAS: Not exactly, I meant more of a physical meeting.

MISS BRAHMS: Oh yeah, a physical meeting. That's a new one, you filthy beast!

MR HUMPHRIES: Mr Lucas, this gentleman's inside leg measurement won't take itself, you know.

MR LUCAS: Oh, Mr Humphries, beneath these tawdry innuendos aren't you really saying that you want to know me intimately?

MR HUMPHRIES: I don't know what you mean I'm sure.

MR LUCAS: You want to touch my wellspring.

MR HUMPHRIES: Ooh, that's better, an innuendo, now I'll do one. Oooh, I feel dizzy. Must be that mince I had earlier.

MR LUCAS: Mr Humphries, are you interested in blut brude chat?

MR HUMPHRIES: Oh, I love anything by Liza Minnelli, that's from *Cabaret*, isn't it?

MR LUCAS: No, it's a blood oath between men. Eternal friendship. To truly know each other as men, spiritually and physically, we must wrestle naked on the floor.

MR HUMPHRIES: Oh well. Anything for staff bonding.
(they wrestle with appropriate noises and gestures)

MR LUCAS: Do you feel it, Mr Humphries? The sheer exhilarating electric fire.

MR HUMPHRIES: Yes, I put the extra bar on.

MR LUCAS: Let's bind our lives together, eternally.

MRS SLOCOMBE: Mr Humphries, I've never seen you like this. Your animal magnificence. Your supernatural energy. My heart beats to the rhythm of nature and yearns for a new honesty between men and women.

MR HUMPHRIES: Oh, that's really good, Mrs Slocombe.

MISS BRAHMS: Great. Good stuff, Mrs Slocombe.

MR HUMPHRIES: No more double entendres then?

MRS SLOCOMBE: And as soon as I've thawed out my pussy.

(a chorus) Oh, Mrs Slocombe!

MRS SLOCOMBE: Oh sorry, force of habit.

Maria von Trapp (interviewee) from The Sound of Music, *interviewed for a position on the Board of Film Censors*

Scene: Famous literary figures being interviewed for contemporary jobs

Maria von Trapp: played by Linda Smith
Interviewer: played by David Stafford

MARIA: (sings) Climb every mountain, hmm . . . hmm . . . hmm . . .

INTERVIEWER: Do come in, Ms . . .?

MARIA: Von Trapp. Maria von Trapp

INTERVIEWER: So, you're interested in joining the Board of Film Censors?

MARIA: Oh yes! Very keen, very keen.

INTERVIEWER: You seem very confident.

MARIA: (sings) Oh yes, you will see I have confidence in me.

INTERVIEWER: Would you mind not singing?

MARIA: I'm sorry, I can't help it, it's a form of Tourette's Syndrome.

INTERVIEWER: Odd. So, first things first. What's your previous work experience?

MARIA: Nun.

INTERVIEWER: What, none at all?

MARIA: No. Nun.

INTERVIEWER: Not even voluntary work?

MARIA: No. Nun. I'm an ex-nun, you see. I used to be in a convent.

INTERVIEWER: How sweet. So when did you first become interested in cinema?

MARIA: When I was in the convent, we had a little film club. Actually, that's also where I first became interested in censorship.

INTERVIEWER: Oh really?

MARIA: Yes. You see, obviously not all the films we got sent were suitable for, shall we say, Catholic tastes, so Mother Superior would censor them but without compromising their artistic integrity of course.

INTERVIEWER: Of course. That's interesting. So what films did you see?

MARIA: Well, I particularly enjoyed the Texas Chainsaw Mass. A heart-warming tale of God-fearing lumberjacks. A very exciting film was *The Nuns of Navarone*. Of course, the classic *Nunfight at the OK Corral*, I enjoyed that a lot.

INTERVIEWER: These films must have been butchered.

MARIA: No, no, no, not at all.

INTERVIEWER: Well, do you at least have any new ideas about, say, film classification?

MARIA: Oh yes I do. I'd introduce a whole new system of classification based on musical notes. For example, Doh – a film, a Simpsons film, Ray – some filth with Ray Winstone.

INTERVIEWER: That's enough. That's enough. Quite honestly, whoever told you you'd make a good film censor gave you very bad advice.

MARIA: (sings to the tune of 'Edelweiss') Bad advice, bad advice . . .

INTERVIEWER: Will you please shut up, Miss von Trapp. Please send in the next candidate, and I only hope to God they're nothing like you. Your ideas are mad, your voice gets right up my nose and you've got no dress sense. OK. Next candidate. Miss Widdecombe?

I Claudius *in the style of* Casualty

Creating a new soap opera based on a literary theme. Hopefully, my soap will soon be developed by Channel 4 TV

Scene: The Casualty Department of Holby General Hospital
  Theme music and background noise of a hospital
  It's a busy night; CHARLIE the charge nurse takes charge

Charlie: played by David Stafford
Duffy: played by Linda Smith
Sonny: played by Stuart Maconie
Sam: played by Mark Thomas

CHARLIE: I want all available staff to Casualty right now. We've had an intake of serious trauma cases from Rome.

DUFFY: But Charlie, Rome's 2,000 miles away.

CHARLIE: I know, Duffy, but we're the nearest Casualty Department that's open. It's a disgrace. This is no time for one of my impassioned speeches about the NHS. The porters have the first of the injured. Sonny, what's happened to this patient?

SONNY: Young fella named Caligula, sports injury you might say. He was stabbed on the way to the match at the Coliseum. He doesn't even know that his team, The Lions, won easily.

DUFFY: BP 90 over 60, pulse 140, looks bad. Sam, you're a nice but nosy gay nurse, what about family? Does he have any next of kin?

SAM: Umm, yes, he does, most of them frequently!

CHARLIE: Give him two units of uncrossed matched blood.

SAM: Uncrossed matched? You'll be lucky with this lot, they're all inter-related. Talk about duelling banjos. Being a nice but nosy gay nurse, I found out about his family, the Claudians. Talk about toga parties. Apparently, chummy here got jiggy with his sister, married her, then went more bonkers.

CHARLIE: There's no time for your gossip now, son. Here's Sonny with some more cases.

SONNY: I'm only a cheery but dim porter, but this lot look like they've been poisoned.

DUFFY: Poisoned! God, they've not been eating the hospital food, have they?

CHARLIE: No, Duffy, although you are right about hospital food. It's a dis-grace. But this is no time for one of my impassioned speeches about the NHS. Hmm, discoloration of lips, pupils dilated, vomiting. Sam, any more information?

SAM: Mmm yeah, more Claudians – Drusus, Germanicus, Marcellus, Augustus – all suffering from food poisoning. They fell ill after getting a buffet supplied by Lady Livia's 'Food to Die For'.

CHARLIE: Come on, SPCs, and U&Gs.

SAM: Mmm, well, being a nice but nosy gay nurse, I've been chatting to a Mr I Claudius, just arrived in a minibus at Outpatients for speech therapy and a new orthopaedic boot, and *he* says that Livia, his grand-mother, deliberately poisoned Germanicus, his brother, and Drusus, his father, who is also her son and she . . .

DUFFY: Oh, my God! Keep him talking, Sam, I'll phone social services and the police, this lot makes the Windsors look like the Waltons.

CHARLIE: God, I hate Saturday night shifts!

SONNY: Here, hold on, I've seen all this on the telly. This all happened 2,000 years ago.

CHARLIE: That's right, Sonny, and they've only just reached the top of the waiting list. It's a disgrace. At last! It is time to make my impassioned speech about the NHS, the closures, the waiting lists, the crap food
. . .

Mr Stevens meets Hannibal Lecter (the meeting of two fictional characters)

Hannibal Lecter, the psychopathic serial killer from Silence of the Lambs, *played in the film by Anthony Hopkins, and the very, very deferential butler Mr Stevens from the novel* The Remains of the Day, *played again in the film by Anthony Hopkins.*

| Stevens: | played by Linda Smith |
| Hannibal Lecter: | played by David Stafford |

STEVENS: Finding myself in need of a new situation (my previous employer, alas, having become so persecuted for his Nazi politics that he has had to go into hiding as a *Daily Mail* columnist), I have taken up a position as butler to a Dr Lecter, a cultured man, of refined tastes. I believe we are well suited, for like myself he believes in a strict pecking order – in fact he gets quite excited about the pecking order. Dr Lecter has special dietary requirements due to a serious medical condition known as 'being a psychopath'. I have made it my duty to satisfy these requirements. Earlier, I entered his study . . .

MUSIC: Bit of *Goldberg Variations*

LECTER: Ah, Stevens, Bach! Bach!

STEVENS: Woof, woof, sir.

LECTER: No, Stevens! Bach!

STEVENS: Oh, I see, sir, 'Stevens Bach'! Well, thank you, 'Sir Boyo!' but I don't think I should be playing either of these characters quite so . . . Welsh – if you don't mind me saying.

LECTER: The music, you idiot.

STEVENS: Ahh, I see, sir, yes indeed, sir.

LECTER: Has that pizza delivery boy arrived yet?

STEVENS: No, sir.

LECTER: Excellent! Another ten minutes and I get him for free! You can have the pizza if you like, Stevens. By the way, Stevens, don't order me any more of those so-called donna kebabs, what a misleadingly named snack.

STEVENS: Very well, sir – but if sir had seen fit to mention that sir was peckish, there's still most of the postman's leg in the fridge. I could have made a sandwich on a tray.

LECTER: How many times have I told you, Stevens, I don't like leftovers. I won't eat The Remains on a Tray, besides, he was a bit stringy – all that cycling, I suppose.

STEVENS: Apologies, sir.

LECTER: By the way, Stevens, I think this book, *The Little Book of Bowing and Scraping*, is yours. I'm afraid the bookmark has fallen out though.

STEVENS: Oh, sir, not to worry, I think I know my place.

LECTER: That will be all, my good fellow – oh, by the way I am having a few people for dinner tonight.

STEVENS: Bon appétit, sir.

I spent my afternoon off playing my favourite record, *Now That's What I Call Deference Vol. III*, then I descended to the dining room to clear away the Remains of the Fray. This is the scene that met my eyes: the room was splattered with blood and viscera, severed limbs dangled from the chandelier, torsos were jammed in the sideboard; Dr Lecter dreamily spooned brains from a human skull whilst playing Kerplunk with a stack of eyeballs. I froze in horror, my heart stopped beating, I stared like a madman scarcely believing the evidence of my own eyes – my employer, my master, was drinking from a dirty glass! A great smeary smudge of a fingerprint on the rim for the whole world to see! That flighty young parlourmaid Polly was responsible for this, I'll be prepared to wager. I'd be giving her a piece of my mind, make no mistake – the girl was a slattern and would doubtless end up in prison.

STEVENS: Oh, sir, the glass, I am so ashamed, I can't apologise enough, sir.

LECTER: Oh well, no one's perfect, Stevens. Don't look so nervous, man, I am not going to bite your head off.

STEVENS: You are far too lenient, sir . . . by the way, there's a policeman at the door . . . shall I send him in?

LECTER: Oh no, Stevens, I couldn't eat another bite . . .

THE BEATON GENERATION
BBC Radio 4

National Pet Week

My initial excitement about *National Pet Week* – brilliant! A whole
week of re-runs of *Whatever Happened to the Likely Lads* – sub-
sided when I realised it was about animal awareness – animal
awareness – anyone who uses pavements for walking on can't
help but be aware of them! Make the dogshit slalom an Olympic
sport and there's your British gold medal.

Of course, when I was a child it was different – pet owners
were responsible – they collected up their dogs' do's and sent it
off to help the war effort, to build Spitfires and make powdered
egg . . . and now I know some of you youngsters out there won't
remember, but in those days the scariest dog was any Alsatian –
imagine that! Now that every tosser down The Pitbull and Balcony has got a picture of a devil dog in their front window with
the sign 'Break in, make my day'. Ironic really, because a photo
of the owners would be more effective – 'Break in, and I'll bore
the tits off you explaining why Enoch Powell was such a brilliant
man.'

Possibly I'm a bit bitter, because of my dodgy track record with
pets – I've had a few duff ones. First Fluffy, the only cat in the
world that wouldn't wash. The vet gave us some weird Marmite-
type stuff to rub in his fur, which was supposed to be so delicious
to cats that he would lick it off and get the idea of this washing
business. Fluffy completely ignored this fascist interference with
his dirty protest, so now we still had a filthy cat but he was covered
in weird Marmite-type stuff as well. When he walked past it was
like being downwind of Runcorn.

Then there was Tommy the Tortoise, who got stuck down the
side of the shed and turned into Tommy the percussion instru-
ment, a great hit at assemblies. (Kum bay yah, my lord.) I felt
betrayed by the animal world. Still, National Pet Week has some
top events: pet church services; sponsored pet walks; pet *Univer-*

sity Challenge: 'Oh, come on, Fido, what did Elizabethan gentle-men wear round their necks?' 'Ruff.' 'That's right, now Chorley Wood Obedience School, your starter. What kind of trade did Joe Orton like? . . . 'Oh, come on, Bonzo!'

Some of these days and weeks coming up don't sound quite as good: National Parenting Day of 5 May for example. Are the sort of crap parents who think the legend 'Small children can choke on nuts' is a serving suggestion going to turn into Mary Poppins because of National Parenting Day? And *Day of the Midwife* sounds like a low-budget horror movie. *Day of the Midwife* when giant midwives stalk the metropolis delivering babies to people who just haven't got the room. I suggest something less ambitious, a week devoted to a more manageable problem. I announce National That feeling you get that you've left the grill on at home even though you know you can't have because you haven't even used the grill today but you have to go back and check even though you're nearly at the station because you won't have a moment's peace all day unless you do – Week.

CLIVE ANDERSON'S CHAT ROOM,
BBC Radio 2

On Mandelson and Kinnock as EU Commissioners

LINDA (to Neil Kinnock): What was it, that job?
(KINNOCK: I could describe it to you in a minute . . . but I don't think we've got a minute . . . Kinnock begins to explain various roles of a Commissioner . . .)
Is anyone else slipping into a light coma ?
(KINNOCK: I was trying to save the nation . . .)

Nobody knows what they do, this is the problem with you people in Government, no one knows what you do and nobody is inter-ested. Any job where you can't describe it in a word . . . you know – comedian, journalist, broadcaster – whatever . . . Any job where they can start telling you what they're doing and in the meantime you can go off, watch something on telly, make a meal and fashion a lovely origami swan . . . and then at the end of it you *still* don't know what they do – IT ISN'T A REAL JOB!

On Prince Charles's staff and sex discrimination

Could I just put in a word in Prince Charles's defence . . . that I feel a certain amount of sympathy with him over this because it must be very galling to see people promoted all around you when you've fought and struggled and sweated your way to be born and then somehow for fifty-odd years you hit a glass ceiling . . . and you just can't get promoted that extra notch . . .

what provoked him to say this? . . .

Two points . . . the first one is – the thing that provoked this silly memo was that – one woman said what seemed to be a perfectly reasonable thing – people with degrees within his employment, you know, it might be thought that they could perhaps train to move up to another office – that doesn't sound so completely out-rageous, does it? First thing . . . and as for him having been born to what he's been doing and all that – well, I'm not impressed with the fact that he's born to be prince and he's managed to *be* the prince, you know, I was born to be a teenage crack addict with three kids by the time I was seventeen but I'm not. I'm more impressed with that, frankly . . .

On the new TV series, The Sex Inspectors

What's newsworthy about it is that it's another one of these awful things of 'experts' telling you how to do things – these sexperts as they call it – and I for one will not be watching it – it's a horrible idea. This couple saying, 'Well, there's something wrong with our sex life . . . ' Yes! IT'S ON THE TELLY – THAT'S WHAT'S WRONG WITH IT.

On David Blunkett's affairs

In terms of David Blunkett it's actually kind of wonderful 'cos I've always referred to him as Satan's Bearded Folk Singer, as I've always seen him as a dour and forbidding figure. Now it's David Blunkett, International Man of Mystery . . .

On the England cricket team being advised not to tour Zimbabwe by HM Government

Well, I am actually a cricket fan – I enjoy cricket – but what I find interesting is that quite a few of the voices in cricket who are saying, 'No – they shouldn't go, they absolutely shouldn't go. How can they with all the terrible things that Mugabe is doing to the white farmers?', were quite keen to go to South Africa during apartheid, and it's interesting how their view has changed now that the victims are perceived to be predominantly white. That's not true actually, far more black people in Zimbabwe are victims of Mugabe and have been for a long time and no one bothered about it – but as soon as it affects white farmers, about whom of course it's equally terrible that they are being murdered – but you see, I wish that those same voices were raised as loudly against apartheid as they are against Mugabe.

MONOLOGUES
From *The Treatment*, BBC Radio 5

Televised debate

During this year's Conservative Party conference William Hague challenged Tony Blair to a televised debate in the lead-up to the next election. But now Hague's advisers are rumoured to be trying to make him reconsider. Would the sight of party leaders slugging it out on TV add anything to our political culture? Giving the Dimblebys a run for their money . . . Linda Smith:

This is a fantastic idea, originating in America, where it has recently proved so effective in helping the public to make up their minds. That was sarcasm, of course. It is a terrible idea. I could be wrong, but I don't think many people go through the *Radio Times* underlining all the coming week's live coverage from Parliament in red biro so as not to miss any 'debates', so why should they get any extra airtime? Besides, how would politicians like it if Entertainment invaded Parliament the way it's invaded Entertainment? If instead of Parliament on telly, you had telly in Parliament? It would be ridiculous – imagine *Animal Hospital* broadcast from the House of Lords – yeah, well, that's a bad example, but you get my drift. We must have strict demarcation between rubbish, i.e. so-called 'debates' between Blair, Hague and that other one, the fiddle player Kennedy, and legitimate programming.

If these people want to break into showbiz, let them do it the hard way – get an act. Of course, Hague already has a lucrative sideline as a voice-over artist – most famously as Wallace from Wallace and Gromit, 'Oh, it's the wrong trousers, Gromit.' Tony Blair and his pal Peter Mandelson could curry favour in their North-East constituencies by remaking *Whatever Happened to the Likely Lads* with Tony Blair as the socially ambitious Bob, Peter as the eternal bachelor Terry, and Cherie as snooty Thelma Pet. And if they *must* have a televised debate – if they insist upon it – then don't have it chaired by one of the hereditary presenters, The Dimblebys. Have it chaired by someone with suitable gravitas, say Paul Ross.

He could maybe do it – as part of his cable hit *Psychic Challenge*. I think that would be brilliant, where psychics have to guess things about the competitors, but then of course any hapless medium who started staring at Tony Blair for any length of time is likely to start screaming 'His eyes, what's wrong with his eyes?' and crash terrified from the nearest window on to an ironically placed crucifix. But this really is a point with me. I'm sick of these hereditary Dimblebys and I think it should be revealed, here and now this morning, that the Dimblebys aren't even English, they're German.

They used to be the von Dimbleburgs, and to curry favour with the British public they changed it. They do in fact have a tragic uncle – Baron Josef von Dimbleburg – who is languishing in a mental hospital now, not allowed to be seen by us, and I think the truth should come out.

Nick Reilly – caring boss

Nick Reilly at Vauxhall has said that he is prepared to give up his dosh for a year – that's one hundred and sixty grand – if unions agree to a proposed pay deal. With her thoughts here's Linda Smith:

I don't know any Captains of Industry, but I know what they're like from the television. When I was a kid they were always played by that actor with bad skin, Ray somebody; he was dripping with Brylcreem, drank whisky and soda all day long and was head of Multinational Flanges, a vast corporation grown from humble beginnings run by a ruthlessly ambitious family at war within itself, with all the tension that implies. He always had to shout, even on the phone. 'I want those Buenos Aires figures and I want them yesterday.' 'Take a letter, Miss Jones, and drink a whisky and soda for me, I'm just too damned busy.' 'Cross me, Sir John, and I'll break you like a twig. One of those snappy ones, not a bendy one.' 'Jenkins, nip round to my house and have sex with my wife. I'm just too damned busy.'

But this image has been shattered for me now by Nick 'Call me Nick' Reilly, a boss who isn't motivated by money and power, he does it for lurve . . . yeah, he the lurve boss, mm mm. His office is lit by a strange, saintly glow – shy woodland creatures approach his desk without fear. He speaks gently to his workforce: 'Look, team, things are tough, not so many people want Vauxhalls these days, even though we've got an advert where a man says "The Vectra from Vauxhall" as if he's about to be sick. But we're all in the same boat. Huh! The *Titanic*. Huh! Of course, you're in steerage and I'm in first class, so if we hit an iceberg you're well stuffed . . . and I don't like this analogy any more. Anyway, just to show my lurve, I'm going to forgo my salary this year if you'll accept a tiny little pay rise, OK. Ciao! Big hugs! Big hugs! Oh, Miss Jones, make sure that I recoup my lost salary in bonuses next year if this deal goes through and pick up my salaries from the other five companies I am president of. I'm just too damned busy. I could snap you like a twig.'

Gay footballer

Last Saturday Robbie Fowler, Liverpool's golden lad, is alleged to have insulted Graham Le Saux, Chelsea's book-reading intellectual. Why is football stuck in this Neanderthal age where it is deemed acceptable to taunt people in this way?

Reading the *Guardian* and a passion for antiques are not common activities for footballers – except of course for seventies midfield ace Arthur 'bites yer legs' Negus – a notorious hardman, who would goad his opponents beyond endurance with his taunts: 'You know that eighteenth-century barometer you just bought, Rodney Marsh? It's a fake! Ha Ha!' 'Have you read Monday's Arts and Media section yet, Bestie? Of course you haven't, you lightweight!' But *nor* are these hobbies surefire proof of gayness: my next-door neighbours, both devoted friends of Dorothy, wouldn't line their cat litter with the *Guardian* and the only antique they're interested in is Cilla Black.

Of course you couldn't expect the . . . er . . . differently bright Robbie Fowler to know this – or indeed that allegedly offering the free run of his tradesmen's entrance to Graeme Le Saux proves anything about Le Saux's predilictions. Still, my Aunt Val always offers me Battenberg cake – she knows I don't like it. It's just a wind-up. Full marks to Fowler for not starting a rumour that Le Saux is black. There have been other intellectual players. Trevor Brooking had some 'O' and 'A' levels, I don't think anyone called him a poof – but that's probably because they didn't want to send him off on one: 'Well, I don't know, it depends what you mean by poof, I mean on the one hand no but on the other hand maybe, but

I don't really want to commit myself to a point of view if you wouldn't mind.'

No, normal, macho footballers prefer *real* men's hobbies like modelling frocks (David Beckham), girlie hair products (David Ginola) or drenching themselves in perfume (Kevin Keegan – remember those Brut adverts?). We've all got our prejudices, I for example don't like floppy-haired bespectacled ex-MP football pundits who go I . . . I . . . I . . . in a stupid way. But the fact that both Fowler and Le Saux think 'gay' is a terrible insult shows that bigotry will not change until people can be openly gay in all walks of life, not just cat breeding and musicals. Oh, I forgot, I don't like Leeds fans either. But they're a bunch of bigots.

Mobile phones

Up till now the only health risk associated with mobile phones has been the other passengers on the train getting so irate that they ram it down your throat. But perhaps they're more dangerous than we think. A biologist who is convinced that mobiles can cause cancer took his case into the courts this week. Guardian of the nation's health or a nutty technophobe – Linda Smith has the answer.

This is very worrying news if you use mobile phones, but I don't, so as Nelson Muntz from *The Simpsons* would say, 'Ha! Ha!' Oh, none of my mates are in danger 'cos their mobiles are always switched off when you ring, you just get that snooty cow who says, 'The mobile phone you are ringing is switched off. Ha! Ha!' No, those at risk are merchant bankers (in both senses), who keep up this constant sub-Joyceian stream of consciousness on the phone, willing participants in an audio Truman Show – 'Yes, yes, on the train, darling . . . pulling into the station . . . .yes, chuffa chuffa whoo whoo . . . in the car now . . . pulling up outside the house, walking up the path, OK, darling open the door in 5, 4, 3, 2, 1. Hello, darling, can't talk, I'm on the mobile.'

Of course, a mobile is a godsend in an emergency. 'Hello, darling, yes, supermarket, there's no Abbey Crunch, so I got Gypsy

Creams . . . oh, you prefer Fruit Jaspers . . . thank God for the mobile.' According to this same scientist, Roger Coghill, mobiles aren't the only death-traps in everyday life; there's car tyres, TVs, photocopiers (which is great news for those fed up with the office wag who thinks it's hilarious to photocopy his (I'm guessing his) bum), microwaves and even hairdryers, if used for more than ten minutes at a time – cor, that must be causing panic in the world of country music.

Now I'm not anti-research, like those outraged farmers who say, 'How dare these boffins say our meat's rancid and diseased just because it's rancid and diseased – bloody townies!' and I don't subscribe to old wives' bollocks like 'Best thing in the world for you, TB, drives out polio.' And who knows if these findings are true or not, because, like most people, what I know about science could be written, and in fact has been written, on the first twelve pages of *A Brief History of Time* (and that includes the introduction and publisher's name).

But this idea that the world is getting more dangerous compared to what? To the Black Death? The Irish Famine? I think not. True, no one had to worry about getting cancer from the spinning jenny, but that's because they'd already fallen in it and been mangled to death. Your average boy chimney sweep had to have a mid-life crisis at the age of seven: 'Oh, now I've got my own brush and soot bucket, what's the point?' Even amongst the rich, young men died of cravats or syphilis, young ladies died out of politeness really.

So dodgy phones are disturbing, yes, but in the danger stakes, they're hardly the First World War, are they? Wilfred Owen would have had his work cut out trying to be the poetic voice of the lost generation of microwave victims: 'The white eyes writhing in his face, his lolling face, like a devil's sick of . . . *trying to get that shepherd's pie warmed up.*' No, if you're really worried about it, just try a bit of string and two yoghurt pots.

Weather wars

Storm clouds gather at BBC Weather Centre as some of the nation's best-loved weather men find themselves in a deep trough as a warm front of telegenic weather women pushes in – Linda Smith is here to tell us which way the wind blows.

As Bob Dylan says, you don't need a weatherman to tell which way the wind blows – just as well really, as Michael Fish couldn't spot a hurricane if it whistled up his Farrah slacks and ruffled his moustache. Personally, I felt sorry for him in 1987 – what difference would it have made if he had predicted the Great Storm? What would we have done, brought all the trees indoors? Nailed Hampshire down? Chucked a tarpaulin over Kent? But now, thirteen years on, there's trouble at the Met Office again. Firstly, there was the, to the outsider, frankly baffling allegations made by Fish and John Kettley, of bullying at the Meteorological Office. How on earth do weathermen bully each other? Does Bill Giles swagger about going, 'Oi! Kettley! You said there'd be drizzle in the Midlands – didn't happen, did it? You're rubbish, Kettley, and you know you are! Oi! Fishy! Don't say isobars, right? *I* say isobars. Isobars is *my* word, so stop copying me, right, or you'll get a Chinese burn.'

On top of this, Kettley and Fish have now been downsized, replaced by a new, young, almost exclusively female team. Yes, they're your Weather Girls and it's draining men! What a palaver! Just when exactly did guessing the weather become the new Rock and Roll? I mean, one minute they're a bunch of civil servants, the next they're all drama queens! The Met Office must look like something out of *A Chorus Line*, with nervous young hopeful weather people in leg-warmers going, 'The six o'clock weather slot – oh God, I hope I get it. I really hope I get it'. The whole of English culture is steeped in weather. Our great artist Turner with his *Storms at Sea*, Dickens with his descriptions of fog, Thomas Hardy's rain-lashed Wessex, Shakespeare and his blasted heath. We have far more words for rain than Eskimos have for snow – spitting, pouring cats and dogs, scattered showers, on it goes – in fact if Earth,Wind and Fire had been a British band, they wouldn't be Earth,Wind and Fire, they'd be called Cloudy to start, with a bit of drizzle, clearing up later with sunny spells, but quite seasonable for the time of year, mustn't grumble.

Curry scare

Until now the worst you could expect from a curry in the health stakes was summed up in the old joke about putting the toilet paper in the fridge, but it was reported this week that some Indian restaurants have been using illegally high amounts of colouring that can cause rashes, breathing difficulties and even asthma attacks. Could this threaten Britain's love affair with the 'ruby murray' or will we 'pilau' right on? Here, to wipe down our plates, is Linda Smith:

Oh, there's always some health scare, isn't there? Today it is curry – what's next? Fags? Beer? Crazy. Besides, everyone knows that food colouring is where all the goodness is – the E vitamins – E157, E239, E58 all essential. And, with all the panic these days about skin cancer, a quick rubdown with a cube of chicken tikka is a safe and tasty way to a lovely tan. I'm afraid telling *me* that curry is bad for you is like telling me that that Lenny Henry is a fantastic actor or that Jeffrey Archer writes *The Sopranos*. The statements reach my brain only to be told by the little doorman, 'I'm sorry, you're not on the guest list, you're not coming in.'

My very first curry was one I made at school in domestic science – one of those English curries with so much fruit and nuts in it, it was effectively a meat trifle and was as delicious as it sounds. Up to the age of eighteen the only thing I'd ever eaten with spices in it was a mince pie, so my first restaurant curry was quite a shock – it was like the film *Awakenings* running in my mouth. Suddenly, with my tastebuds woken from their years of slumber and looking for action, I was hooked, and over the years I've been to all sorts of Asian restaurants – authentic and anglicised, trendy new places that looked like the inside of Terence Conran's mind and those old-fashioned, tatty places with carpets that seem to have had all the chewing gum in the world trodden into them until their surface resembles black ice, and are full of leery gangs of lads scoffing Vindaloo (which is of course the Indian word for 'You drunken tosser of an engineering student, please try to be sick outside'). And solitary drunks chewing the hot towel complaining that the naan bread's stale.

Actually, you know you're in a tough curry house when instead of a hot towel at the end of the meal, the waiter just spits on his hanky and rubs it all over your face. Here's a little tip for you. The next time you're in an Indian restaurant, here's a little ice breaker – when your cool yoghurt drink arrives, hold it up to your ear, listen, and say, 'What's that, lassi? The mail coach has been robbed? You wait here, I'll head them off at the pass.' Believe me, the waiter will enjoy this as much as you do.

Women in sport

As you were leafing through your copy of the British Journal of Sports Medicine *over the breakfast table the other morning, I expect, like me, that you were fascinated to read that women could compete as sporting equals with men were it not for decades of cultural stereotyping. So will the day come when women play men off the pitch? Linda Smith gets on her marks.*

Victorian scientific theory was strong on theory and absolutely crap on science. Many's the poor wretch transported to the colonies in those days with no more proof of guilt than that their ear lobes were really pointy, or the autumn light fell weirdly on their ugly teeth. Against this murky background of superstition, is it any wonder that Charles Darwin was such a Nobby No Mates? Or indeed that Victorian women were advised to give sport a wide berth and stick to more feminine hobbies like tuberculosis and hysterical visions?

Quite apart from the practical difficulties of running the 100-metres hurdle in a crinoline and bustle (many girls fell at the first fence and had to be shot), the prevailing belief was that if women took part in any sport more strenuous than, quote, 'light bean bag throwing', an event so rubbish even Sky haven't televised it, they would grow beards, pipes, and whiskers and turn into men. Actually, this did happen to one poor girl – she experimented with the heavy bean bag, and sadly Mary Ann became George Eliot, author of *Middlemarch* and the best Olympic shot-putter we never had.

By Edwardian times a few rebels were defying this natural law, like that brave suffragette who tried to enter the Derby – didn't go too well. By the Second World War, women were *still* being discouraged – as in this 1944 propaganda broadcast: 'Ladies of Britain, when you pick up a tennis racket in earnest you are passing military secrets to the Germans – for pity's sake, stop now, you Nazi harlots!' Of course this has all changed now – we've got Sporty Spice and those attitudes seem absurd. Nowadays, it's totally accepted that women are just as good as men are at taking performance-enhancing drugs. Anyone for light bean bags?

The Millennium Dome

Details were released this week of the Mandelson – I'm sorry – Millennium Dome. Linda Smith is beside herself with excitement . . .

This week, as we were being told off by Tony Blair for lacking 'Dome Keenness' (where was our positivity? Have the Spice Girls taught us nothing? Did they die in vain at the Brit Awards?) everything went all wavy and I was into a flashback . . . I was six years old, in Miss Coles's class, listening to a similar warning about what happens when people just can't be arsed: 'If you children don't bring in cabbage leaves and apples, Tufty the guinea pig will die!' A frisson (a word we couldn't understand or spell) passed through the room – how horrible! And yet how thrilling! The power of life and death!

The very same power that we all have over the glorified school trip that is the Blunderdome. Just look at these plans! The Dome will house, wait for it, 'The Learning Curve', 'Licensed to Skill', and better still, 'Time to Talk!' (with an exclamation mark!). Were these titles dreamed up by *Look and Learn* readers, snorting Ovaltine while listening to the *Tomorrow's World* theme? Now, don't let me put you off – perhaps you'd enjoy struggling over to Greenwich on the as yet unfinished Jubilee line, or in a taxi – 'South of the river, this many years after the birth of Christ? You're having a laugh!' Or sell your home to pay the rail fare from anywhere north of Watford in order to crawl up the bum of a giant statue into a theme park of internal organs! 'Liver World.' Whizzing down the intestinal flume into the bladder complete with wave machine.

Before you do it, just ask yourself, is it worth it? Just to get to a party organised by Tony Blair, a man whose idea of fun is taking a tambourine into church, and that other noted knees-up meister, Peter Mandelson? No, I say let's have some real fun – let's watch Peter Mandelson's guinea pig die!

I-VILLAGE

Linda wrote the following pieces for a short-lived website called I-Village.

The Oscars

The Oscars are universally acknowledged to be the most prestigious awards in the film industry, the ceremony watched by millions across the world – so how many of last year's winners can you name? Best Actor? Easy, Kevin Spacey. Best Actress? Er, is it that woman I've not heard of, before or since, in that sensitive but dull-looking film that I didn't fancy? Best Supporting Actor, now I *know* that was Michael Caine, although the idea of one of the few genuine film stars in the world, in fact the only English one, being described as a 'supporting actor' and winning an Oscar for one of his unfortunate forays into pretending to be someone other than Michael Caine . . . well.

As for Best Supporting Actress . . . not a clue . . . I'm afraid. So assuming my vagueness on this matter to be typical, why, after all the pre-Oscar hype and razzmatazz, are the results so ephemeral?

Well, partly, it's the proliferation of awards these days. As in boxing, there are too many titles. At one time there was just the Oscars and everything else meant nothing. There was Cannes, of course, basically a nice little holiday, where Hollywood, like an indulgent parent watching their child dance, pretended that foreigners knew about movies. Every year they'd watch a bunch of smoking, drinking cholesterol-drenched European weirdos give gongs to films that wouldn't make dollar one. Times have changed though, the BAFTAS, for example. Until recently, the BAFTAS meant as much internationally as a swimming certificate or a cycling proficiency test. American winners would always express their polite thanks via satellite, even if they were in Britain at the time. But now, these Cinderella awards are newly glamorised and hip.

There's the Golden Globes, the Emmys, Venice – not to mention all the other non-film-related awards that performers are up for. Did Jack Nicholson win a Bear for the most outstanding human performance in a Latvian animation at the Berlin Film Festival, or 'Rear of the Year' in *TV Quick*?

The Oscars ceremony itself is a bit of a turn-off. Before it was televised everywhere, it seemed so glamorous; now we can see it for what it is – a recruitment video for Scientology, with dancing. The tone is relentlessly anodyne – in an experiment in astringency, the Academy once asked David Letterman to host the show. Never again: horrified by a smattering of New York cynicism, they immediately reverted to a safe and schmultzy Whoopi Goldberg / Billy Crystal job-share. And why so long? Are the Oscars directed by Oliver Stone? The endless categories: 'Best performance by an actress pretending that her leading man isn't old enough to be her grandfather.' 'Best attempt by Keanu Reeves not to look like a computer-generated graphic.' If only the acceptance speeches were more entertaining; way back when Marlon

Brando was still feasible as a land mammal, political protests provided a bit of fun – film stars supporting Native Americans, stopping wars and saving whales by not accepting a small gilded statue.

What have we got now? Tom Hanks invoking God and Gwyneth Paltrow tearful and trembling like Fay Wray expressing a kind of gratitude that might have seemed excessive if she had just been rescued from a giant gorilla, let alone given a prize. Every year I watch in the vain hope that just one winner will have the gumption to stand up and say, 'I'd like to thank the Academy for this award, which, if I may say, I have won in spite of the efforts of the following people: my family, who mocked my dreams and constantly undermined me – still laughing, trailer trash? My old teacher, Mr Johnson, who said I'd never amount to anything – you're an old man now, Mr Johnson, but hopefully still sufficiently compos mentis to find my triumph bitter. Indeed, my ex-agent, 'freshening up our client list this, my friend!' and don't get me started on my ex-wife – how's the rehab, honey? I'm sure to have missed people out, but so many have stood in my way it would be impossible to mention them all, that's why I've taken out a full page ad in *Variety*!'

One day maybe. Until then, just as Roman Emperors had someone whispering in their ear, reminding them of their mortality, maybe Oscar winners should have someone reminding them that Martin Scorsese has never won an Oscar, and he's a genius – so don't get too carried away.

Railtrack

A long time ago, before rail privatisation, I sat trapped on a freezing, buffet-less Manchester to Sheffield train. We had just, literally and metaphorically, crawled through Hope: now we were sunk in the despair that is 'points failure outside Chesterfield'. To add another layer to this mille-feuille of misery, it was Sunday. I remember thinking then, given that privatisation always results in poorer service to the public, whoever took on British Rail would have their work cut out making it any worse than this. It would take an act of destructive genius. Well, hats off to Railtrack, you've done it, and then some. Just as successive Labour Party leaders make you nostalgic for the previous clown, so Railtrack make the British Rail years seem a paradise lost.

Some of the differences, of course, are a question of presentation. In a misplaced spirit of 'least said soonest mended', British Rail didn't go in for explanations of poor service. Railtrack on the other hand seem to delight, Reggie Perrin-like, in inventing ever more bizarre excuses for delays: the wrong kind of snow, the wrong kind of leaves. This suggests the trains themselves are queeny, demanding prima donnas screeching, 'What's *this* supposed to be? I ordered snow, *snow*! I'm an artist. I can't work with this . . . sludge! If anyone wants me I'll be in my *shed*!' A Martian watching this torment would find it hard to believe we are actually charged for it. Even the Emperor of Japan didn't have the gall to charge prisoners of war for building the Burma Railway.

This shambles is nothing beside disasters like Ladbroke Grove and Hatfield. Apparently, the crack in the rail at Hatfield was visible 10 metres away – 10 metres? How do they explain that? Just dizziness? 'Oh, what am I like, if I don't make a list, nothing gets done,' or were they leaving it there deliberately so passengers could tick it off in their *I Spy Book of Murderous Neglect*? Railtrack chief Gerald Corbett has expressed a noble determination 'not to rest until rail safety is assured', conveniently forgetting that he was meant to be doing that all along. Or, in his eagerness to get to the salary, did he skip over that part of the job description? Anyway, with the scale of repairs needed it's a foolish promise. As it is, every rail journey for the next two years would be quicker by Spacehopper, so Corbett wandering around half mad with sleep deprivation, seeing the wrong kind of giant lizards on the line, is hardly a help. He's offered to resign, but the board talked him out of it – what did they say, I wonder? 'Come on, Corby, be a sport, stay on for just one more tragedy.' I think I preferred Mr Corbett when he was running *The Sooty Show*. He was almost up to the job.

Blair, of course, with his passion for Partnership with Business (partner being the PC term for whoever's screwing you on a regular basis), is trying to play down any connection between privatisation and abysmal safety standards. This is about as convincing as someone standing over a stabbed body, holding a bloodstained knife saying, 'Honestly, this isn't what it looks like.' As ever, he has misjudged the public mood. If, when he won the '97 election, he'd promised to renationalise the railways, the nation would have cheered. Now, if he stood up and said, 'My Government has decided to use the entire board of Railtrack for vivisection, then pile their still-twitching bodies by the banks of the River Ouse, to save on sandbags', people would just say, 'Oh well, I suppose new shades of lipstick don't test themselves. Now, where's that Spacehopper?'

Comic Relief

It feels as if we've had Christmas now, what with the shops having been crammed with Yuletide tat since August, so the next religio-commercial festival looming up in the calendar is Comic Relief; an event that makes me as uneasy as the news that BSE has crossed over into dry white wine. Why? Because Comic Relief is charity, worse than that, it's New Charity; it has the gloss of change, of being different from what it's replaced but just like New Labour, in effect it is exactly the same. Why is charity a bad thing? Because like the National Lottery (and who can walk past a line of pasty-faced paupers queuing for Lotto tickets without wanting to shout, 'Like opera, do you? Get down to Covent Garden much, do you, you dopey bastards? What's your favourite zone in the Dome?'), charity is a tax on the poor. It's no coincidence that Mrs Thatcher (a former Prime Minister of Great Britain as very old people may remember) was really keen on charity.

Poorer people give a much higher proportion of their income to good causes than do the better off. How sickening then to see some clapped-out old rock star standing in an African village explaining earnestly that just £5 will water the crops for a month, knowing full well that if he scraped the surplus coke from his snout, left over from the previous night's revels, the money raised would irrigate the entire Sudan. Now that's a Red Nose Day I could really get behind.

Meanwhile, back in the studio, there's the question of corporate donations. A grinning suit from some rancid multinational – Farm Fresh Pharmaceuticals or something – thrilled to be rubbing shoulders with his TV favourites, proudly hands over a giant cheque, live on prime-time TV, to a grateful charity. You just can't buy publicity like that. Except that he just did – really, really cheaply. Oh well, people think, charity's not perfect, but what would happen without it? The Government just wouldn't pay for those things. Hmm, well, it's interesting what Governments choose to pay for, and what they leave to charity.

The Kosovan war, for example, was a very dear do, but I don't remember Nicholas Lyndhurst running a marathon dressed as a Teletubby to raise funds for it. The Government knows full well that Hale and Pace live from Belgrade saying, 'This Chinese Embassy behind us has never, ever been bombed. Isn't that sad? But, you know, with your help we can change that!' just wouldn't tug the nation's heartstrings. So perhaps if the amount of energy that goes into the North Kent Round Table's sponsored Cross-dressed Bridge Night in aid of the Lifeboats went into pressuris-ing the Government instead, we might not need charity in this country. And some marriages in North Kent might be saved.

But what about globally, the developing world? Now, I admit I don't fully understand Third World debt – I've always thought that the skint countries should just brazen it out. Turn the lights out, hide behind the sofa and pretend they're not in when the World Bank comes knocking. I mean, what are the IMF going to do, for God's sake? Repossess Brazil? However, I do know that by wiping out this debt, the lot of the poorest people on the planet would improve enormously at a stroke. Their confidence would rise, and they'd be better placed to tackle the corrupt regimes that saddled them with the debt in the first place.

This is, I know, a huge project, and obviously involves a masterly strategy. It could not be achieved with Comic Relief's frankly piss-poor night of TV. A 'Let Them Eat Cake' special or Ben Elton's unique comedy stylings might frighten us, but world bankers are made of sterner stuff. No, the threat has to be serious. We need Greg Dyke, in close-up, delivering this grim-faced warning: 'If all Third World debt is not cancelled immediately, I'm afraid I shall have no alternative but to give Lenny Henry another series of *Chef*!' Please give generously. Please.

I'M SORRY I HAVEN'T A CLUE
Tim Brooke-Taylor, comedian, actor, writer and Goodie

Now I've got to be honest, my first reaction to Linda was a negative. It wasn't that she wasn't funny, it was that she was too funny
for too long. She was on the *News Quiz* and no one else seemed to
get a look-in. It was later that I discovered that in that particular
show no one else really shone, so the edit made it look as if she was
a loud-mouth who wouldn't let anyone else get a look-in. Once I'd
discovered that, I asked our producer on *I'm Sorry I Haven't a
Clue*, Jon Naismith, if Linda could be my doubles partner. 'What
a good idea,' he said and couldn't wait to book her. She was a natural for the show and made me giggle with almost everything she
said. We had devised a Sound Charade between us, 'Six Feet
Under'. The device was to pretend that Linda was under the table
and she was trying to guess the others seated at the table: 'The
Beverley Sisters – six feet'. 'The Three Stooges?' 'The Goodies –
seven feet, oh no, that's a table leg.' But Linda didn't just pretend
to be under the table – she dived down there and eventually
emerged with a smile on her face, saying, 'Are you sure you can
get me on to *Just a Minute*, Tim?' Funny and smutty, just what we
like on *Clue*. Humphrey Lyttelton adored her and you can't get
much funnier or smuttier than Humph. But it wasn't just the
smuttier moments that really endeared her to all of us. It was the
quickness of wit. There was a moment during the recording of *I'm
Sorry I Haven't a Christmas Carol*. After the sound effect of knocking and a door opening, Humph as Ebenezer Scrumph was due to
say, 'May I come in?', and Linda as Mrs Crotchet was to reply,
'Why, it's Mr Scrumph! And his arms are laden with gifts.' In the
event, Linda forgot to wait for her cue and after the door-opening

sound effect both she and Humph said the lines, 'May I come in?' and 'It's Ebenezer Scrumph!' simultaneously. Linda immediately added, 'I knew it would be you' to a huge laugh from the audience. Humph repeated the line, 'I knew it would be you' with a chuckle for some time after the recording had finished.

Here are some of Linda's contributions to *I'm Sorry I Haven't a Clue*. It will be difficult to replace her as the ideal mixed doubles partner.

Tim Brooke-Taylor, 2006.

New definitions

CONTEXT — prison library book
CONTRABAND — US-backed counter-revolutionary orchestra
DEGLAZE — to stop watching neighbours
INDELIBLE — a person who cannot be persuaded to eat bagels
MAISONETTE — a very small Chief Constable
MARGATE — the 'mother of all scandals'
MUSHROOMS — what Laurence Llewellyn-Bowen does
PALISADE — what the Queen drinks
PENDULOUS — when you can put a pen under it and it stays there
POSTULATE — new name for Royal Mail
SCARF — to eat in Knightsbridge

Spanish Radio Times

The Man in the Iron Basque
Seville, Tapas and Huntas Club
Man about the House of Bernarda Alba
Juan Foot in the Grave

Mottoes

The Association of Norfolk Bakers
'Two Hundred Years in Bread'

IKEA
'I'm sorry, you're going to have to put your own slogan together'

British Telecom
'Putting you on hold'

Daily Mail *Readers' Songbook*

String 'Em Up Before You Go-Go
Working on a Chain Gang – is too good for them frankly
Strangers in the Night – feel free to shoot them
The Times They Are A-Changin' – but not for the better frankly
Wishin' and Hangin' and Floggin' and Taggin'

Hirsute person's film club

The Italian Bob
Tashablanca
Sweet Beard of Youth
Whiskers Galore
Hairy Queen of Scots

Victorian news headlines

Jim Davidson to Entertain Troops in Crimea: Light Brigade Volunteer for Valley of Death
Mrs Beeton Quits Lucrative Cookery Gig to Buy Norwich City
Arriva Trains Apologise for the Late Arrival of Stephenson's
Rocket – This Is Due to the Wrong Kind of William Huskisson on
the Track

Victorian novelty catalogue

Ladies! Are Your Lapdogs Always the Wrong Size? Then why not
treat yourself to a set of Adjustable Spaniels?

ODE TO LINDA
A LOT OF LAUGHS

Oh, what a happy day to think of Linda
I am so old, I remember Tommy Trinder
You may say: "Who?", that will not hinder
My verse, because dear Linda
Was in the family line, kith and kinder
That she carried on - Linda Smith
No false memories, no transient myth
She was there, upon the News Quiz
Doing the business, doing the biz
Full of fun and full of fizz
Then thoughts turn to Just a Minute
Who but our own Linda in it
Could fill the seconds with such thoughts
Any context, any sorts
Of reactions were just hers
So many, now my memory blurs
But that's irrelevant, forget the blur
When we remember Linda, it's just her
Funny, natural, endlessly inventive
I don't need any further incentive
To say that you were one of a kind
I can never lose from my mind
Your wit spontaneous, seemingly unplanned
Your album of whalesong, that turned out to be
a dolphin tribute band
just one and so were you
You always, always had a clue
And now, my friends, I end this rhyme
Hoping it wasn't a Short History of Wasting Time
With all here, I'm one who has
Lovely memories, love Uncle Baz.

To Linda from Barry Cryer

'A COLLECTION OF ECCENTRICITIES', BBC RADIO 3

A Series of Talking Heads Inspired by Hogarth's *Rake's Progress*.
Nibbles on Arrival in the Sequoia Room.
Written and performed by Linda Smith.

LINDA: (as the organiser):
'Welcome to the Hawley Thorne Country House Hotel, Berkshire, where guests can enjoy full conference facilities, corporate entertainment in our Redwood Suite and the lowest background levels of radon gas in the Home Counties. Will the party from the Amalgamated Trading Bank of Barrow, Buoys and Toffs please make their way to the Sequoia Room where your 'Down Argentine Way' South American-themed company Christmas dinner and cabaret is under way. Nibbles on arrival, stand-up comedian during pudding. Polite management request: please refrain from throwing glasses, as fragments of crystal tend to clog the Dyson.'

LINDA: (as herself):
Oh, marvellous. Nothing says 'festive season' quite like 500 investment bankers dressed as gauchos in a hotel near Bracknell, waiting for me to entertain them with a sideways look at life. Over pudding. So, if they do open their great maws to laugh, I'll get pebbledashed with tiramisu. How's that caught on – tiramisu? It's horrible, like eating an alcoholic's mattress. Should count my blessings, I suppose. At least tiramisu's soft. I did a corporate once, a group of mobile phone salesmen on a team-building weekend in the Forest of Dean, and they were served crème brûlée. Well, they were so gee'd up after a day of competitive rambling and ritual humiliation – if they forgot their kagoules they had to do it in their vest and pants – they went barmy with the brulée. Started tearing off shards of caramel and spinning them at each other like ninja stars. It was like *Crouching Tiger, Hidden Dragon* – only with a load of wankers.

Oh, just look at this mob; they are already half-cut and they're only on the nibbles – tiger prawn tails. Hmm, what else are they having – seafood vol-au-vent followed by a medley of ocean treasures?

Ha, I suspect the chef had a sack of scampi with a few too many miles on the clock hanging about in the freezer – not off exactly, but a bit ambiguoso, ha, ha, ha.

As usual, they've asked me to join them for dinner before my set. Yeah, right, put my name down for that one – I'm sure before they were ripped limb from limb in the arena the Christians liked nothing better than to share a finger buffet with the bloody lions. Eat with them! They buy your services and these people think they've bought you. Just because they have. Oh, don't start with the self-loathing, not this early. You're already talking to yourself, let's just keep it at that, shall we?

Even the good-looking ones are ugly – you know, that ugly kind of good-looking – like the sons of Jeffrey Archer. I wonder how many of this lot will end up in choky. Not nearly enough. How can they not be fraudsters? Their whole job's a fraud – waving their arms about, shouting, 'Buy! Buy! No, Sell! Sell! Get me Tokyo! No, I said – Buy!' If you took them out of the Stock Exchange and put them on the street they'd just be nutters. By the same token, if you gave nutters a mobile phone they'd be bankers.

Here, I recognise that one there – the porky, angry-looking one – suit by Giorgio Armani, face by Francis Bacon – he's the Managing Director. I've seen him on the news, doing the old number – 'Downturn, what downturn? It's just a little blip, the ATBBBT, we'll ride it out. We're moving forward to meet the future, so there isn't a gap . . . between now and the future, the fact that we've just laid off 500 workers shows how confident we are in that figure.'

That explains why the mood out there's so extra poisonous. They've just had their Christmas bonus, but it's a bit down on last year's . . . and next year, who knows? So they're drowning out the thought that this might be the last dance on the *Titanic* by stuffing their brains with cocaine, the powdered form of money, and of course, a noted cure for paranoia. Settling that queasy, uneasy feeling in the pit of the stomach, not entirely due to dodgy langoustines, with jugs of champagne and Red Bull. They're bigging themselves up, throwing money around – wearing it, drinking it, eating it, smoking it, snorting it – just to keep out the deadly idea that it might not last. Here, blimey – my cheque better not bounce – I'm not doing this one for love, that's for sure. Just as I don't think that woman there is doing the Managing Director for love.

Or perhaps I'm being cynical – perhaps she's always subconsciously admired his flabby puce face and masterful way with a redundancy notice, and all it's taken to bring this attraction to the surface is for her to drink her body weight in tequila. Watching businessmen at play can make Andrea Dworkin seem like Tammy Wynette. Mind you, these hard-bitten City women aren't that appealing. That one over there with the power cleavage, either she's overdone the Botox injections or she's had her face stuck in a Corby trouser press overnight. Why would you want your face paralysed unless you're a professional poker player? I suppose logically, then, her ultimate beauty treatment would be a massive stroke.

Mad. No such luxury for that working girl trying to turn a trick, she's looking a bit past her best – oh, the manager's throwing her out. Ahh, her dumpy little legs look a bit tragic in fishnets from behind. That reminds me, I must buy a bag of satsumas. Oh, come on, cheer up – if you get all morose you'll end up going down about as well as Anne Robinson at an Eistedfodd. Remember, twenty minutes, big wad of dosh and it's over. Right, what will I kick off with? This lot are a hard bunch so something cruel, maybe the Mary Whitehouse with Tourette's Syndrome routine? Right, I am Gladiator and I will kill tonight.

Good evening, a delight to be here . . . I see the Managing Director's pulled – blimey, they're on the dance floor now. I can't quite tell if she's doing the bossa nova or doing the boss a favour . . .

JUST A MINUTE
Claire Jones, Radio producer

What was Linda like on *Just a Minute*? Playful, competitive, skil-ful . . . all in all, a tip-top panellist.

Linda and Paul Merton occasionally ganged up on Nicholas if they decided one of his decisions as chairman was ludicrous. They would return again and again in a kind of verbal relay race to the subject of, for instance, whether herbaceous borders could outwit somebody . . . until Nicholas finally gave in.

And then there were those frequent moments when frustration and/or the competitive bug got to Linda and we'd be treated to her sustained wrath on the subject of golf or bungalows or the Alexander Technique.

There was always a sublime moment from Linda in every show where she'd 'fly'. Once it was when she was on stage with Sir Clement Freud and was seated next to Stephen Fry. Both of them were sounding posh and erudite and suddenly Linda turned into a cockney flower girl and started trying to sell them violets. The balloon of pomposity was pricked and the audience loved her for it.

Linda had warmth and common sense, so you weren't worried she was going to be prima donna-ish about the state of the back-stage green room; where she was sitting on stage; the menu at the after-show meal or the accommodation on one of our many out-of-London recordings.

She was great fun, a lovely person and the perfect booking for *Just a Minute*.

Claire Jones, 2006.

PEAR-SHAPED
Nicholas Parsons, actor, writer, comedian and broadcaster, chairman of *Just a Minute*

I first met Linda when she guested on *Just a Minute* in November 1998. It was a recording at the Lyceum Theatre in Sheffield, which must have been poignant for her because, as I discovered later, she had studied at the university in that city. Once Linda had really settled into the show and gained her confidence, her contributions over the years were immeasurable and always delightful. There was one occasion which stands out in my memory and that was a recording in 2001 at Cardiff, when Linda started with the subject and went for the full minute without hesitation, repetition or deviation. This is very difficult to do when you have three talented, keen and sharp minds waiting to pounce and gain points for themselves if you break one of the three rules of the game. The subject, I remember, was 'Pear-shaped', and Linda stormed ahead with style and panache. Her humorous comments and inventiveness on a subject which offered limited scope were magnificent. She was very funny and duly received a huge round of applause.

Linda was one of those rare people who gave out to everyone. She was charming, unassuming, with a delightful sense of humour, and after being in her company for a while you felt you had been with a very special person. She will be greatly missed by all those who had the pleasure of knowing her, and particularly by those who had the joy of working with her. She is a sad loss to our profession; she had yet to achieve her full potential. I will always treasure the memories of those occasions when we worked together, and recall how her gentle and humorous personality could light up any show in which she was involved.

Nicholas Parsons, 2006.

EXCERPT:
Cardiff, 7 August 2001

NICHOLAS PARSONS: And Linda, your turn to begin. The subject is 'Pear-shaped'. Tell us something about 'Pear-shaped' in just a minute, starting now.

LINDA: Pear-shaped is an expression people use when something has gone horribly wrong in any kind of way. For example, the Jeffrey Archer trial from that man's point of view went pear-shaped really quite early in the proceedings and I cannot help but feel for poor Mary his wife because now that he's in prison she'll have to see him on a regular basis (applause) which is not really how they have conducted their union so far. And one can understand why. Pear-shaped is a strange shape to choose as something that is bad because pear-shaped is a lovely shape. I think a better fruit to choose to denote disaster would be the star fruit. What on earth is that? It's a mess – it tastes of nothing – it looks scary (whistles and applause).

THE NEWS QUIZ
Simon Hoggart, journalist and broadcaster

Linda first came on to the *News Quiz* in 1998. She was nervous at first, but then most people are. The show can be terrifying, not because the other panellists are anything other than friendly (it's one of the strengths of the programme that the panellists get on well). But would you want to match wits with Andy Hamilton, Jeremy Hardy, Armando Iannucci, Alan Coren and the rest? Or know that if you bombed it wouldn't be in front of fifty people in a comedy club drunkenly yelling, 'Taxi for Miss Smith!' but two million radio listeners?

So she tended to arrive with routines ready sketched out in her mind which she then downloaded. Like her superb take on the Ron Davies walk on Clapham Common, when he claimed to have been taken in by a Rastafarian who offered him a meal. 'You know what it's like,' she said, 'you go for a walk, you think, ooh, aren't I doing well, I'm in the Cabinet, I'm about to become the first Prime Minister of my homeland. On the other hand, I could murder a dish of rice and peas.'

As the audience roared, I learned two things from that gag. One was that the listeners didn't just like Linda, they loved her. In the following years, when I went out to introduce the panel each week a sigh of happiness would roll up towards the stage if I announced her name. Or a slight, courteous, Radio 4-listener frisson of displeasure if I didn't.

The other thing was that she had an extraordinary way of relating the news of the week to everyday life. Many women comedians – Victoria Wood, French and Saunders – are most interested in character and situation. The wisecrack is an essentially masculine art, being aggressive and assertive, used as a weapon. Linda managed both at the same time. Take her classic routine about the missing WMDs in Iraq. She started out, as she often did, as if she was rambling, talking to a friend at the bus stop, perhaps. She felt sorry for Bush and Blair, she said, looking for those weapons. It was like her scissors, she often couldn't find them, even though she looked everywhere! She let the audience's laughter grow, then added, almost as an afterthought, ' . . . but at least I know my scissors exist.'

She was endlessly generous with her comic gifts, and would put as much effort and art into something she knew would be cut as she would into an answer that was certain to stay in the finished show. We adored her routines in which she was visiting Alan or Jeremy in a retirement home. 'His daughter's wonderful. She comes every week, and it's two buses . . .' 'No, dear, I'm sure the nurses aren't stealing your clothes.' Her ear for the way real people talk was faultless. She was also kind and outgoing to fans, or to other people's guests who had come to the recording, getting involved and interested in the conversation of people she'd probably never meet again.

Invidious to pick out one finest moment from so many. But this would be mine. The question was about a new French version of Viagra. Alan's joke, 'Can you get it over the counter? Only if you take two,' was well enough known for the audience to laugh before the punchline. Sandi Toksvig mentioned that it was National Condom Week. She had just been sent in the post a plastic condom sizer with three holes in, marked 'large', 'medium' and, hilariously, 'trim'. It looked, she said, like those devices that let you measure how much spaghetti you need.

I asked if it measured a chap before or after you put the spaghetti into the boiling water. Sandi began to lose it, as she sometimes does, and her whoops of laughter moved the audience to laugh even more. Linda waited for the perfect moment, that slight pause, which she could detect like a surfer launching into a wave, then said, 'I think Simon's trying to ask if it's *al dente.*' The tidal wave of laughter almost physically buffeted us.

Simon Hoggart, 2006.

Linda on the *News Quiz* A–Z

'A' levels

This is the proposed scrapping of 'A' levels. They're being replaced with some sort of diploma sort of thing. A document that's a bit broader than 'A' level results that talks about all the things that the kid might be good at . . . social skills and other little interests they might have, and I think it sounds like a good idea, really. Probably a lot better than the document I left school with, with the words, 'has contributed little to school life, I only hope her attitude changes in the future'. [Pause] Yes, that's a great thing to go out into the world with, isn't it, Jed Leicester, you evil old camel. I would have to say that, sadly, my attitude hasn't changed and it's provided me with a pretty good living. Rather better than the little typing job that I'm sure you had in mind for me. I don't know why they just don't scrap school altogether, it's a complete waste of time in my opinion. I don't know how many years of Geography I did; I can't get from here to Euston . . . I spent twenty years colouring maps of the world. South America and its produce. Colouring in little tubs of palm oil and maize. Maize. It comes from everywhere, goes everywhere, then you never see it . . .

Aristocracy

The Duke and Duchess of Hamilton are boycotting Jenners, which is a department store in Edinburgh, because they stock foie gras, which is apparently a cruelly produced goose liver. Sounds disgusting. But anyway, fantastic bit of class war from the Duke and Duchess, direct political action, and they're standing outside the shop going, 'Here one doesn't go, here one doesn't go, here one doesn't go,' and generally having a right go about this goose liver thing. And there's a lovely quote from the Duke who said, 'I've tried it once, and it wasn't good enough to justify the cruelty.' That is marvellous . . . this scale of cruelty that he's got for some things. 'For a bacon sandwich' – for example – 'I'd hand my entire family over to the Stasi.'

ASBOs

People knock ASBOs but you have to bear in mind, they are the only qualifications some of these kids are going to get.

BBC strike

What a marvellous day it was. It was full of surprises. I wish I'd seen the picket line. Jeremy Paxman standing there, going, 'What do we want? Go on, answer the question – What do we want?' No, it was all very jolly. This man on the telly reading the news, Steven Cole? I normally see him on BBC World reading the news, so I always associate him with hotel rooms, like little sewing kits . . . funny to see him out in the wider world. And who's that anonymous man reading the news on the radio? Peter Jefferson? Who's he then? The scabs were rather charming, weren't they? Terry Wogan said he wished them luck, but obviously he couldn't deprive eight million listeners of the Commodores.

Biometric Identity Recognition Software For ID Cards

It doesn't remember people and it doesn't recognise people? This computer is based on my nan. What's the good of that? A computer that's going, 'You're not my grandson . . .'

Birds

Scientists claim that birds are as clever as mammals. They haven't got a great sense of time, though, have they? They don't know the difference between 4 a.m. and the morning.

Church of England

If you're going to insult a religious group, the Church of England might be the one. What are they going to do? Give you a sherry that's not at the right temperature?

Climate change

There's a conference of scientists in Exeter about global warming where they've actually worked out a timetable for it. So we now know that in thirty years from now the world is – officially – too hot for me. 'Cos I don't like it too warm. Actually, I think this is something I got from my mum, because the weather would come on the TV and to inject a bit of humour into the proceedings the forecaster would say something like, 'And the hottest spot on the earth tonight was Riyadh which was 130 degrees!' And my mum would go, 'Woah. Too hot for me!' And of course we'd have to phone up Mrs Mohammed and cancel that fortnight in August at the Desert View Guest House. Climate change – it's a bit of a worry, I suppose. Polar bears. What can you do if you've got a great big fur coat on, you can't get it off? They're already thinking because the Antarctic is shrinking and the sea's getting bigger, you've got relatively young polar bears going, 'You know, when I was younger, I'm sure Antarctica was bigger than this. It was all ice floes. You could jump from one to another . . . now I'm too hot to eat a seal. I just want a salad.'

Curling

England have a gold medal in curling. Sorry, England and allied countries – Scotland. It's housework on ice, that's what it is. They throw a paperweight across an ice rink and then these ladies furiously dust in front of it, to clear the path because they like a tidy ice rink. Anyone could drop round and see your ice rink in a state and that would be awful. I think we're also doing quite well in defrosting the fridge, and we're doing marvellously in the free-form bath cleaning. They've invented things for us that we're good at, tidying up.

Delia

Dame Delia . . . just astonishing pictures of her in this paper from this football match – Norwich City, who she's chairwoman of, and she's saved them and given them loads of money. To be honest, I don't want to cast aspersions, but from the look of her in those photos I think she might have sucked the rum out of about 2,000 babas. She looked like your auntie at Christmas. She looked like she'd been on the port and lemon big style. 'Ahl help them win. Ahl cheer them up . . . give me that microphone. Get it here . . . get out of here, all of ya . . . Ya don't know me, Ya don't know anything *about* me. Right. I love you. You're the bes' fans in the worl'. An' I got a luvverly recipe for apple crumble. And I'm not givin' it to ya until ya start singin' . . . *sing* . . . *ya* . . . *sing* . . .' And that was it, really.

Depressed MPs

Apparently, MPs are in danger of being depressed. (audience laugh) Yes! You see, that's probably the sort of reaction that makes them depressed. You try and explain that they're in mental torment and everyone just laughs. Yes, apparently they might need a bit of counselling. I imagine that *would* cheer you up, wouldn't it? Some dreary woman in a dress made of Quorn sitting there going, 'Yes . . . yes . . . yes . . . yes . . . mmmm, I know . . . yes.'

Disarming

I was quite bemused to read that Gerry Adams was going to be disarming the IRA. I'm not sure how you do that. I suppose you go up and say, 'What's your name? Declan? Why, that's beautiful. Give me the balaclava, Declan.'

Dunkirk

The re-enactment of the Dunkirk evacuation for the sixtieth anniversary, which was to happen on Thursday, didn't because the weather was a bit murky. Hardly the Dunkirk spirit. There's an honorary Commodore who's in charge of the flotilla who said, 'Getting this lot across this shipping channel is a bit like getting a bunch of geriatrics across the M25 at rush hour.' A bit of an unfortunate phrase, I thought. But also, you've probably not seen the M25 recently at rush hour, because you'd have no trouble getting a bunch of geriatrics across. They could do a jigsaw in the middle, actually.

Estelle Morris

The teachers at their Easter do. It was quite stormy, especially for Estelle Morris, the Minister for Education. They weren't very impressed by anything she had to say. Not surprisingly, because they were coming up with things like a 'Mum's Army' of helpers to come in and help. This is how they deal with the shortages of teachers and staff, they get volunteer mums in to come and help them. What a nightmare for the kids, they don't want to be sitting there in class chatting with their friends, texting each other, suddenly their mum comes up, spits on a hanky and wipes their face. So what's going to happen now, are we going to have people conscripted into teaching? It's so hard to get anyone to do it that we're going to be press-ganged. You'll be sitting having a drink and a load of people with elbow patches come up and clump you round the head. Next thing you know, you're teaching a bunch of fifteen-year-old crack addicts.

EU

Do you actually read these articles about the EU? 'Cos I find, this week I was reading the paper and I thought, 'Oh, this is probably going to come up,' and I started reading it. Next thing I know I wake up, freezing cold, it's the middle of the night, I've got drool all over my face, and it's *Celebrity Love Island – The Director's Cut* . . .

Foot and Mouth

I must say, I'm glad that the killing's stopped. It was getting ridiculous. They were killing every living creature on the face of the land. You daren't go out in a fleece.

Franklin Mint

The Franklin Mint have issued a set of commemorative plates of topless Sophie Rhys Jones. I don't understand this Franklin Mint thing. You collect all these weird things like sets of thimbles with great twentieth-century war criminals on them, whatever, and you collect them, but you don't really collect them. You send away the money and they send them to you, which isn't collecting really, is it? You collect things over a period of years – that's just buying something, isn't it? You could say that British Gas have a collection of my cheques.

Freemasons

Do Freemasons get their clothes from the Freemasons' Catalogue?

Funeral arrangements

This peer of the realm – Lord Newborough – was a war hero. He wanted his ashes to be blasted from a cannon on to his country estate. He was quite a lad in his life; he escaped from Colditz. So you wonder if he's even really dead or he's half-way to Switzerland with his papers forged by Donald Pleasence. I suppose it would have been even more appropriate if he'd had all mourners put ashes in their pockets and wander round the grounds trickling them out of the bottom. A very novel funeral.

Golf

The problem with golf is it encourages people to go outdoors who really should stay indoors. Publicans in bulging Pringle pastel jumpers. They're in the same category for me as gardens full of conifers and bungalows – they're not low-rise buildings, they're high-rise coffins.

Grey power

Q. 'Who detected a victory for grey power?'
A. (JEREMY HARDY) I haven't the slightest idea. I've never seen you before. I don't know any of these people.

LINDA: Jeremy, you do know.

JEREMY: I don't, Linda.

LINDA: You do because it's an elderly detective who's become the head of the Association of Private Detectives. You remember because you've hired a private detective that time you thought the nurses were stealing your clothes.

JEREMY: Oh yeah!

LINDA: It's just an elderly woman (Mrs Sorrell) who is at an age where most old people are solving mysteries like 'What did I come in here for?' She has rather impressively become the head of private detectives in Britain – it's fantastic. Down these mean streets a woman must walk – wearing K-Skips. So it's a top result. A very heart-warming story.

Guidelines

The CPS have guidelines saying the exact amount of force a householder may use against intruders. The thing I find baffling: *yes*, you're allowed to kill them, but you're *only* allowed to kill them. It's just political correctness gone mad.

Handy hints

Have you ever tried using one of those giant Toblerones as a toast rack? Works once.

Happy hour

The Government are going to ban 'Happy Hour'. Apparently we can't cope with 'Happy Hour' at all. It causes too many fights and violence, so we're going to have a 'Mustn't Grumble Hour' where the drinks are full price – but still mustn't grumble. I think alcohol can prevent a lot of crime certainly in my own case, because if it wasn't for the availability of drink I'm sure I would have killed my entire family several Christmases ago with a two-pound tin of Quality Street. That's another thing they are thinking about, raising the age at which you can buy alcohol to twenty-one. How can you get to the age of twenty-one without a drink in this miserable New Labour Britain? Good God, it's not humanly possible.

House of Commons

I spy as in 'I Spy Strangers'. This is about the modernisation of the House of Commons. They aren't going to knock through into a through-lounge, downstairs toilet, sauna – nothing so sensible as that. They are going to get rid of all those funny things they say and do. Like, if you are bringing up a point of order, you have to hold an opera hat, and if you're asking a question you have to hold a brown paper envelope full of money. All these strange to-dos and also this thing that's been particularly upsetting the 'Blair Babes' is that when they are obviously reading a prepared question the Opposition will shout 'Reading' because they've never seen it before. Reading – they think it's the work of the devil and no good will come of it.

Human cannonball

This is a very sad story of a man who was a human cannon at the circus. He'd wanted to do it since he was a kid and he'd practised and done all sorts of special skull-toughening exercises and he did it, and he was great at it, but he hurt his knee. Just a little knee injury. And they said, 'Well, no. There's a health and safety issue here. It's a surprisingly dangerous job, being fired from a cannon, and you'll have to go on a special safety course – in Brazil.' Which apparently is a centre of excellence for the human cannon industry. But he said, 'Ooh no. I can't fly.' So they've sacked him! And he's heartbroken. And he's suing them for wrongful dismissal. But I think they need to take a lateral approach here. OK, so he's frightened of aeroplanes; many people are. (pause) He likes the cannon. (pause) A bigger cannon. That's the idea. Get him to Brazil. But he doesn't want one of those cheap economy ones. He doesn't want to go on EasyCannon.

Islamic dress

The ever-hilarious subject of Moslem dress. This is about a young girl in Luton who took her school to court. She was wearing the jilbad, because it only shows your hands and your face. It seems to me that the salwar kameez does the same thing if you wear a scarf. So I'm not sure if this was a religious thing, or whether it was just 'Teenager doesn't want to wear school uniform'. I can understand that. Because I would have rather worn that jilbad than worn my school uniform and it would have probably been more practical. I had this really stiff blazer made out of really unyielding material – totally stiff – and you could turn round inside it and it would stay there. And it had this crest on it like you were all little midget Alan Whickers. In the middle of winter with the skirts and little white socks – absolutely freezing, goosebumps on our legs you could grate nutmegs on. Just so cruel. Of course we needed to wear the school uniform so paedophiles could find us.

Isle of Wight dentists shortage

Apparently there aren't many dentists on the Isle of Wight. They're not very good, some of them. Apparently they just fill your teeth with coloured sand. Anyway, the people of the Isle of Wight can't get their teeth done so they're going on what they call the 'Tooth Ferry', they're going on these dentistry trips to France. And it's a bit

like a booze cruise really. You go off on the boat, you become unconscious, and when you wake up you've got a few teeth missing.

Jeffrey Archer

Norman Stanley Archer has been released to the somewhat cryo-
genic embrace of, er, Mary. The body language! You didn't really
have to be Desmond Morris to read that, really, did you? He went
forward for that big snog and she just swerved in a way that none
of the England cricket team appear able to do, and I think the message was loud and clear. 'You've heard this many times from pros-
titutes, Jeffrey . . . NO KISSING.'

Ken Clarke

Been quiet for a few years, hasn't he, in politics anyway, Ken
Clarke. But for two years he was actually co-hosting *Two Fat
Ladies* . . . very thinly disguised. And when he's not doing that
he's going all around the world taking baskets of cigarettes to
poor people, which is very kind of him. No, it's good if poor
people smoke because it takes the edge off their appetite. Tiring
of this good work, he's decided to stand for leadership of the
Conservative Party which I believe is some sort of golf club – I'm
not sure really why we should be interested in this. They're an
unappealing lot. He's described as the left-wing candidate, isn't
he? And then there's two nondescript baldy blokes, and then
there's the *other* one, Mr Portillo, who seems to have his lips on
inside out. And they got rid of Ann Widdecombe as she's no use
because she's only audible to sheep dogs. No, really. She's like a
demented Clanger. She has a swannee whistle stuck in her throat.

Kilroy Silk

Don't you think he's got the most extraordinary face? It's so
golden and crumbly, it's like his head's made out of Honey
Crunch.

Lampreys

The robot lamprey. I'm sure you've seen this. Scientists, not just car mechanics, scientists, have wired up the brain of a lamprey to a computer, a robot thing . . . well, wheel actually. And the computer is powered by the lamprey brain. But the terrible thing is they've chosen an evil lamprey . . . an evil lamprey with a bad brain that was about to be hung for murder and only Peter Cushing can save it. I've seen this film, definitely. That's what it is, at last an end to no lamprey robot misery.

London mayoral elections

When I went to vote there was a very keen woman standing there with a Labour rosette and she said, 'Can I ask you how you're going to vote?' And I said, 'Yes, I'm going to vote for Frank Dobson.' Her little face lit up, and I went, *'Joking!'*

Lottery

I don't do the lottery, which means I'm marginally less likely to win it than someone who does.

Maltesers

Maltesers have the less-fattening centre. Yes, but they are covered in milk chocolate! That's like saying – 'I'll have a mineral water, please. Can you put some cubes of lard in it?'

Married life

Misery loves company. I find married people, they're always encouraging you to get married if you're not. And the next thing that they do is assume that you, as a child-free person, are inevitably going to have kids. So they'll be changing some stinking nappy and they look at you and say, 'Oooh, you've got all this to come.' I always say, 'No, when my boyfriend's incontinent he's going straight in a home.'

Michael Jackson's trial – 'trial of the century'

Can't help thinking, can you, that Nuremberg might have had the edge. (pause) It was of another century, as someone just pointed out in the audience. I do love that about our Radio 4 audience. 'Dear *Points of View*, I was appalled when I recently went to a recording of the popular radio show *News Quiz*, when one of the panellists inaccurately described a *century*! Children may have been listening.
P.S. Is Andy Hamilton getting shorter?'

Middle East

It's rather annoying the way *our* oil's ended up under *their* sand.

Millennium Dome

It sounded so good at the time when somebody said, 'On this toxic wasteground we'll build a big shed with nothing in it.' How could it fail?

Murdoch

This wasn't actually published in any Murdoch paper, an unusual fit of shyness for Mr Murdoch. But he was actually made a Papal Knight, which is causing a bit of a fuss really from Catholics who see him as having bought this favour, which is unprecedented in the Catholic Church. The Catholic Church do their best to make Father Ted look like a documentary, don't they?

New home

I've just moved house recently and the problem wasn't so much with the estate agent but the people we bought the house from who were just mad. They seemed to have this idea that if they left as much as a curtain rail in the house, somehow we would capture their soul. When we got to the house we found they had actually pumped all the oxygen out of the rooms and taken it with them, so that's another new thing we've got to get. And they took the battery out of the smoke alarm.

Norfolk

This woman, June Wilson, who lives in Norfolk, wrote to the paper to say just how rubbish Norfolk was really – to say there was a certain element of pointing at aeroplanes going on. Basically, I'm treading carefully here. That it was a bit like 'Deliverance' with little power cruisers and people wrote in to the paper saying this is outrageous – 'Backward? Us? Burn the witch!' Didn't go down well at all. 'Boring? Norfolk, boring? Good God – we've got a gas museum in Fakenham!' This woman is under a bit of a fatwah now which apparently in Norfolk takes the form of unwanted pizzas being delivered to you. It's not too scary but I do feel a bit for this woman. Because a similar thing happened to me when I made a joke, perhaps unwisely, about my home town of Erith, implying that it wasn't exactly 'Manhattan of a Friday night round at Liza Minnelli's house'.

Offenders

David Blunkett has plans to tag troublesome teenage offenders. Don't you think it's silly? Teenagers. You don't need to tag them. Just shove them in front of a PlayStation with a bucket of sugar. They're not going to move.

Pandas

I think the female pandas try a bit too hard. They end up looking a bit tarty with all that eye make-up. Men prefer a more natural look, I think. There was a list of things they tried to help them that included letting them watch television. When has that helped *anyone* have sex? Nodding off in front of *Newsnight* . . . They're creatures of habit, aren't they? They only eat bamboo. 'Oh no . . . don't want anything too spicy. No sex, no. Got to be up early. Got a bamboo to eat tomorrow. I don't know *where* the days go.'

Papal tour

The Pope's been off on one of his little adventure holidays. I mean, all credit to him. I mean, most people at his age, they just go and visit some friends that live in Alicante, don't they? But he's been to Greece, and he's been to Syria, and then he's off to Malta. Quite impressive. He's saying sorry to various religions. He said sorry to the Greek Orthodox religion for crimes that the Catholics had done against them, he said sorry to Islam . . . do you think he'd do better doing a round robin letter? Or maybe just putting an advert in the *Syrian Bugle* or whatever . . .

Pavarotti

Pavarotti is a UN Ambassador – hopefully to nowhere where there's famine. That would be a cruel joke. Unless they're sending him as a bouncy castle to cheer things up a bit.

Penguin

Penguins are dying of the heat because it's getting too hot. Because they are like pensioners. They won't take their coats off, will they? 'No. I feel comfortable if I'm smart.'

Pinochet fights extradition

This is General Pinochet, and I know, Simon, you have explained that it is in fact pronounced Pino-*chette*, but I just want to annoy him by mispronouncing his name – it must be torture! Well, what's happened with General Pinochet is he's just lost another round in his fight against extradition, which means that unless this bout is arranged by Don King, extradition must be well ahead on points by now, I should think. Should win hands down. There's been quite a lot of moaning from the people of Wentworth in Surrey, hasn't there? About them not wanting him there. But I think they're being a bit dog in the manger about it really, because it must brighten up the Neighbourhood Watch a bit – you know, 'We've had a prowler at the golf course, there's a bit of dodgy street lighting we're worried about, that might lead to break-ins and oh, there's a murderous dictator at number 33.'

Plans to kill Bin Laden

I think I can clear this up. I've not been on the show for a couple of weeks and that's because I've been on covert operations within Afghanistan. Not happy with my disguise. I'm not sure it was that convincing. I was an Avon Lady in Kabul. (pause) Didn't shift much gear, to be honest. A couple of tubes of beard-styling gel and that was it. House is full of lip gloss. No, but it is baffling, this policy. They're now saying they're going to kill him, but I thought, the way things were going, their policy was to kill everyone else and the one left standing would be Bin Laden.

Prescott

I suspect language isn't his first language.

Prozac for pets

This is Prozac for pets. Apparently dogs get depressed. I don't quite know how they found this out as you can't really take them to the psychiatrist because they are not allowed on the couch.

Queen

She's worn herself out, waving for Britain, hasn't she? One of her hands is really big from waving. It's like one of these big hands they have at football matches . . .

Questions

Do you know what, Simon? I reckon that in the morning when you've had a good night's sleep, all these questions that are troubling you so much won't seem so important.

Rabbits

Rabbits are becoming popular with adults as a pet because they're not much trouble as a pet; they don't keep the neighbours awake at night with their barking. And you can also eat them . . .Cats are basically psychopaths, they would kill you if they had the chance. If they figured out how to open a tin, that would be you dead. I've had a terrible do lately with the cats in my garden. My garden pond, or as they call it *Yo! Sushi*. Carnage. I came out the other day, there were five dead frogs all around the pond, all lying in twisted, mutilated positions. I did a little outline of them in chalk and taped that bit of the garden off. The police weren't interested at all. Just tried to frame up a black cat down the road. I don't think it was him. It was this big ginger bastard. Cats aren't very good. But rabbits are a bit dull. They would be no good at that Lassie kind of thing. 'What? Bandits up at the pass?' They'd just trot towards you, then say, 'Oh, sod this. I haven't had a shag for two and a half minutes . . .'

Recorders

Apparently playing the recorder puts children off music for life. I find children playing the recorder puts me off children for life, actually. Once you've heard 'Father Hear The Prayer We Offer' off-key several times, the urge to re-enact a scene from an Hieronymous Bosch painting becomes quite overwhelming. Just lucky they don't play the bagpipes. Could be even more serious.

Reverend Lee Rayfield

Reverend Lee Rayfield of Maidenhead told his Christmas congregation – that included many children – that it was scientifically impossible for Santa to deliver presents to all the children of the world. I would have thought the old scientific proof was an unfortunate thread for a vicar to start pulling on, really . . .

Royal revelations

This new book about the Royals by Penny Junor has all sorts of astonishing revelations, like the fact that Charles and Diana didn't really get on. And the Windsors, they're all mad. So a right old turn-up. Things like the Queen not wanting Diana to have a state funeral and saying, 'No, the Co-op and a meat tea, that's all she deserves.' But there was one astonishing thing which was the allegation that Diana was some sort of Mafia hit woman who wanted Camilla 'to sleep with the fishes' and was going to have her bumped off. I suppose you can't really threaten a member of the upper classes by putting a horse's head in their bed. Business as usual really.

Royalty

Imagine the Queen meeting Camilla.
  'You're my son's mistress? That must be interesting.'

Rugby

I don't understand rugby at all. It's like a really boring fight that someone keeps breaking up.

Shell suit

Do you know that if you hold a shell suit up to your ear you can hear Romford?

Shyness

Apparently scientists have discovered a drug that overcomes shyness. Now, I thought we already had a drug that overcomes shyness. It's called alcohol. It works very well. It's never failed me, especially at this time of year. You can see people rolling down the streets with overcome shyness.

Small men

Research suggests small men are less unfaithful. That's because the small man is about bosom height with women, so he's happy for about fifty years. The taller man can actually look around. 'Oh look, there's some more over there.'

Soaps

This is people watching soaps on television and then going along to their doctor's, thinking they've got whatever illness the character in the soap opera has got. So, like, there's that man in *EastEnders* who's had a brain tumour, so lots of people here watched that and thought, 'I'm watching this – there must be something wrong with my brain, I'd better go and have it seen to.' And they watch *Emmerdale* and they go to the doctor's and say, 'I seem to have lost the will to live . . .'. Basically their viewing habits affect their health. If you listen to *The Archers*, you get run over by a tractor . . .

Songbirds

There was a story in the papers this week about British songbirds having to sing louder, because of noise pollution. They've had to make their little birdsong louder and higher. They're all sitting there going, 'YES, I'M ON THE TREE!'

Tatchell

Peter Tatchell. He's gay, you know. I'm told. Apparently on Easter Sunday he got up in church, him and some mates in Canterbury Cathedral, and disrupted the service, started shouting about gay weddings, and the Archbishop of Canterbury said, 'Go on, get out of it, you can't come up here, you haven't got a frock.' The moral majority get outraged about gay people's promiscuity. Of course, you let them get married and they'll be celibate in a year like everybody else.

Teachers

Teachers have been told this week that they can now restrain unruly pupils, they can now put a hand on them and push them or hold them but not hurt them. In fact, there's a lovely little phrase in the report, 'They can shepherd them from the room' (spoken in a rural accent). 'And here's Mrs Crabtree, thirty-five, been a teacher for ten years. And we've got Craig, a drug-crazed thug (whistles to a sheep dog). Come by, come by, come by, Craig. Oh dear, oh dear, oh dear, Craig's stabbed her with a craft knife. She'll lose points for that.'

Tony Blair

He's never had the populist touch. He's like the Geography teacher at the school disco. Everyone wants him to leave so they can start enjoying themselves.

Tories

The Tory Party, they've come out with all these policies saying, oh, we can drive the car really fast if we like on the motorway, they're going to change that; they're going to stop speed cameras unfairly speeding; they're going to let us have drugs if we want drugs. Basically they're like a divorced parent, really. They don't see that much of us so they're trying to win back our affection with these lavish gifts. And they're saying, 'Remember, Tony Blair isn't your real dad.'

Tory leadership

This has been running for so long now, this question, you can get a bursary for answering it. Michael Howard was apparently humiliated on a vote on how they're going to choose the new leader. He got four votes for his idea of what should be done – which was him, his best friend Francis Maude, a cleaner who felt a bit sorry for him, and Ann Widdecombe in a spirit of irony.

Toxic carpets

Fitted carpets act like toxic sponges, containing dangerous levels of pollutants. 'Apparently, children are something like twenty times more susceptible to these toxins . . . so put them in first, like a canary. If they croak, rip that carpet up.'

Tracey's cat

Tracey Emin's cat Docket went missing. It wasn't such a happy ending. Docket was found – but he was found by Damien Hirst. Nasty business.

Unsuitable name

I rather question the phrase 'Happy Hour' when you look at the people availing themselves of this facility. It's more, 'I'm trapped in a loveless marriage which is why I'm drinking tequila at thruppence a flagon instead of getting the 8.33 back to Chislehurst, bloody hell I never wanted to live there anyway' Hour.

Viagra

Where are all these impotent men appearing from? For years it was 'No. Never, never happened before . . . never happened to me before.' Suddenly there's millions of them.

Wedding bells

This is a very sweet story. This is a church in Wales where they can't afford bellringers. You just can't get the bellringers these days – it's a dying art. And people obviously like bells for their wedding, so what they've got people to do is, they've got the con-gregation . . . they've got half of them to be the dings and the other half to be the dongs . . . and they do the lovely wedding bells, *ding dong ding dong*. Although sometimes there's a bit of anarchy and some people are dinging when they should be donging and dong-ing when they should be dinging, but generally it's very jolly. They make their own entertainment. It all sounds rather lovely, actually. I quite like the idea of it. I think more people should take this up. Police cars should have somebody sitting on top going *ner ner, ner ner.*

Women's brains

A neuroscience conference in San Diego says that women's brains are denser than men's. Well, better packed . . . because men can't pack. If you fold the brain cells properly you can fit more in.

Women's drinking habits

The organisation to encourage women drinking beer has come up with this idea that it might be more attractive to women if – instead of having a pint – they served you with a third of a pint and they got it in a wine-glass affair. When I was a student in Sheffield they used to be called 'a lady's glass'. 'Can I have a half of bitter, please?' 'Is it for you, love?' And you'd say, 'Yes.' 'Ah, you'll want it in a *lady's glass*.' Which was like a normal glass, only it had a doily underneath. Smelling salts on the side in case it was all a bit too much for you. This is the case now – that you'd prefer a third of a pint. That is not a drink! That is homeopathy. If there's this great upsurge in binge drinking, how can there be correspondingly a decline in beer drinking, or are all these out-of-control teenagers drinking an interesting Beaune wine?

Xenophobia

Asylum-seekers in Dover, I think, we're talking about, aren't we? There was a bit of a to-do, in Dover . . . big fight broke out, I think it really was, the people of Dover – all fighting over who was the most helpful to the asylum-seekers. 'No, I'm the best Samaritan,' 'No, I am,' 'No, I'm the most welcoming to strangers,' 'No I am.' It was a big fight, it was a dreadful business . . . no, if only that were true. No – they don't want them there in Dover, and People's Princess Ann Widdecombe has come up with this extraordinary rationale for why they don't like asylum-seekers in Dover. 'Well, you know, it's a small town and they're not used to foreigners' . . . IT'S A BLOODY PORT! Have they not noticed a certain moisture round the edges? It's the sea! It's where the foreigners come in – in big boats.

Yoda

Scientists have bred the oldest laboratory mouse. Now, the mouse is called Yoda, and the little mouse that looks after this old mouse, its carer I suppose, is called Princess Leia. So I think that tells us *quite a lot* about the scientists in question. He keeps going, 'I'm four. I'm *four*. I've seen some changes here. Oh, it was all fields. I remember you could leave your cage open all day and no one would fit electrodes to your genitals. Oh, it was lovely round here. I'm getting one of those Stannah exercise wheels . . .'

Zero tolerance

Don't you think modern teachers are sort of missing a trick? They quite often find their classes disruptive and naughty and noisy. But you see, when I was at school, the teachers had a weapon – boredom. I don't think teachers know how to use boredom like they used to. They'd drone on about the Gross National Product of Brazil, maize, corn . . . by the time they'd got to palm oil you'd drifted off . . . the light smell of ink from the Gestetner. So by the time it was playtime, by the time you were ready for your milk, you were in a light coma. Discipline wasn't a problem.

Zzz

You notice no matter how hard it is to go to sleep at night, you always want to go to sleep once the alarm goes off, no matter. Awake all night, alarm goes off: 'Uhh . . . five more minutes.' So what you *should* do is set your alarm for five minutes *after* you go to bed; eight hours' refreshing sleep.

'LEAVE IT TO ME'
Corrie Corfield, newsreader, continuity announcer and party animal

I once confided in Linda that the worst part of doing the *News Quiz* for me, was giving microphone level to the sound engineers before the recording began – because I was so unused to being glibly off-the-cuff and not reading a script. There we'd all be, sitting on the stage and Simon Hoggart, the chairman, would whizz round the table to the panellists – 'Jeremy . . . how are you?', 'Francis . . . I see you've joined the *Evening Standard*,' 'Alan . . . what delight awaits you in the oven when you get home?' etc., etc. And they would all reply with some pithy one-liner or comic diatribe against a politician and the audience would laugh and the engineers got their level and I'd get more and more nervous, thinking, 'What on earth am I going to say?'

So I told Linda. 'Don't worry,' she said, 'leave it to me.'

So, whenever she was on the panel with me, she would ask me a question or make some comment that relaxed us both, was invariably hilarious, and made me feel a real part of the team. My favourite is one June when I had just returned from a holiday in Greece and was rather suntanned.

'Corrie,' she asked, 'have you been away, or has your liver packed up?'

It brought the house down.

Corrie Corfield, 2006.

PART FOUR

'Why, Lord Onslow, You're a Tease!'

Linda Live and on TV

1998–2005

ALL THE FUN OF THE MAYOR
Jeremy Hardy, comedian and writer

I do not have the kind of encyclopaedic memory that Linda had. I'm afraid I can't remember meeting her for the first time. I got to know her gradually through work. She and Warren were living in Sheffield, and I would stay with them whenever I had a gig there. When they moved to London, I was glad they lived nearer, but annoyed to find myself having to stay in hotels in Sheffield.

One thing I do remember being struck by early on was what nice hair Linda had. At some time or other she decided to cut it off because someone told her that the way she kept flicking it out of her face was distracting to audiences. I don't know who this Mandelsonian figure was, but I doubt he or she was crucial in her success. For my money, there are plenty of comics, but hardly any with really nice hair; and the cut-throat, cut-hair world of comedy could do with a lot more physical beauty

As I say, there are lots of comics, and a lot of those are very good. I can't remember the point at which I realised Linda was unusually talented, but she was additionally unusual in that her talent seemed to grow continuously for the whole of her career. She just got funnier and funnier. At any rate, over time, a combination of admiration and friendship made me start suggesting her for things, like the *News Quiz*.

It soon became obvious that Linda was going to be consistently brilliant and increasingly popular on the show. So I then went through a phase of feeling jealous about the fact that Linda was funnier than me and everyone knew it. Then I felt guilty because she was not only funnier than me but also my friend and someone

I should be glad for. After that I just enjoyed every moment of working with her.

The BBC is both a wonderful and terrible organisation, capable of wonderful and terrible decisions, sometimes from the same person. For a while, in the nightmare days of Birtian madness, there was a policy of separating Linda and me, as though we were two disruptive pupils in a Geography lesson. A guideline was cascaded from the Head of Cascades down into the Humour Resources pool to the effect that Jeremy Hardy and Linda Smith must not appear on the same *News Quizzes* because they were 'too similar'. How true that was. How often when brushing my teeth would I catch sight of the mirror and think, 'Fuck me, Linda's head's in the bathroom cabinet. And she's got rabies.'

I don't think we were very similar. We enjoyed each other's company and we laughed at a lot of the same things. We also agreed about a lot of things. In fact, we were once accused in a *Times* article of being entrist cadre of the revolutionary Left, using comic skills to infiltrate Radio 4 as part of a wider plot. The article wasn't nasty about us, in fact it was quite complimentary about our comedy identities. We were just fascinated as to who, in the author's fevered imagination, could have sent us.

Anyhow, I doubt that the BBC executive who ordered that we be kept in separate shows was worried that we might use the programme to pass coded messages to one another. I think it was just a daft decision by someone whose job it was to make decisions. In a target-based world, if people are rewarded for the number of decisions they make, they make as many as they can, so it follows that a lot of those decisions will be daft. The fact was that Linda and I worked well together and enjoyed it. It probably seemed like we were having too much fun.

True, Linda worked well with a lot of people. I'm not sure she was on better form if I was around, but I do know I much preferred her being around. I'd like to think I kindled funny thoughts in her the same way she did in me. But apart from bantering together on the *News Quiz*, we never really got down to much serious work together, which is a shame. I think we'd have made some really good TV programmes if we'd applied ourselves.

We appeared on a few things together but the only thing I could call 'ours' was a one-off show about the first election for Mayor of London in 2000. It mightn't sound like a promising subject; and the title, *All the Fun of the Mayor*, was not of our choosing. But someone has to come up with names for things and we couldn't come up with one ourselves. I think the programme turned out surprisingly well.

The genesis of it was when Linda joined me and Paul Foot on an even less promising-sounding Channel 4 programme about the NHS in 1998. Paul and Linda took to each other immediately, and from that time onwards we would all meet up with Mark Steel for lunch in the Star Café, round the corner from the *Private Eye* offices. They were lovely occasions. When Paul died in 2004, Linda was already acutely aware that her own life was in danger.

We decided to do a kind of spoof news programme, slipping in and out of presenter characters. Looking at it now, I can see that Linda succeeded far more than I did. In fact, her performance was almost flawless. There was always something so open about Linda that people could tell when she was being genuine and when she was being heavily ironic or lightly tongue-in-cheek. She had that twinkle. My performance was a bit clunky. I also raced through the script, which was so complex and densely written that I've had to watch it twice in a row just to make sense of some bits. The writing, in which Linda and I were equal partners, isn't to blame. The bits Linda delivered all make perfect sense.

Jeffrey Archer was problematic for us, because his case was sub judice, and there was a lot of last-minute rewriting, but the idea of presenting his story in the style of a bad novel served us well. Archer held a special place in Linda's contempt, and he later inspired one of her best ever *News Quiz* riffs when he came out of prison.

But the real issue was what to do with Livingstone. He wasn't a hero or a villain to either of us. The party hierarchy's attempt to block him was so blatant it didn't need exposing. And they had made such fools of themselves that they hadn't left us much scope. So we decided to construct an elaborate conspiracy theory using our mountain of archive footage, to the effect that a Livingstone victory was exactly what the Labour leadership wanted. Mandelson was orchestrating events and had been grooming Livingstone since the seventies, with Thatcher, Major, Kinnock, Blair and Jim Davidson all in on it. We also had some fun with the idea that Livingstone might be even more of a villain than he was painted, a proper villain living in a hollow volcano protected by an army of newt-like Amphibo-People. And on a more serious note, we predicted he'd be rehabilitated by the Labour leadership in no time, but that bit didn't make the edit.

The Mandelson conspiracy theory was our big set piece and I think it was a good use of telly. Most of what I've done and Linda did on telly could also have worked on radio, but this was like proper telly. I think the way we sourced and used all that footage showed we had the makings of a really good series. But we were a bit knackered once it was over and neither of us was driven enough to try to take things any further. Not that that matters greatly in the scheme of things. I'm just glad to have a bit of video of me and Linda together.

Jeremy Hardy, 2006.

Excerpt from:

All the Fun of the Mayor

Written and presented by
Jeremy Hardy and Linda Smith

BBC Television
4 May 2000

ITEM 13 (STUDIO + VT): EVIL KEN

JEREMY: So, apart from his fondness for newts, what's Ken Livingstone really like?

LINDA: There has been no shortage of attacks

VT
Blair and Boateng

on him from colleagues./

OUT: . . . a big responsibility

DUR:

75. 4 _____/
MS LINDA

LINDA: Perhaps the clincher is the evidence of people who used to be his friends but have gone off him, as this *Times* article

VT
Times headline, 'Livingstone has no shame'

shows./

76. 4 _____ (Tony Banks quote on screen)/
MS LINDA

You see, 'He has no shame', and that comes from none other than serious politician Tony Banks and he should know the sting

VT
VT *Sun* front page, Banks in Union Jack hat

of humiliation./

77. 2 _____/
MS JEREMY

78. 4 _____/
MS LINDA

LINDA: Another former GLC colleague was Paul Boateng, who we heard from just now. What fuels his hatred, you might wonder? Well, look at what a young barrister was expected to do if he wanted to get

VT INSERT 34

anywhere in the GLC./

clip of Boateng
pooving about
something chronic

OUT: . . . music

DUR:

79. 2   /

MS JEREMY

JEREMY: You might be too young or too provincial to remember the GLC. So does Livingstone deserve the name

VT INSET 35

Red Ken?/

Clip of Cutler

OUT:

DUR:

80. 4   /

MS LINDA

LINDA: (I/V) His most heinous of crimes of course was the Fares Fair policy, a system of fares that were quite literally fair. Livingstone cheapened the whole business of travel in order

VT

to popularise the Tube,/ a seedy

Neutral busy
Tube footage

underground network of trains operating in the demi-monde of London's twilight underbelly which existed to carry gays

81. 2   and lesbians all over London./

MS JEREMY

JEREMY: (V/O) And not only them but also buskers, strap-hangers and other passengers who were fellow travellers along

VT INSERT 37   for the ride./ Clearly this

Dismantling ticket   madness had to be stopped, but
machines/   the strain of destroying the
Denning   policy turned Lord Denning, a progressive and idealistic law lord, into a drooling old bigot.

LINDA:

VT INSERT 38   And what about policing?/ But

IN: The only   poor old Dobbo doesn't realise
thing . . .   just how anti-police Ken is.
OUT: . . . in the city
DUR:

OUT: . . . in the city.

DUR:

82. 4   /

MS LINDA

LINDA (cont'd): As mayor, he will

VT INSERT 39   force them into gay marriages./

Mr Leather   Look what he's got planned
beginning with   for our brave boys in blue.
three guys cuddling
and as much more
of the cop-hat bits
as we can justify

Here's a preview of Ken's

VT   new-look traffic cops./

Rollerblading cops

JEREMY: That's not all. He is also planning to give young black men the right to make police cars pull over and say to the driver, 'Is this your car, son? Smart car for a young fella.' This bobbies-on-the-beat thing is a ruse to get the police out of their cars and stop them running people over. Livingstone would stop the police doing what they do best, unarmed combat, which means

shooting people who are

83. 4   unarmed./

   MS LINDA   LINDA: I mean, it's like stop and search. If you can think of a better way of investigating crime than harassing black people, we'd like to hear it. Yes, the trendy lawyers might say police should get an actual description or evidence as the in-crowd call it. But these things take

84. 2   time and brains./

   MS JEREMY

                       JEREMY:

                       Why do you think the police fit up innocent people? It's not malice; innocent people are easier to catch because they're not expecting anything

                       and they're generally more

85. 3   compliant./

   2-S + VIDEO WALL

                       LINDA: In fact, not only is Livingstone anti-police and pro-drugs, he has a sneering contempt for

   ON VIDEO WALL   all the emergency services. He is
   VT INSERT 40   anti-fire brigade and pro-fire./

Red smoke clip from Save GLC rally	And I wonder if Millbank are aware that his ability to travel through time enabled him to start the Fire of London, while free-basing.
	LINDA (V/O): He also caused the plague by
ON VIDEO WALL	having unprotected sex with
VT INSERT 41	rats./ Left light on in the Blitz.
Rat Library pictures	And caused Pea Soupers by pouring pea soup into London's air vents. (All these clips v. quick) He was also Raffles the Gentleman Jewel Thief, only common.
	JEREMY (V/O): The legend of his support for the IRA is a distraction from the real truth that he is on the Army Council of EA and secretly led the Baader Meinhof Gang alongside his old oppo Douglas
VT INSERT 42	Baader-Meinhof./
Douglas Bader	

86. 3 _____ /

    2-S

LINDA (STUDIO):
Clearly Ken is a criminal mastermind. So, we decided to doorstep

87. 1 _____ him at his campaign HQ./

    CU TRACEY ISLAND

88. 3 _____ TRACEY ISLAND./

    2-S + PROP

JEREMY: Which turned out to be a

secret island which is one of those ones that looks like a volcano but is really a hinged island, so that the top can come off and a rocket come out. It is guarded by half-newt Amphibo-People who have machine guns painted silver, which is very effective.

LINDA: They agreed to speak to us in their

89. 2 _____ quavery newt voices./
   MCU JEREMY

JEREMY: We thought they'd be like (in a Darth Vader voice) 'You poor fools – ha

90. 4 _____ ha ha!'/
   MCU LINDA

LINDA: Yeah, but they were more like, 'Good morning, can I help you?', more newty. They told us they still support Ken but think he takes them for granted after

91. 3 _____ wooing them to begin with./
   2-S JEREMY/LINDA

JEREMY: Ken's consort is a beautiful lady with long floaty hair and eyes full of sadness who swims but can't talk.

LINDA: Anyway, we only just escaped the island after Ken, laughing like a maniac, pulled the self-destruct lever and we only got away because a boat was tied up outside and even then it was touch and go because bits of the blown-up island landed quite near and the molten lava nearly caught up with us as well but luckily the currents were in our favour.

JEREMY: Sadly we got none of this on camera because the light was bad and we just didn't think we could do it justice.

LINDA: Yes, they'd had a lovely week, apparently, but it was really overcast that day. They were as disappointed as we were./

92. 2

MCU JEREMY

JEREMY: So you'll have to take our word for it but the gist of it is, Ken is definitely hungry for power and perhaps a little bit vain./

93. 4

MCU LINDA

LINDA: And he might have an army of newt Amphibo-People but probably not./

94. 3

2-S JEREMY/LINDA

ITEM 14 (STUDIO): OUTRO/
GOODBYES
JEREMY: In any event, wherever you are tonight will be a bad night for New Labour. Why? Because people are disappointed, when Labour got in there was celebration because the Tories had gone and now people feel let down. They feel like some-one who waited eighteen years for a

transplant and a successful operation only to find out the other bloke
had the same thing as them. So will
Livingstone become the champion
of these people?

LINDA: No, shouldn't think so.

JEREMY: Why not?

LINDA: Well, it's more likely that
he'll be rehabilitated, rejoin the
Labour Party and knuckle under.
So he'll turn out to have been no
more than a harmless release for
people's anger and frustration, just
like one of those rubber bricks you
throw at the telly.

JEREMY: That's depressing.

LINDA: It is, but try and keep it in
perspective, Jeremy. All over the
world tonight there are people who
are homeless, stateless, poverty-
stricken, facing floods or droughts,
driven to the very edge of despair,
but they keep their spirits up by
saying, 'Could be worse, at least I'm
not Frank Dobson.'

HAVE I GOT NEWS FOR YOU
David Quantick, comedy writer and journalist

'Why, Lord Onslow, you're a tease,' she said. The elderly peer beamed, peerishly. 'And you're lovely,' he replied. Linda looked back at him, almost approvingly, and said, 'I must say you're the only lord I've ever met and you do not disappoint.'

That was very much Linda Smith on *Have I Got News for You*. She had a genius for suddenly latching on to one of her fellow guests – particularly if that guest was a peer or, say, the unsuccessful former leader of a major political party – and talking to them in a manner which would be, initially, frankly coquettish, and then increasingly barbed. She would begin with a measure of apparently puzzled interest – 'I know you!' she said to William Hague – and end with them ruined, on the end of a big hook. By the end of a brief conversation with Linda Smith, many public figures would be wishing they had considered some other career, possibly something monastic.

Linda's appearances on *Have I Got News for You* and *Question Time* were not as frequent as her splendid voyages through the *News Quiz*, but they were always unforgettable. From her HIGNFY debut, where she made a memorable comment about Jesus and his relationship to eggs, to her serious appearance on *Question Time*, where she looked mightily fed up with some bloke from the *Independent*, Linda managed to combine composure with criticism and humour with, oddly, a slightly regal quality. She was, in this as in every other area, dignified and hilarious.

She was also a slightly surreal commentator on these shows. Whether it was Christ and his eggs, the *Doctor Zhivago*-like quality of modern rail travel, or just the invisibility of David Dickinson in front of mahogany, Linda had the kind of surrealism that's normally referred to as 'gentle', except that there was very little that was gentle about Linda when she sank her teeth in.

TV also brought out Linda's political side. On *QT* she made serious points and didn't play to the gallery; she wouldn't be the Token Funny Person. At the same time she was funny. In among the editors and the Blair babes, she was direct, clear and a one-woman jugular-seeking missile. You see her on *Question Time* and her comments on the hollowness of Tony Blair aren't a joke, they're a strong belief. Her digs at William Hague barely conceal a powerful contempt. And her all-out devastation of Neil Kinnock on *HIGNFY* is rooted in anger as well as the sheer joy of having the opportunity to rip the living piss out of a man who, she clearly believed, single-handedly wrecked socialism's chances of winning an election.

Linda was also, by the way, a brilliant team player. This is rare on television panel games, where guests don't have the time or the ability to bond with their team-mates. But Linda was superb in that context, especially when her partner in malice was Paul Merton, whose own downbeat surrealism fitted well with Linda.

The following is a small selection of Linda's best television moments. We see her particular genius in mixing the domestic with the grandiose. We see her toppling the self-styled great and good. And we see a great topical, political, surreal comedian doing what she did best; enjoying being funny.

David Quantick, 2006.

LINDA ON *HAVE I GOT NEWS FOR YOU*

On eggs

Jesus didn't like eggs. He gave rise to the Easter Egg but tragically never got to try one.

On the 2000 US elections

They want to get Anne Robinson out there. She'd sort it out. 'George W. Bush, you are as thick as shit – goodbye.'

On the British Government selling off air traffic control

You sometimes wonder if they're drug addicts. They just seem to be selling things off. If you went round 10 Downing Street, there's probably not a stick of furniture.

On the idea of the gay mafia

What is a gay mafia anyway? 'Peter? You wearing those pants with that shirt? Forget about it!' 'Hey, you know what would brighten up this hideaway? Some scatter cushions.'

Missing words

POLICE SAY SORRY FOR . . . 'Walking on the Moon', and all their other crap singles.

On Steven Byers, the Minister for Transport

You don't often get a Minister *Against* Transport.

On the new, faulty five-pound notes whose serial numbers rubbed off

They're like a scratchcard, really. And you win five pounds.

On Richard 'Dirty' Desmond, pornographer and publisher, being invited by Tony Blair to tea at Number Ten

He comes round for tea and Tony says, 'Oh, you must be so hot in that suit. . . I'll pour the tea, it's getting quite steamy. . .'

To David Dickinson

LINDA: I think you should be minister of suaveness. The tan is so fantastic – it's a beautiful mahogany stain, if I may say so. When you're at a furniture sale, when you stand in front of a wardrobe, you disappear, don't you?

DAVID: Can I tell you how I do it?

LINDA: Please do.

DAVID: I go abroad several times a year, sit round the pool and I take in the sunshine.

LINDA: And you end up looking like Judith Chalmers' nan. . .

Missing words

KILLER DORMOUSE THREATENS . . . Haywards Heath.

On Abu Hamza's hook

Abu Hamza couldn't be a Bond villain because no cat's going to let him stroke it with that.

Missing words

GEORGE LED AN UNASSUMING LIFE UNTIL HE BECAME . . . assuming.

On Blair's heart treatment

Do you not think it would have given Blair a bit of a rosy view of the Health Service? He turns up, in there, five hours later, bish bosh, he's out. He must be thinking, 'What are all these old biddies moaning about? Trolley all night waiting for hip replacement? Rubbish! It's marvellous!'

To the Earl of Onslow

LINDA: You've got ever such a lot of names. I was looking you up on the internet. You've got about twelve names.

EARL: I've only got five.

LINDA: Oh no, it was more than that. Michael William Pebbledash Tarmac . . . you know in the House of Lords when they're deciding which hereditary peers to keep you have to describe in twenty words why you should be a peer? Just writing your name would use up your go.

There's going to be another cull of the hereditary peers. You have to do it . . . and they respect you for it!

On the Tories

I think they've got to stop having these supply leaders who can't keep order. Iain Duncan Smith doesn't seem to have held down a job in his life. Do you think he needs Restart?

On David Gest, fourth husband of Liza Minnelli

He does seem to have quite a lot of plastic surgery done – but not by a plastic surgeon.

To Neil Kinnock, guest presenter

In 1992 do you think you'd have won if, instead of campaigning, you'd just pissed off on holiday for three weeks? Just gone away, kept your gob off the telly, maybe replaced yourself with, say, a lovely little kitten. A ginger kitten, if you wanted to be a bit rebellious. A jar of ginger marmalade. Something like that. Do you think you would have sailed in? I mean, I realise you were up against the mighty charisma of John Major. That's a tough old one, isn't it? The man who ran away from the circus to become an accountant.

On Princess Diana's voice coach

He vowed that he would never sell the tapes until he felt like it. She said Charles only wanted sex every three weeks. Well, that seems a very odd thing to say to a voice coach. Normally it's your Henry Higgins – you know, 'The rain in Spain falls mainly on the plain.' Not 'My husband only shags me every three weeks.'

Missing words

LONG-TIME READERS OF WINDSOCK WILL ALREADY BE FAMILIAR WITH . . . Windsock Readers' Wives.

LINDA ON *QUESTION TIME*, BBC TELEVISION

On Cherie Blair's apparent sympathy for suicide bombers

I could not believe – I'm not a fan of Cherie Blair – but I could not believe the amount of furore that this caused. I thought at least that she was going to come out as a member of Hammas or something. All she'd said was that suicide bombing was the product of hatred. It's not the product of wild optimism or joie de vivre, is it?

On Government/press relations

I think the Blair Government and the press are in a sort of abusive relationship. They both know they should leave it because it's never going to get any better. They're like Burton and Taylor, really.

On the England flag

If everyone uses it, it loses its voodoo power. It's just colours on a bit of material.

On retrials

Yes, of course it would be better if it were easier to convict people . . . Now that brought to mind the Stephen Lawrence case where I, and many other people, thought justice wasn't done. Would I want another trial? Yes I would, but that would probably be wrong. How many times could you go on retrying people? You'd just end up with a nation of rich and powerful lawyers and we'd just be their human slaves. You do have to come back to those basic tenets of civil liberties, no matter how painful it might be.

On speed controls

Yes, speed does kill, but on the other hand if some hard-working tax payer – a tall, female comedian, for example – were driving back from Brighton in the middle of the night and, just say for example, she were stopped for speeding just as the motorway becomes the Purley Way by a traffic cop just cynically waiting to pounce on her, then that – just as an example out of the blue – that's wrong.

ROOM 101

Extracts from Linda's appearance on the BBC 2 show, hosted by Paul Merton. First transmitted on 17 November 2003.

PAUL: All right, well, let's have a look at your first choice then, illustrated by this charming collection of people here. I'll stick him there.

(Stills of men in bow ties – props)

LINDA: Oh, lovely.

PAUL: And I'll put him next to him.

LINDA: Oh, Gawd!

PAUL: The most alert of you will find a recurring theme. And here's the last one at the end, oops, if I can just sort of put him in there. OK. So what do these people all have in common?

LINDA: Well, apart from the obvious, they are wearing bow ties.

PAUL: Bow ties?

LINDA: Yeah.

PAUL: So what have you got against bow ties?

LINDA: Well, it's just a sign of the psychopath really, isn't it? I think, you know, no one good, with the exception – there's always an exception that breaks a rule – with the exception of Frank Muir, no one who wears them in real life is anything but a psychopath or a . . . just a twat really. That's . . . I'm sorry, there's no other, well, there is another word, but I can't really use that.

PAUL: But how can you describe Russell Grant . . .? Oh, I see what you're saying, yeah. This is the weirdest police identity parade in the history of the Metropolitan Police, by the way, this one here.

LINDA: But the great thing is, you could pick any one of them and they would have done the crime.

PAUL: Yes. Do you think we should create a bow tie-wearing register, so like you should have the right to know if somebody wearing a bow tie moves in next door to you?

LINDA: Yeah, absolutely. I think they should be registered at police stations and there should be big vigilante groups outside their house, you know, forcing them off the estate, definitely.

PAUL: People wear bow ties because it's show business, isn't it? I mean, there's Bernard Manning there, I mean, obviously he is in show business, and Neil Hamilton desperately would like to be in show business. But that's the idea, isn't it?

LINDA: I don't really like you saying his name, because it gives him the oxygen of publicity and I'm not that happy with him having the oxygen of oxygen.

PAUL: Would it help if I just sort of turned him around, because that really isn't giving him the oxygen of publicity?

LINDA: No, that's good, that's better really.

PAUL: But I mean, it's show business, isn't it? There's something about the bow tie that says: I'm eccentric, I'm wacky, I'm slightly individual.

LINDA: Yeah, that's the thing, it's that contrived eccentricity really, it's like people wearing, you know, novelty T-shirts and things, it's a contrived thing. And it's not only show biz, it's even worse when people not in show biz wear them, because I think it's really offensive when you see doctors wearing bow ties. I think that's just disgraceful, like you're, no, it really is, you're at a hospital, you see a consultant, they're the worst, the higher up the doctor food chain they are, the more likely they are to wear this ridiculous neckwear.

So you're there in the hospital and they're saying, well, I'm afraid these results don't look very good. They're dressed like Coco the Clown! You know, it's just insulting, isn't it, don't you think, they look like the organ-grinder's monkey. Well actually, that's another thing, I was actually bitten once by a monkey wearing a bow tie.

PAUL: A monkey wearing a bow tie? I don't think I've ever seen a monkey with . . .

LINDA: Yeah, it was a formal occasion, but you know.

PAUL: Yes. And was the monkey there on its own, or was there an owner?

LINDA: Oh no, there was someone, a very irresponsible owner with them, obviously, that's at Blackheath, at the funfair, you'd get these, you know – did you used to get them when you were a kid? little dressed-up monkeys that photographers sort of thrust at you.

PAUL: With a little fez.

LINDA: Yeah, little fez, little cardigan, and in this case, bow tie. You know, and the photographer threw it at me, photo of the little girl, BITE, in my neck. Down Casualty for a tetanus injection. That was a lovely day!

PAUL: Well, then you go down, you see a consultant who's also got a bow tie.

LINDA: Bow tie, exactly.

PAUL: So this is what it is. But I think the hospital consultants, they just wear a bow tie to soften the bad news, don't they? And if it's really serious, the bow tie spins around like that and lights up. 'You've got three weeks to live.' You get a laugh out of it, don't you, you get a laugh. Something was . . .

LINDA: But then other doctors, you know, I mean it is the sign of the psychopath. Peter Sutcliffe was a bow tie-wearer. That is another clue the police missed. I believe Harold Shipman was.

PAUL: Yes, yes, he also wore a bow tie.

LINDA: You know, they're wearing bow ties.

PAUL: Not the most serious of his crimes, but he certainly was wearing one.

LINDA: Well, I think it wasn't unrelated. I think it would have been a bit of a clue for the police, you know, he might as well have been wearing a T-shirt saying 'Serial killers do it till they're stopped' really. Because the bow tie is a sure sign of guilt, to me.

PAUL: Well, maybe we should tell the police secretly that if there's any old unsolved crimes you've got, look for the guys who are walking around in a bow tie and then bring them in for questioning. But if we tell the bow tie-wearers that, then maybe they'll just sort of like, you know, get rid of it and start wearing cravats.

LINDA: It wouldn't be a big disguise, would it, from bow tie to cravat?

PAUL: Do you see it as a symbol of kind of . . .?

LINDA: The cravat is a gateway drug, yes.

★ ★ ★

PAUL: Let's have a look at your next choice, as illustrated by this.

VT: Man in newsagent's

MAN ON VT: 'Oh, this is just so, my wife is going to be ecstatic about this, because she's read every book, and you know, every book is cherished and I'm just making a dream come true.'

PAUL: Now, I'm not convinced that man's got a wife, but he says . . .

LINDA: I'm not convinced he should be there on his own.

(Harry Potter prop)

PAUL: No. I'm not convinced he lives with anybody in fact, apart from Auntie Betty that's probably in the wardrobe or something. But what's he talking about there?

LINDA: Oh, he's talking about Harry Potter and he's talking about buying it for an adult.

PAUL: Yes.

LINDA: Namely his entirely fictitious wife.

PAUL: Yes. Called Reginald. So it's adults who read Harry Potter books.

LINDA: Absolutely. Adults. No problem with children reading it, no problem with adults reading it to children, that's fine. But adults, shamelessly and openly reading Harry Potter as if that were normal!

(Applause and boos)

LINDA: What is wrong with them? What is wrong with them? I look at them, you know, on the train and they're reading it and they haven't even got the grace to disguise it with pornography or something. They're just sitting there reading it, and I think, oh, the lack of ambition. You think, you could do better than that, surely. I always feel like going with a big bag of books, you know, *Madame Bovary* or something and just swopping them over and saying, just try it, you're thirty-seven!

PAUL: It's not really doing any harm though, is it?

LINDA: It is doing them harm, it's doing society harm, it's doing the world harm. It's a tiny minority of people who should not be allowed to vote. I really feel that. Because . . .

(Applause and boos)

LINDA: It's just wrong, isn't it? I mean, for God's sake, I know what it's all part of, it's part of this culture of middle youth, you know, this idea that we never, you know, we don't grow old.

   And in a way it's a good thing, you know, I can see a positive side to that, because in the past that was everyone's ambition, to be as old as possible as soon as possible. If you look at photographs, like family photos from the 1950s, an entire family group, everyone looks old. You've got little babies with sort of pipes and trilbys and moustaches reading seed catalogues. But now I think we've gone too far the other way now. And people think their childhood lasts until they're sixty.

PAUL: I mean, well yes, I mean we can all remember that time when babies wore trilbys and smoked pipes, it seemed like that day would never end, but do you think these adult versions of these books, I've not seen the adult version, but is he called Harold Potter in the adult version?

LINDA: He's called Harold Pinter in the adult version and I advise people to read him.

PAUL: But you don't think adults should be reading these books at all?

LINDA: Well, I think it's fair enough if it's people with sort of reading difficulties who are learning to read. But no, I think that's fair enough. But not all of them are, not all of them are John Prescott are they, when you see them?

PAUL: No. Is *Lord of the Rings* a children's book, do you think?

LINDA: Oh, for God's sake. *The Lord of the Rings*, that is a book for engineering students called Dave.

(Applause)

LINDA: It is a rubbish rubbish, well, not even one book, he wrote one rubbish book and thought, well, this is rubbish, I'll write some more of this. He kept turning out this rubbish, with these ridiculous rubbish made-up names. Oh, this is the Hobbit called 'Drurin' and 'Gerndolf'. It's just rubbish.

PAUL: But all names are made-up though, aren't they?

LINDA: Yeah, but some are better than others, Paul – I'm convinced.

PAUL: Yeah. Linda, fine, that's a good name.

LINDA: Yeah, yeah, 'Grenoon'. No. He's just got a load of Scrabble tiles, thrown them down and picked his names from that. It's not that I think Harry Potter's a bad thing, it's a brilliant thing, it gets kids reading and they love it and it's great for kids. But it's not for the grown-ups.

PAUL: Yeah. Well, maybe there's a couple of things that we could do, because you're talking about sort of people reading it on the Tube and it's very embarrassing.

LINDA: Yeah, that's terrible.

PAUL: Maybe there's a couple of things that we can do here, that sort of like, to make it less embarrassing. They could, for example, wear one of these . . .

(Child mask prop)

Right. So, and you could just sort of like have the book in front of you, and you're on the trip and nobody knows.

LINDA: Yeah, no, that fooled me. It's brilliant.

PAUL: Yeah, well, exactly. Well, I mean, if you think that is a simple way of doing it, but to really sort of get away with it and so people don't suspect at all, what you could do is carry an artificial boy with you, right. I'll show you what I mean. An artificial boy. Here he is.

(Artificial boy prop)

And what you do is, he's got a little hole in the back there, you see. So you can sit him on your knee and look through his head.

(Applause)

If you have this on the Tube, believe you me, nobody's looking at the book. So I mean, what do you reckon?

LINDA: Well, I reckon that is fantastic, but the fact that someone has to go to those lengths, rather than buy a grown-up book, just shows you that something has gone horribly wrong in their life, doesn't it really?

PAUL: But don't you think it would cheer up the Northern Line immensely if there was twenty people in the carriage, all just sort of like, you know, turning to each other and talking about school and stuff, and just reading the book? I've got to say, this is the best prop we've ever had.

LINDA: It is fantastic.

(Applause)

LINDA: I'll tell you what, I'll do a deal with you.

PAUL: Yeah.

LINDA: I'll do a deal, I'll take the prop home, if the adults reading Harry Potter can go in. If I can have the prop.

PAUL: Oh, no no no no no. If you want the prop, then the adults who read Harry Potter books have to stay out.

LINDA: Oh, that seems hardly fair.

PAUL: No, it is fair.

LINDA: Oh.

PAUL: I assure you, it's completely fair. Isn't it? Yes it is, yeah. It looks a little bit sinister, but . . .

LINDA: Now say that while drinking a glass of water.

PAUL: I'd rather not, isn't that funny? Now I'm going to ask the audience. First of all, all those who think adults who read Harry Potter books should go into Room 101, put your hands up.

(A lot of the audience put their hands up)

Oh, that's a lot. That's a lot. Ok, well let's have a look . . . and those people who don't think they should go in?

(Audience put their hands up)

PAUL: Oh, I think the first lot have it, so they're . . .

LINDA: Yeah, definitely, by miles.

PAUL: Going into Room 101.

(Applause and boos)

LINDA: What you're hearing there, Paul, you're hearing the sound of literacy.

PAUL: Yeah, well, you've got me convinced, so they're going into Room 101. Say goodbye to the eyeless boy, in he goes. Cheerio.

(Adults who read Harry Potter go into Room 101)

(Applause)

★ ★ ★

PAUL: All right, let's have a look at your last choice, Linda, it's in this drawer if I can get it out. Let's see, here we are.

(Horned helmet prop)

Now, what does this represent?

LINDA: Well, that represents opera. But it's a specific form of opera that I'm opposed to really and it is the comic opera.

PAUL: Ah.

LINDA: The light-hearted opera. I mean, I can see a purpose for the tragic opera, you know, because tragedy doesn't date really, does it?

PAUL: No.

LINDA: You know, a tragedy hundreds of years ago is a tragedy now. But a joke dates. Jokes in opera just are not funny, but people laugh at them, annoyingly. I was once, through no fault of my own, I was at the English National Opera watching *Falstaff*, and it's just so annoying, because there's all these ridiculous things, like he's in disguise so he puts on a big hat. All these people who've known him thirty years, suddenly, you know, oh, they don't recognise him because he's got a big hat on. And then he's got to hide. So he's a big fat bloke and he hides behind a little tree, and they're supposed to not see him. And there was a bloke next to me, in a bow tie, chortling away at this as if it were actually funny. And it's just wrong, that's just so pretentious. It's not funny. And also this whole thing of them singing the bits in between the songs. They'll sort of go, you know:

(sings) 'Would you like a cup of tea? Would you like a cup of tea? Would you like a cup of tea?'

And on and on, going:

(sings) 'Would you like a cup of tea?' 'Only if you're having one, don't make one just for me.'

(Applause)

PAUL: Well, you're on to a winner!

LINDA: You know, it's just stupid, isn't it?

PAUL: Technically it's the musical, you're on to a winner here. But I mean, you say that thing about people singing the same thing over and over again. We've got a clip here of Chris Searle on *In at the Deep End* for the BBC. Let's see if it's true, this is him learning how to sing opera.

VT: Chris Searle

(Chris and others singing opera)

PAUL: He can't go in, does he know that?

LINDA: Can't go in. It would be better if at the end he said; oh, go on, go in.

PAUL: Yeah, exactly, that would be a genuine laugh. Maybe they need more audience participation, they should start making panto opera.

LINDA: Well, I don't know, panto . . .

PAUL: He's behind you, you big fat bastard. You know, things like that. What do you think?

LINDA: Maybe, I don't know. There's another thing that they do, opera singers, that annoys me, which is sing pop songs.

PAUL: Oh yes.

LINDA: Oh, that is just evil, isn't it, when opera singers sing popular music. That is terrible. And it's like Kiri Te Kanawa, you know, Oasis or something, I don't know.

(sings) 'Because after all, you're my Wonderwall.'

PAUL: So what's becoming clear, Linda, I think here, is that going through all your choices, Tim Henman, Harry Potter, bow ties, opera, you don't like posh people.

(Top hat prop)

Maybe what we should do is just make this last item all about posh people, so if I bung that on there, OK, that's balanced quite nicely. So I think, OK, posh people are going into Room 101. All posh people, would you be happy with that? A social revolution.

LINDA: I mean not all posh people.

PAUL: But I could just . . . and they're all gone.

LINDA: Oh, go on then.

PAUL: I think this is going in.

LINDA: Fantastic.

PAUL: Posh people are going into Room 101, in they go.

(Posh people/comic opera go into Room 101)

(Applause)

★

LINDA LIVE ONSTAGE
2001–2003

A little tip

My advice to you, always turn up to shows at theatres with a packet of raffle tickets, because they've always got them by the interval drinks orders. You think that looks nice, three gin and tonics – what's that, 58? – that's me! Thank you. Thus saving pounds.

A miserable tip

The place I come from is appalling – it's a miserable tip. And that's actually what the town slogan says: 'Come to Erith, it's a miserable tip'.

Art galleries

Art galleries are set up to make you feel inadequate. There's millions of them – as many paintings as you ought to see over a lifetime, not over an afternoon. Really and truly. Really, one painting and a tearoom would be enough. That would be my idea of a gallery. A lovely *Crying Boy* and then a tearoom.

Australian Rules football

Rugby is not as violent as Australian Rules football – blimey, what are the rules? No guns in the penalty area, of a Wednesday, I should think.

Blair the mourner

Tony Blair loves to get into that black suit – he's got more than Elton John. He's always got one handy. At least he looks the part. I suppose at a time of crisis – at least he looks sombre. But every time you saw him he seemed to be in a blacker and blacker suit.

What's next? Is he going to walk on and make a speech dressed as Queen Victoria in a big black veil?

Blunkett

It looks scarily like David Blunkett is going to be the next leader. He's Satan's bearded folk singer. How can someone who looks so much like a jolly fisherman be such a miserable bastard?

Burton-on-Trent

Burton-on-Trent is like an almost mythical place, a town built on beer. It's fantastic – town motto, 'Welcome to Burton – you're my best mate, you are.'

Bush and Blair

The international crisis. Now we've got George Bush with his axis of terror or pretzel of death or whatever it is. Tony calls him George and George calls Tony 'Yo! Bitch. Here.'

Sat next to Tony Blair we would all look like Einstein, wouldn't we? Tony and Cherie going round the world in fancy dress – off to India in a Nehru suit. They do look so strange with those Halloween lantern smiles.

Celebrity chefs

What a strange phrase, celebrity chef – it's as much sense as Superstar Dentist. It's only cooking, isn't it? Ainsley Harriott, is there anywhere in the world that that man has not been? Every possible permutation of naff cooking shows. How about a show for inept cannibals – *Can't Eat me Mates,Won't Eat me Mates*.

Chairs

To be honest, once you've decided you've got a favourite chair, you don't like change of any kind.

Countryside

The last time the Countryside Alliance marched on London, it was like carnival time on the Island of Dr Moreau. It really was. A festival of inbreeding. Three faces shared by about 500 people. They're always moaning, 'You try and stop us foxhunting because you don't understand country ways.' Yeah, we understand your ways – they're staring and killing. We reject them in favour of pavements and drainage.

Crime

I like to leaf through my local paper, the *Newham Murderer,* every now and then. There's another thing, coming round to small towns, you tend to forget how violent East London is. You get used to it, I suppose. The other day I was in this little place near Bristol, Thornbury – and they were saying to me, 'Oh, we've had an awful lot of trouble with crime lately.' So I thought – have you? I had a look through the local paper and there was the crime reporting and it had 'Hi-Fi Stolen' and there was a column underneath it saying, 'A hi-fi was stolen from somebody's house. Police are investigating.' I thought, for me as a Londoner . . . the layers of irony in *that*! Police are investigating . . . oh yes! – I'm sure. I thought if they reported that in the *Newham Murderer* every time a hi-fi was stolen it would be as thick as a telephone directory. Within a couple of weeks they would have to put it on microfiche.

Desert Island Discs

Desert Island Discs is a big favourite of mine – I don't know if you heard it last week. Chris Tarrant – surprisingly shallow choices. Surprised me. My favourite from the past, I've listened to it for years – a brilliant one – I don't know how many of you heard this one – John Lee Hooker. That was a corker. Because the bizarre thing with Sue Lawley was that she was actually a lot happier talking to Diana

Mosley than the great bluesman John Lee Hooker. Didn't really find any way of connecting with him. She was sitting there trying to chat to him and he had a record by Bobby 'Blue' Bland or, as he pointed out, *Mister* Bobby 'Blue' Bland, and it was this great record, and at the end of it he went . . . 'Mmm mm, he got it!' And Sue went, 'He got what?' Priceless, innit? Her top effort, I think, was when she had the Reverend Iain Paisley on. I couldn't believe it when I tuned in to that. She was sat there chatting to the Reverend Iain Paisley as if he were a normal person! Takes a bit of doing, doesn't it? Sitting there going, 'Ah well, Reverend, that's a very amusing story about the Anti-Christ. But enough of your showbiz anecdotes. Let's hear your records. I believe you would like to hear that rather beautiful old hymn, "Die, You Fenian Bastard". Played eight times.'

East London

Last night I was in Cirencester, a very dinky town in the Cotswolds. That place is so quiet and sedate. I live in East London which has a nice community feel to it. All it takes is a Kray funeral to get everyone out on the street – all coming together in warmth and happiness to mourn the criminally insane. Fair warms your heart, it really does.

Erith

Erith – not exactly a city that never sleeps, more a town that lies awake all night staring at the ceiling.

Football

It was the world turned upside down, England winning against Argentina – have they got the worst hair in the world, that team? They're either from the seventies or they're porn stars. I will never ever complain about David Seaman's hair again. It is positively classical isn't it, compared to those? It seemed to have a Samson in reverse effect on them, didn't it?

It seemed to weaken them of their footballing powers. It was a fine effort and not what you expect from England. Nice change. Don't think we should get too used to it, that's all I'm saying. You know, least said soonest mended. Not to get carried away.

Gordon Brown

Of course in the Labour Party, Gordon Brown is meant to be the clever one, isn't he? I think he's clever in the way Carol Vorderman is clever. Because she's sat next to Richard Whiteley. Same principle, it's all relative.

Gordon Brown is a bit more impressive than Tony Blair – I suppose because he's Scottish. I don't know why. Why do we trust Scottish people? Even when they've got a can of Tennants Extra you believe them – even if they're driving a train at the time. I don't know. Weird thing – we just think it's a trustworthy accent.

Health

You must try to keep yourself healthy. I do try to go to the gym but I'm put off by the bodybuilders. You get these blokes who are bodybuilding, doing steroids and the rest of it, and their bodies get pumped up, pumped up and pumped up. But their heads stay the same. There's this great big body with a marble rolling about on the top.

It looks ridiculous. Not to mention their genitals, which in comparison, are very disappointing. Great big body and then it's like very discreet jewellery. Nothing showy.

Hecklers

I'm never rude to hecklers, I don't believe in putting down hecklers – I favour a system of vaccination. It's more humane on the whole.

Madonna

I have noticed, since announcing my tour, Madonna has been goaded into doing a few dates. But I notice she's not doing Frome. So that town is mine. Swivel on that, Madge.

Makeover shows

People are constantly redecorating their houses now, aren't they – like little caddis flies always building little bits on to their shell. In the past people would go twenty years without decorating their house. The idea of a makeover in the forties was taking down the blackout curtains after the war.

Neighbours

There's nothing so annoying about a place than it being down the road. As we find with India and Pakistan.

Parents

My parents were quite old when they had me. Not in the modern sense of old, where you get these ninety-year-old women from Milan who scrape a bit of DNA off a cardigan of a bloke in Périgord and produce this weird little William Haguey-looking funny baby thing.

Politics – Jo Moore burying news

How are we going to manage without Jo Moore ? (Stephen Byers' Press Manager).

First of all she wanted to bury news on September 11th. Well, you're a psychopath woman, aren't you? It's no good saying sorry, is it? You can't help it if you think like that – you're just a psycho, just go . . . now! Have treatment, be with your loved ones – something! Then you realise that she is not only horrible, she's really stupid.

Because she thought she could bury news on the day Princess Margaret was buried. It's not like September 11th. No one gives a fuck about Princess Margaret – the family could hardly be bothered. They hadn't even put by for the funeral. There was hardly a flower in the world, was there? No, you can't bury the problems of the British transport system over the funeral of some poor old slapper who's been running a beach bar in the Caribbean for the last forty years. Dear me!

Pot-pourri

Funny stuff, pot-pourri, it's one of those things that suddenly appeared in the eighties, wasn't it? Suddenly a gift choice – oh, thank you, some dead flowers. People started putting little bowls of it all over their house, which is fine of a daytime. If you went round of an evening in a social setting, a few drinks involved – I've been through three bowls of that stuff before now before I've realised it's not crisps. There could be posh ones from Waitrose – you never know now, do you? Breath smells lovely . . . shitting twigs for days.

Queen Mother

They wheel the Queen Mother out at every opportunity, the Windsors. They're getting really desperate, they think, quick, wheel her out because she's old and everyone's just really impressed by her ability to stay alive. If that were an Olympic sport she would be a gold medallist, wouldn't she? People would think, ooh, ain't she marvellous? She's over one hundred and she still does her own breathing. And I've totally lost count of how many hips she's had, it's certainly more than there are corners on people, isn't it? I think she's hoarding them to make a coffee table. Bit cheeky, really, when other people are going short.

Radio 4

(To audience . . . who respond en masse to Linda's inquiry about the number of Radio 4 listeners in the theatre) . . . Oh Lord! Oh now! That's not listeners. That's a beige jihad! The beige army out in force. That's almost a frightening number . . . Good for you to get out though really. Nice to see you out of the house – I know you don't like to be away from your crystal sets too long. Probably recording *The Archers* on a wax cylinder.

Roots

I must say if I had realised the rake was so steep here I would have had my roots done.

Royal Family

It's been a rocky time for the Royal Family lately. I mean, more than usual. Prince Philip with his remark about aborigines chucking spears. Not his most inventive racist slur though, is it really? I was a little disappointed – spears, aborigines, it was fairly obvious. He's had some wonderfully rococo ones in the past, like the one about the fuse box. Saying, 'Did an Indian put that in for you?' You would have to think for a long time about how he arrived at that. What could have happened to make him say that? Well, have they had a very bad experience with an Indian electrician? I don't know.

What happened? Did they get a flyer through the door offering very reasonably priced electrical work from a Mr Patel and they've thought, 'Yeah, we'll have that, it's a lot cheaper than we've been quoted.' And then Windsor Castle burned down. And that's why he's so bitter. Dodgy fuse box? I don't know.

Sport

Something we English people are going to have to get used to now is being reasonably good at sport. A bit of a shock. Not too bad at sport at the moment after a period of being terrible for ages. I believe it was Winston Churchill who once said, 'Gagagagagagahh' because he was pissed and mad. But in a more lucid moment he said, 'Sport is the continuation of war by other means,' well, that would have made the entire England cricket team conscientious objectors. Up until quite recently, but now we're doing quite well in the cricket. I quite like cricket.

I say I like cricket but I don't like the one-day matches very much because I don't like the stuff they wear. It's not very nice, it's not very attractive. For the Test Matches they wear the lovely white trousers and the cotton shirts, and loose fitting flatters all sizes. Floppy hair, honey still for tea, all that romantic sort of thing. But in the one-day matches they're wearing shell suits really, aren't they? No romance in that.

And the football now, with Sven Goran Eriksson as coach we are doing quite well, aren't we? He's obviously quite good but I think he is a bit dull, to be honest. He's a bit like IKEA really, clean and reliable but not very exciting. What a disappointment at IKEA – because the names of things are always so much more exciting than the actual thing, because they're foreign, they sound exotic, they're Scandinavian. Ooh, this looks exciting . . . it's called SVEN. This one's called BJORN. This one's called HORST. There's quite a little frisson really, isn't there? You get it home and you think it's going to be really exciting but it's . . . well, just a unit for your books. Thought it was going to be some kind of stripped-pine sex toy. I imagine a similar disappointment happens all over Scandinavia with people going . . . (told in a Scandinavian accent), 'Oh, it's just a unit for my books. It seemed so exciting in the shop – it's called Colin.'

Swallow

Tonight it's been quite nice, a bit sunny on the way here, there was a bit of a rainbow but it's still very rainy and cold. So tonight, a little bit of advice for you – wrap up warm on your way home – coat on, because one swallow doesn't make a summer . . . though it can make a man's day.

The Garden of England

Romney Marsh in Kent is famous now for Derek Jarman's Garden. I don't know if you've been to Dungeness? If it was a council house he would be evicted, wouldn't he?

It's just a load of scrap metal in the garden. It would be a hard-to-let house. There's no tea rooms, no tea towels to buy. Nothing. It's quite famous now but when I was a kid it was even more remote than it is now.

The Scream

Edvard Munch's *The Scream* – you wouldn't want that staring at you would you? Would be quite appropriate in this setting – impressions of Expressionist paintings (pulls a facial expression to look like the painting of *The Scream*). Apparently it was stolen from the art gallery in Norway. Blimey, someone's gone into that art gallery, looked at every painting and thought, 'I'm having that one.' Probably wanted to put it above the mantelpiece to keep the kids away from the fire.

Tony Blair

I know socialists are often accused of preaching to the converted but Tony Blair's preaching to the loft-coverted. And he and Cherie are such an unappealing pair. You don't want to go staring into their eyes, I'll tell you that. You'll drive your car off a cliff.

Tories

William Hague, what a pitiful figure. Recently forty, meant to be this thrusting young politician. Forty! That's never forty human years, is it? The state of him. He must be a replicant, ageing like Rutger Hauer in *Blade Runner*, isn't he? He's seen all the moons of Venus but he looks really shit. There's probably a painting of him in the attic that looks fine.

And this racism business isn't going to go away. This man Townend. He's said something else again, this is how scared he is of the leader. He's said something else about race. You think, well, William Hague is in a weird position here, because how can he tell them off about racism? – it's ridiculous. It's like he's going, 'Igor, Igor, I told you to keep that monster in the laboratory.' And what must these Tory MPs feel who are getting these letters round, warning them to refrain from racism? I bet they feel like they've joined a golf club and been asked to refrain from golf!

Village violence

What sort of crime do you have here? Is it rival gangs of antique dealers – turn a bit nasty, do they? The Cravats and the Tie Pins. Implacable gangs who stalk the streets once the lights go down, getting into great big fights about the provenance of some Scrimshaw work. 'Tarquin, leave it, you'll kill 'im. Just walk away. Crispin, I'll close your fucking eyes all right!' 'Yeah, fucking buy me off with a cream tea? Outside! You toilet!'

A lot of dinky towns have that Jekyll and Hyde quality. By day . . . cream tea, cream tea. By night . . . suddenly, squaddie town. Violence, drinking . . . I was in Taunton, a regional centre for under-age drinking. We were thrown out of pubs for being over eighteen.

Windsor Arts Centre

Windsor Arts Centre used to be a fire station. I suppose that explains why Windsor Castle was razed to the ground. Not very useful if there's a fire, just chucking mime on it . . .

Windsor's a very posh town – you would be if you weren't right next door to Maidenhead and Bray. This is all relative really. The first time I went to Bray I thought it was the name of the town . . . apparently it's an instruction. (In a high-pitched posh accent) 'It's just a very little town and it's not really suitable for asylum-seekers, they wouldn't be happy here.'

Windsor must be the very epicentre of the pot-pourri industry. There's work for twenty people in that pot-pourri mine there. It's not a proper present, is it, just a bag of dead flowers? Costs more than live ones. I don't know how they work that out.

I had thought Eton College was very privileged but apparently all the computers are bought with collected loyalty cards – from Fortnum and Mason.

WRAP UP WARM
Andy Hamilton, writer and comedian

'Are they as funny offstage as on?'

It's a question that, to be honest, you come to dread; partly because you don't want to shatter someone's world by revealing that their favourite comic is a drunken, shoplifting cat-torturer, but mostly because you know it would be bad for the profession if it became widely known that we're a bunch of miserable bastards. Indeed, some comedians are exceptionally miserable bastards. No need to mention any names. They know who they are.

But whenever this question was asked about Linda, the answer was always very easy – 'Yes. She's every bit as funny offstage.' She never disappointed. She made you laugh each and every time. Even during periods of the most terrible adversity, Linda's extraordinarily inventive comic mind kept ticking over. She never lost that. It was her.

The other quality that I remember about Linda offstage was she was one of the most socially at ease people I've ever met. Her secret, I think, was that she treated everybody the same. She showed a genuine interest in them and had perfect manners. It sounds quaint and old-fashioned, doesn't it? But I think manners were very important to Linda. The first time my wife, Libby, met Linda was after a *News Quiz* recording. We were chatting in the bar about that eternal showbiz topic – is there any point in having an agent? Sensing, I suspect, that my wife was feeling a little left out, due to her husband being a rude git who wasn't including her in the conversation, Linda asked her who her agent was.

'I don't have an agent,' replied Libby, 'I'm a housewife.'

'Well, you still need an agent,' said Linda instantly. She then proceeded to improvise a brilliant portrayal of a housewife's agent, ringing up husbands and informing them that 'My girl's not going anywhere near the Marigolds for that kind of money.'

Yes, Linda was a very kind person – with just the occasional lapse into viciousness. As an illustration, here's one of the last jokes I heard her make. Mark Steel was describing the rather surreal experience of appearing on a chat show alongside Joan Collins.

'How old is Joan Collins?' I asked him.

'Ooh, not sure,' said Mark, 'I reckon she must be about seventy-five.'

Then, in a frail voice, Linda asked, 'How much is that in human years?'

On the same occasion, with lots of friends gathered round her bedside fearing the inevitable, someone asked her if she'd read *The Da Vinci Code*. With a tired but mischievous smile, Linda replied, 'I'm saving that for later.'

Occasionally Linda abandoned wit in favour of good old-fashioned Anglo-Saxon. At the Sony Awards one year, some bright spark thought it would be *terribly amusing* to have the Best Comedy award presented to the *News Quiz* team by . . . Neil and Christine Hamilton. Like reluctant teenagers, we trooped up on stage to receive our gong from that macabre pair of attention-seeking mutants (sorry about the vitriol, but it's what Linda would have wanted). As the audience applauded, photographers asked us to cluster together for a group shot. The Hamiltons reacted to the cameras in the way that hyenas react to a limping wildebeest. Suddenly, they were squirming their way into the group. Myself, Simon Hoggart and Alan Coren smiled awkwardly as Neil Hamilton posed alongside us as if he was our new best mate. Christine Hamilton pushed herself in next to Linda, who prompt-ly told her to fuck off. (Christine didn't oblige, by the way – I think she's heard that expression so many times that it's probably lost all meaning for her.)

Linda was seething because the Hamiltons embodied almost everything that she hated – from their politics to their revoltingly acquired status as 'celebrities'. It was an anger that somehow ran side by side with the playfulness in her work. She was always at her funniest when she was launching into attacks on the corrupt and the stupid – or, as she liked to call them, the 'differently bright'.

The other great weapon in her comic arsenal was her joyful use of the English language. She seemed to be able to conjure up any linguistic technique at will. Simile, metaphor, hyperbole, comic euphemism, understatement, parody – you name it, she could do it. All delivered with immaculate timing and exceptional speed of thought. She had the complete game. In fact, sitting alongside her in the *News Quiz*, I always felt it was the equivalent of a tennis player playing doubles with Roger Federer.

You can find all these qualities in the next piece. It's a transcript of a performance of a one-woman show that Linda gave on 6 May 2004 at Sudbury in Suffolk, as part of her *Wrap Up Warm* tour. Now, a transcript of this kind of show is quite an unusual thing to read. Not as unusual as a José Mourinho apology. Or a Jeffrey Archer novel where the dialogue sounds like it could actually be spoken by a human being. But pretty unusual, nonetheless. Stand-up is not really a literary form. But you'll find it a surprisingly easy read, because you cannot help but hear Linda's unforgettable voice.

(By an astonishing coincidence, you can actually hear this very performance on one of those new-fangled CD-type things – *Linda Smith Live.*)

This show represents the peak of Linda's development as a stage performer, effortlessly holding an audience in the palm of her hand for an hour and a half. Elsewhere in this book you'll find examples of Linda's early stand-up, where she's playing sometimes raucous houses with hecklers (male, invariably). But by 2004, she no longer played bear pits. She had found a huge national audience that included people of every age and class. All her dates were packed out. In every corner of England.

So read on, and hear Linda delighting the good people of Sudbury, making them laugh at the absurdities of the world and making them laugh about themselves and their sleepy English town in a way that is quintessentially Linda. She teases them, she plays games with them about the ritual of pre-ordering interval drinks, she mocks them for their English reserve – and they love her for it. Audiences felt completely at home in Linda's company. We all did. Which is why we will miss her so much.

Andy Hamilton, 2006.

'WRAP UP WARM' TOUR
Sudbury, 6 May 2004

Hello – that's a nice friendly welcome . . . well . . . yo! Sudbury – they say you play Sudbury twice in your life – once on the way up . . . it's good to be back! It's good to be back in Sudbury at this lovely theatre – what a lovely little place it is . . . really gorgeous, isn't it? The only mistake I've made here, I think, is wearing black trousers, I think that was an error – I know it's not very big, but to the people at the back I must seem like a rather hazy satellite link from Israel.

Slightly worrying thing is – this is the comedy set . . . wouldn't want to see it when they're doing Chekhov would you? People would be topping themselves . . .

But it is a lovely venue . . . really friendly, and they are not all like that – venues – not all of them, you know, this is a lovely little theatre . . . sometimes arts centres can be . . . not so good . . . some are love-ly – but some are a bit . . . soulless, but it makes a difference – a wel-come when you arrive somewhere . . . you know you get somewhere like (softly) – Telford . . . there you are, travelling all day . . . and there to meet you is this woman, standing at the door like this – you know those people, semi-filleted . . . weakened by thirty years of veganism . . . consequently, hardly got the strength to support her own skeleton . . . standing there in a dress made of Quorn . . . pre-vious job: administrator in a vegetarian circus – where the most exciting thing that happened . . . was a man placing his head into the mouth of a live yoghurt . . . standing there . . . 'Oh, hello, you're here, are you? – I'm afraid nobody's coming – I don't know why – Marjorie's put a leaflet in the library' (laughter) . . .

How could it fail?

Well, Sudbury – I find it quite a groovy little place actually, with Gainsborough House and everything . . . a bit of an artistic community – where there are artists there are always allied trades, aren't there? – all sorts of alternative-y things . . . you know, dingly dreamcatcher-type things . . . sort of malarkey – we are

probably not far from a bit of colonic irrigation . . . I don't know
when that became a leisure pursuit . . . you turn round and all of
a sudden people are having that . . . I don't think it's right, I don't
think your colon should be a flume . . . it's basically CenterParcs
for sweetcorn . . . the British holiday the weather can't spoil.
(laughter)

No, I like a bit of an alternative place, me . . . I go up to
Glastonbury – last time I was at Glastonbury I was really ripped
off – bought a CD of Whale Song, got it home . . . it was a tribute
band of dolphins . . . 'Hey, hey, we're the minkys', what a swizz
. . . mind you, I LOVE tribute bands – I was in Yorkshire recently
and there was a fantastic local version of Bon Jovi – called By Jovi
(laughter) . . . lovely, isn't it?

It's posh round here . . . to avoid the roadworks we went the
very scenic route – we came through Clare and Cavendish . . .
very nice – very posh – you know when you're in a posh town
when you see the local drunk lying in the gutter holding up a
placard saying, 'Anything but Chardonnay' – quite smart, isn't
it? Well, thanks for coming tonight . . . look upon it as a personal favour . . . and it is nice to get out, isn't it? . . . of a wartime,
isn't it? . . . it's important to keep going, isn't it really . . . like in
the Blitz – I suppose I'm the modern equivalent of Vera Lynn
(laughter).

I was in the dentist the other week and there was a copy of *Saga*
magazine and flicking through it I came across an interview with
Dame Vera Lynn and the interviewer said, 'Dame Vera, do you
think there will ever be another you? – do you think there will ever
be another Forces' Sweetheart?' and she said, 'No, I don't think
so – these days the wars don't last long enough for an artiste to
establish themselves' (laughter).

But we are living in very weird times, aren't we? . . . with just
the one dominant superpower in the world, with the threat of
international terror, and our only hope is . . . in the President of
the United States. A man whose eyes are drawn on. Badly drawn
President, basically – just, basically, two currants shoved in – nothing happening there. I mean, I'm a liberal soul – I'm all for the

challenged having little jobs . . . perhaps not that one just something in a supermarket really, just to boost his confidence to begin with (laughter).

I don't know, I think we could stop all these wars in a minute really – if we gave George W. an atlas and said, 'There you are, George – anything on there you can spell – you can attack.' I think we'd be all right, but Austramania would be bricking it, wouldn't they? (laughter)

Of course it wouldn't be quite so terrifying if our own Prime Minister, Tony Blair, didn't have some kind of pathetic schoolboy crush on him (laughter) – the only thing I can put it down to is that Blair was bullied as a kid and now he really likes hanging around with the tough kids – 'cos with Putin he's beside himself – he's like a teenager going . . . 'Oh God, he was, like, in the KGB and he's so totally my mate!' – 'I mean, like, he's had people killed and he texts me!' His relationships with these thugs . . . he's like Barbara Windsor with the Kray twins – you know . . . 'They were gentl'men to me . . .' (laughter)

But Bush is his number one squeeze, isn't he? – he's his favourite, and I imagine that at conferences, Gordon Brown shoves Tony Blair in his path . . . you know, like your mates used to do at school when you fancied someone . . . you know, they would shove you in his path . . . 'Oh, get off . . . oh, Gordon – duhh . . . ! Sorry about him. . . tsk! Anyway, er . . . hi–iy! Er . . . hi-iy, fancy meeting you here! – Didn't expect to see you here at this Anglo-American conference, oh well . . . yeah . . . so, er . . . what do you like doing then? . . . OH, WAR! YEAH . . . I like doing that as well! . . . Probably see you there then! . . . Brilliant – OH, HE LIKES ME! OOOEEE!' Oh dear . . . I think Blair must be some sort of negative genius – I had absolutely no expectation of him – and he's let me down . . . desperately . . . (laughter)

You should never moan . . . you never know when you're well off – I have moaned about every Labour leader there's ever been – Neil Kinnock, I thought was an absolute idiot . . . now he looks like Spartacus – oh, you don't know when you're well off.

And the Tories now with their pitiful relaunch – oh, Michael Howard, we're supposed to have forgotten him from before because he's had this Trinny and Susannah makeover and you imagine them with him saying, like, 'We think you'll like what we've done, Michael, just have a little look in the mirror – oh no, you can't really, can you? . . . We've stitched you a lovely little shadow on – we think you'll really like that' . . .

No surprise they got rid of the last one . . . Ian Drunken Doobry or whatever his name was – Wilson, Keppel and Betty . . . talk about anonymous – he'd come on the news and I'd be thinking . . . oh tsk! . . . err . . . HIM?! Oh God, my memory, honestly, oh, what was he in? . . . *Midsomer Murders*! – yes, he was the third corpse!

Turns out he was . . .

The only one you vaguely recognise out of that lot is Ann Widdecombe . . . yes, she's got some sort of profile, hasn't she? God, yeah . . . but she's confused us all by going blonde – I was watching *Question Time* for half an hour, thinking . . . Christ – Sue Barker's slapped on a bit of weight!! – I don't think Sir Cliff would be interested now, Sue!

On the international scene, the whole Europe thing rumbles on with the new countries coming in and now . . . will we join properly or not, what are we gonna be? Are we going to join the single currency? I mean, I don't know really – Sudbury, what do you think? What does Sudbury think of the single currency? Who's against it? Ohh! . . . firm but polite – well, we DON'T like it – we've got to put our hands up here . . . so all right then . . . who's for it? . . . equally civilised . . .

I like that – we've got a basic difference here, but we're not going to get too excited about it. A few of us agree, a few of us don't – but I don't know – I can see both sides really – I can't help noticing that as a general rule, just as a very broad rule, people who are not so keen on the single currency come from what you might call 'the older end of the audience' – without wishing to be rude in any way . . . let's just say – putting it another way . . . the section of the audience that's probably no stranger to *Watercolour Challenge*. Fair? . . . would that be fair? Who could blame you? What a

cracking show! – *Watercolour Challenge* . . . *competitive* water-colours . . . think about that for a minute. . . exciting AND relaxing, I suppose, at the same time – presided over by Hannah Gordon . . . the younger older man's Joan Bakewell.

I can see both sides of this really – I can see why people DO support the single currency . . . it's sensible . . . and I can see why people aren't so keen on it – because it's sensible . . . but you can be a bit too sensible in this life, can't you? I don't think you want to go around being sensible – there's something unromantic about the whole of Europe having the same money – not changing your money up when you go abroad . . . I like doing that – it makes it feel like the world's all the same, doesn't it? I mean, good God, when I'm in Rome . . . I want to pay in lire for my Big Mac. Do as the Romans do.

It would be a shame if everywhere got to be the same, wouldn't it? Dear me! The old single currency thing has got to be quite emotive, I expect there are people out there who didn't raise their hand for the single currency because they would rather reinstate the Groat . . . but people do get a bit worked up about it . . . but on the other hand – other things from Europe haven't caused such a fuss really – the metric system – you know, kilos instead of pounds . . . oooh NO!? We don't like it here in Sudbury – well, OK! – I would normally think that kind of thing is more into Essex really, that you get a bit of that . . . er, normally Leigh-on-Sea, normally butchers . . . greengrocers who are metric martyrs basically – who so hate metrication – who so loathe it . . . that THEY WOULD RATHER GO TO PRISON . . . than sell bananas by the kilo. You've got to think . . . the quality of martyrdom has fallen off rather over the centuries, hasn't it really? You can't get a martyr like you used to . . . they're not interested in being broken on a wheel, are they? Shoved full of arrows – no . . . they're just a stroppy greengrocer from Leigh-on-Sea – that's all. (laughter)

And another thing occurs to me . . . who catches them at this? What area of the police is responsible for this heinous weights and measures crime? It isn't really a very glamorous part of police work, is it? . . . can't really imagine a mini-series with David

Jason – 'the maverick Inspector Appleyard of the metric police
solving metric crime . . . it's the victims he cares about' – or Nick
Ross leaning over at the end of *Crimewatch* . . . 'Remember, most
shops display in metric AND imperial so . . . don't have night-
mares.' (laughter)

Funny thing with metrication – some things have been metric
from long before metrication was brought in for other things – for
example, drugs . . . ooh! drugs . . . don't talk to us about drugs . . .
we're already quite racy by being the only people in a 5-mile
radius not actively making chutney! Drugs! . . . well, I'm going to
alienate you a bit further now by saying, cocaine, for example – so
bad people tell me – is always sold, apparently, by the g . . . well,
mind you, you'd do well to avoid cocaine really, because it's a stupid drug, very expensive . . . turns people into idiots and also,
more to the point, keeps you up all night which I can't imagine . . .
is a great benefit really, in Sudbury . . . and why you'd want
that . . . really? I don't want to be rude, but for God's sake that
could be a bit of a curse really, couldn't it? Five o'clock in the
morning, laying there thinking . . . oh, for God's sake! Hurry up
and be light! – maybe Long Melford will be open and I can go and
. . . browse . . . I can browse, really aggressively, amongst some
antiques. (laughter)

I've become very paranoid about the world lately, about crime
and horrible things . . . happening outside – I think the fear of it is
greater than the reality, and I'll tell you something that has given
me a more miserable outlook on life . . . getting satellite television.
Now, I don't know what the reception is . . . I mean, I was talking
about this somewhere and they couldn't get Channel 5 – unless
they set fire to a priest or something . . . Satellite TV – I don't know
if you've got it, but if you haven't got it and you're thinking about
it . . . don't, just stop now – it's the road to hell – it's just miserable
. . . it's awful – there are a million channels, literally a million channels, most of which are history channels, all of which are obsessed
with the Third Reich – if there had been no Nazis they wouldn't
have a programme to show you, really. It's the same with Channel
4 and Channel 5 as well, with the documentaries – if there had

been no Hitler they'd be stumped, completely . . . so you'll be watching some quality channel like UK Nazi Gold, the cream of the Nazi programming, and it'll be something like . . .

'Adolf Hitler, His Secret Role in World War Two.'

'Bunker Wives' or, 'When Nazi Facelifts Go Wrong.'

'Your Top Twenty Nuremberg Moments with Graham Norton.'

And between this top-quality programming are the most miserable adverts in the world – I don't know if it's because it's cable or because it's daytime, but they're seeping into the evening now . . . miserable, miserable adverts . . . aimed at people watching obscure channels in the daytime, and it builds up such a horrible picture of the world, and your future in it. It starts off with June Whitfield nagging you to pay for your own funeral – I don't know how she ever makes a sale – and it moves on to John Stalker . . . former Mancunian top cop John Stalker trying to sell you sun awnings . . . trying to get you to blot out every ray of light from the world for those in the grip of manic depression . . .

'Hello, I'm John Stalker – are you, like me, tired of the pitiless glare of an English summer? Maddened by the relentless gaze of cruel Helios – sick of lurking in your house all summer long like a mad bloke in a siege situation – such as I would have dealt with in my high-flying career? Well, suffer no longer – install Gloom Master sun awnings – summer, bang to rights!' (laughter)

Terrible . . . then it all gets worse with those terrible loan adverts – those terrible people, Ocean Finance and the like . . . these awful, tragic, hollow-eyed wraiths come on, telling you these awful stories – 'I'm up to my eyes in debt – and, curiously, no reputable company would give me another loan! Then I discovered Dodgy Bastards – they've given me a million pounds! . . . and all they wanted in return are my kidneys . . .' NO, DON'T DO IT!

And then, worse than that . . . the accident insurance adverts – 'Where there's blame, there's a claim' – when people who've had these accidents come on like medieval beggars, and wave their stumps at you for money – it's unedifying, isn't it? – with these outlandish stories – 'I slipped on a banana skin and successfully sued the Dominican Republic' – and then by the time

that the man in the wig and the swimming trunks in the bath with
the door in it comes on . . . why doesn't the water come out? I
don't understand . . . why should the laws of physics be turned
upside down just because it's time for *Countdown*? – by then
you're just a gibbering wreck and you're lurking in your house,
totally paranoid.

Awful . . . and I phoned up one of these adverts from the telly,
for security consultants – consultants . . . I don't think they can
operate on you or anything . . . because I've moved house and I
needed a new lock, so I had this bloke round, I'd made an appointment . . . knock on the door, I opened the door . . . 'Look at that,
look at that . . . I could walk straight in there – why do the public
make it so easy for the criminal?'

'Yes, well, you knocked on the door.'

'Yes, I knocked on the door . . . and you opened it . . . '
(laughter)

'Dear me – I can see I've got my work cut out here – and anyway, it doesn't matter much, you might as well have your door
wide open, with a big pile of jewellery on your doormat with a sign
saying "HELP YOURSELF BECAUSE I LOVE CRIME"
because with that Mickey Mouse lock you've got on there you're
virtually the criminal's accomplice – you've virtually got a little
mask and swag bag yourself, madam – your dabs are all over this,
you want to get rid of that and get a good, sturdy Chubb lock –
you want a Chubb lock really and a dead-lock – to be honest, you
want a Chubb lock, a dead-lock and a mortice lock, and that's not
really enough – you want a Chubb lock, a dead-lock, a mortice
lock and locking bolts . . . really I would recommend a Chubb
lock, a dead-lock, a mortice lock and locking bolts and a little
chain so you can peep out and see who's there, . . . really that's
woefully inadequate – you want a Chubb lock, a dead-lock, a mortice lock, locking bolts, a chain you slide across so you can peep
out and see who's there, and shutters that come down your windows every time you go out – make your house look like a sub-Post
Office, lovely it is . . . but if you want to go top-of-the-range,
madam, you want our "Crimestopper package" . . . you'll have a

Chubb lock, dead-lock, mortice lock, locking bolts, a chain you can slide across so you can peep out and see who's there, shutters that come down your windows every time you go out, make your house seem like a sub-Post Office, lovely, and 500 Chinese terracotta warriors ranged about your living room – of course that won't keep people out – it'll just slow them down a bit on the way out.' (laughter)

I had a friend who did this – it didn't make any difference . . . his house was still repossessed.

So now, I've got so much bling on my door, I've got so much jewellery hanging off the door, it sounds like P Diddy shaking hands with Jimmy Savile. Ah! There's people out there thinking . . . who is P Diddy? There might be a few thinking . . . who the bloody hell is Jimmy Savile? Probably some people out there who think J-Lo is a way of referring to John Lewis . . . should be really, shouldn't it?

I think people have an idea about crime, there was once this golden age when there was never any crime and everybody just fluttered about like butterflies and society was marvellous – and my nan was a terrible one for this – she would say, 'You can't trust no one nowadays – they're all after you, like when I was a girl, it was all lovely – you could leave the door wide open, no one would steal anything' – and I'd think, yeah, Nan, because they'd have to be quite creative to steal something in your house, because you didn't have anything, did you? That's why they didn't steal anything – I don't think there's more crime – there's just more stuff.

Really, looking at the state of your house, Nan, you probably left your door open in the vain hope that something might waft in. I can imagine Raffles the gentleman jewel thief, breaking into your scullery . . . heh, heh, heh . . . and dragging out the mangle . . . heh, heh, heh, having it resprayed, changing the number plate and selling it in Amsterdam. (laughter)

As I said, I had a little scenic drive around the villages of Essex and Suffolk to get here but I quite often travel on the train and last night they told me that your train provider is called ONE . . . nice,

isn't it . . . it doesn't even give you hope, does it? Just the one, yeah
. . . be round next Thursday. (laughter)

I like Virgin, that's a great name for a train provider really,
Virgin . . . never done it before, heard there was some money in
it!

But it doesn't really matter who serves your area with trains,
they are all rubbish, the whole transport system of Britain is col-
lapsing . . . the train system is so chronic now that any journey you
undertake by train in Britain is identical to the one taken by Omar
Sharif in *Doctor Zhivago*, that's what it's like – the same drama and
misery.

Ancient, knackered rolling stock limping painfully across the
land, shuddering to a halt for no apparent reason with the lights
flickering on and off – everyone running up and down – What's
going on? What's up ahead? I don't know . . . is it Rod Steiger with
the White Guard? . . . Desperate women in headscarves running
alongside the carriages throwing their babies into the train, shouting, 'I'LL NEVER SEE PURLEY OAKS BUT MY CHILD
MIGHT!' (laughter) – miserable!

And you're stuck there with that miserable train buffet, when
you go along and have a cup of tea or 'leaf tea' as they style it . . .
as if the rest of the time we're having dead rat tea or something –
gives added value, 'leaf tea' . . . and these horrible-looking sandwiches with weird combinations of cheese, pickle and rawlplug,
and 'Sandwich of the Week' and you think, I bet tuna mayo are
gutted, aren't they? It should have been me – I should have been
sandwich of the week!

And everything is the wrong size – giant bags of crisps – this
supersize idea – that's not a packet of crisps, it's a pillowcase –
the idea is it's an airbag – and you clutch it to your chest in the
event of an accident – biscuits as well, biscuits, great giant biscuits THAT big . . . giant chocolate chip cookies, the size of a
satellite dish . . . you could slap it on the side of the train and pick
up UK Nazi Gold . . . get back to your seat to find a whole family nibbling their way to the middle of one, like Borrowers.
(laughter)

No different really if you travel on the motorways. You're crawling along in a jam and you'll stop off at a services for a break – first thing you see is all your fellow road users playing violent video games – that's encouraging . . . you think, aah, they'll be joining me soon, after they've killed a few thousand aliens . . . and into the Food Court, cheerily optimistic, rustic-sounding outfits like Red Rooster, Granny's Pantry, Country Kitchen . . . I'm not sure which country that would be – Albania possibly, judging by what's on display.

If you just want a cup of tea, to find it, you've got to go around this slalom like a stripped-pine Nordic sauna shelf which goes on forever so that by the time you actually get some soup, it's stone cold or as I like to call it . . . English gazpacho . . . and very expensive, as my mum would say, 'for what it is'. I'm not sure what things are what they're not really – everything is what it is really – but expensive 'for what it is', er . . . 'I'll have this cold cup of tea, please, and could I have a scone, please, and I'm very sorry . . . I've only got a ten pound note'. 'Well, you'll have to put that scone back then.' (laughter)

You can't really blame the poor little kids that work there, can you? . . . normally these teenagers who are just terrified to be talking to an adult and they're not even allowed to use their own words now – they've got to use these terrible corporate phrases – all these terrible bits of language that they are forced to use and you'll be standing there and you'll say, 'Can I have a small coffee, please?'

'DON'T DO SMALL.'

'What do you do then?'

'ER . . . GRANDE AND . . . REGULAR . . .'

'What is regular?'

'IT'S LIKE MEDIUM . . .'

'Well, how big's that then?'

'QUITE SMALL . . .'

So I end up usually living on tinned stuff . . . lager mainly. I find it's good to keep a few cans in the glove box – breaks the ice at the scene of an accident. (laughter)

But you can't help worrying about what you eat these days – there are so many food scares, so what I tend to do, just to keep healthy, I tend to live almost exclusively on Bernard Matthews. Oh, they're fantastic . . . they're really, really good for you . . . I can consume, say, one turkey burger or one of his more novelty lines like . . . reconstituted, mechanically recovered turkey fragments, formed into the shape of stegosaurus lips – one little portion of stego-lips contains a full course of antibiotics – I haven't had a sore throat in years, I head them off at the pass – but it's very important to eat every nugget . . . if you don't finish the course they don't work.

And I think all the vitamins you need are in a glass of Sunny Delight. All the major E group vitamins are in there . . . E27, E136 – well, you can see the goodness in it, the way the kids are bouncing off the walls when they've had a glass!

I love that one they do in summer . . . Sunny Delight with a hint of Ventolin.

There's GM foods to worry about now – that's something new, whether they're safe or not, and there's someone who is not at all keen on GM foods – Prince Charles is very against them, he's all for organic foods, isn't he? In fact he was quoted recently over the GM maize controversy – he was quoted as saying . . . he 'feared genetic disaster' . . . bless . . . oh, but it's nice of him to worry about us though – but a bit late for him really, shutting the stable door after the horse has mated with your entire family. Can't help feeling a little bit sorry for him . . . he's kind of the Private Pike of the Royal Family . . . STUPID BOY . . . he's desperate for our love – which is more than you can say for Camilla because she's given up on public affection really – I think she's come to the conclusion that she's about as popular as Anne Robinson at an Eisteddfod. Ooh . . . Anne Robinson's new face . . . Gawd – she looks like a recently surprised Siamese cat, walking into a gale . . . terrifying!

But no, Camilla – she's realised now that we don't like her . . . she's just brazening it out, isn't she – she says, 'People don't like hunting – good, I'll do more of it – I'll tell you what, get

Gloucestershire floodlit – I'll hunt at night' – 'top floodlit hunting action . . . no foxes? – I don't care – cats! – Persian cats – they look a bit pleased with themselves . . . get those running – guinea pigs, terrapins – I don't care – I'll hunt anything.'

I tell you what, these people are psychopaths. I was in Leicestershire recently – there's a bloody Quorn hunt! Where's the sport in that? A harmless edible fungus!

They're not normal . . . but it's funny times for the Royal Family, isn't it? Edward and Sophie, how the hell do they live? I can only imagine they're doing something like catalogue fraud, just sitting at home ordering stuff from Littlewoods, then moving before they have to pay . . . they do actually make the Duchess of York seem quite classy in retrospect – she looks like Grace Kelly now – she must be bitter because she's been kicked out of the Royal Family, off the civil list, not living in Andrew's mansion . . . single parent, basically . . . trying to get by doing little single parent jobs – Ann Summers parties and ambassador for Weight Watchers as well, which I didn't realise was a country . . .

'Aah, ambassador – with this Ryvita you are spoiling us!'

'The ambassador was famous for his cottage cheese' . . . (laughter)

No, she's living in a hard-to-let council flat in South-East London – Kidbrooke, it's awful . . . I saw her on television the other day, moaning about the conditions – awful, graffiti all over the walkways, people chucking televisions off the balcony, standing there saying, 'It's terrible here, terrible – dangerous dogs runnin' everywhere . . . I had enough of that at bloody Sandringham . . . do wivvout it 'ere, and that lift – that never works and when it does it smells of polo ponies an' 'er, Eugenie – shut it! Shut your face – I'll give you summink to whine about in a minute . . . 'er, Eugenie, I've no shoes for 'er, I've no shoes for 'er . . . I've got to send her to school in skis! Luckily she goes to school in Switzerland but that's not the point, innit?' (laughter)

So, I mentioned the Gainsborough connection here. I myself live in East London which is a centre of a different artistic community – the Brit Art community – it's just all modern art round

there now, it's all so trendy, it's so gentrified – everything's a gallery or an atelier or a designer furniture workshop. They all live round there, all the Tracey Emins and the rest of it, and it's a bit confusing really – you don't know if things are real or art any more . . . I walk around, I go into a pub and I think, is this a real pub or an ironic pub? – don't really know – there's a big jar of pickled eggs on the bar . . . and I say, 'How much are those?' And the barman says, 'Three hundred thousand pounds. They're Damien Hirst – if you cut them in half that's half a million . . . and leave that ashtray – that filthy ashtray, that's a Tracey Emin – don't empty that.' Oh my God, this used to be gangland, used to be rough, it used to be run by Ronnie and Reggie . . . now it's run by Gilbert and George. (laughter)

But I do enjoy art – had I got here earlier today I might have had a look at Gainsborough House if it had been open . . . there's a few paintings in there, yes? Not too many though, yeah, because I don't like too many paintings in an art gallery. Just too many, most of them a bit overwhelming, because you go in with good intentions – that you'll look at a few picture – and you think, oh blimey, I'll be here for the rest of my life! It's just too many, isn't it?

My attitude to art is, I like it, but not for very long, because it's interesting for a minute, then . . . boring for ever! You go in thinking, 'Oh, look at all these, I'd better whip round here quickly . . . I walk into the first one, here we are . . . Van Gogh, *Field of Corn with Crows* – obviously that wouldn't be here, would it? *Field of Rape Seed* . . . or *Crop Sprayer* . . . So you're looking at that and you're thinking, oh, look at the brooding quality he's got into those crows – yeah . . . that's it, you've done it, you're off . . . what was that, ten seconds? And I'm thinking – ten seconds . . . I'm doing well here, and then I notice a whole load of people . . . Quorn woman and her mates from the arts centre, who were there before me . . . who are still looking at the same painting . . . so, no, I'm a bit insecure, I'm thinking – aah! I clearly didn't understand that, I'll just sidle back – make it seem like I was just trying to see it from a different angle – well, a different room actually – let's have another look, see what I've missed – what have I missed? . . . Nothing.

Nothing at all . . . it's exactly as I first thought – a field of corn, some crows, that's it.

Well, what's the matter with these people – have they got slow eyes? What's up with them? Is this a special day for the slow of eye? No . . . they seem to be moving quite normally – well, I dunno, maybe there's a caption somewhere that says: 'Our artist has made several mistakes . . . can you spot them? Mr Van Gogh has hidden twelve buckets and spades in this picture . . . and if you find them, you get a bunch of sunflowers.' (laughter)

So I stomp off to the gift shop, because I always like that, and the gift shop, really, should occupy the space the gallery does, and the gallery should be the size of the gift shop, really, because the gift shop is great, with all your little Gauguin pencils and all the pretty cards of the paintings – and this is another thing I don't understand, like 'Sandwich of the Month' – who decides what painting gets to appear on greetings cards and which paintings don't make the grade? Is there some auditioning process? What happens? You've got the Laughing Cavalier standing there going, 'I hope I get it, I really hope I get it' . . . it must be heartbreaking if you don't . . . and some of them seem obvious – the Impressionist paintings, obviously they're very decorative, they're going to be cast – some seem less obvious . . . a card that you often see, a painting that often appears in greetings card form . . . Edvard Munch's *The Scream*. What occasion . . . ? Apart from a wedding, what occasion is that one suitable for? Who are you sending that to? Who wants to get that through the post? What are you writing in that? . . . 'Best wishes on your third nervous breakdown'. (laughter)

No, I mentioned, Van Gogh there – I do admire Van Gogh – I do think he was one of the greatest geniuses that ever lived – but he was a bit of a soppy date, he really was, because he did some very silly things . . . top of the list, famously, the stupid thing he did that everyone knows about was that after a row with Gauguin – absolutely ripped to the tits on absinthe, completely off his tree – girlfriend had left him . . . so, chopped his ear off and sent it to her . . .

Do you think she came back?

Do you think that did the trick?

Hasn't really caught on, has it? 'Say it with ears' . . . For a start, you wouldn't try that trick today with our post, would you? Six months later she'd be saying, 'Ooh . . . a sun-dried tomato!' And what was he thinking? What was the girl going to do? Open up this package, fish out this lug and go, 'Ooh, Vinny – I thought you were all mad and driven and weird and a loner and our relationship was doomed and you go and do a lovely thing like this – oh, you know how to get round me . . . I SAID, YOU KNOW HOW TO GET ROUND ME!' (laughter)

Well, I think we're moving on to the interval section of the show where you can have some beer-flavoured drinks out in the bar . . . and I can't help noticing that this is quite small but the bar – even smaller . . . I always think bars should be exactly the same size as the auditorium, really, for any sort of comfort, but I'm sure they've got that pre-ordering thing that you can do, so some of you have already got a drink ordered, haven't you? How many of you have got a drink lined up? Again the hands . . . the politeness! . . . If there was some sort of a fascist takeover in Britain, you'd all just walk in an orderly fashion into the trucks – you'd be going in there saying, 'Well . . . here's a turn-up . . . yeah, he did stab me with his bayonet – but you don't like to say, do you . . . we just won't come here again . . .' (laughter)

Who's pre-ordered their bloody drinks? Yes, lots of you have . . . who hasn't? Yes . . . quite a few . . . now those people who have pre-ordered – I reckon you're the very people who could be nagged by June Whitfield into paying for you own funeral because I don't approve of this pre-ordering . . . it's too sensible – you might change your mind, you might get out there and think, I wish I had something else . . . and if it's a gin and tonic, the ice cubes will have been melting in there like the polar ice caps from the minute you sat down – you know that, don't you? You can't live your life in advance like that . . . let's see the people who didn't pre-order – aah yes, prouder now . . . Spartacus moment – now – 'No, I didn't!' Yes – because you're the rebels, you're free spirits, you're bohemians . . . you're Sudbury's Latin Quarter, you are . . . you can't be hemmed in by the MAN with his fascist drinks thing . . . brilliant! – free spirits.

Mind you, on the other hand, you've got bugger all chance of getting a drink! That's the downside of rebellion. (laughter)

So I like to create a little level playing field . . . what I like to do is to make sure that you've got a fighting chance of getting a drink, I have a staggered interval . . . the interval doesn't start just yet, for people who've got a drink ordered. They get to sit here for a few minutes and think about what they've done.

The rest of you – I keep them talking for a bit while the rest of you get a chance to sprint out to the bar . . . just gives you that little extra yard, if you know what I mean – but there will still be a bit of a scramble, to be honest. Some of you . . . will DIE, (laughter)

But . . . it's Darwinism that keeps the herd strong. It means – my audience in the second half – leaner, meaner, sharper . . .

So OK – at my word – and the rest of you sit still – we know who you are, we've seen you put your hand up twice now . . . the refuseniks . . . the interval starts for you . . . remember I keep them talking for as long as I can . . . the interval starts for you . . . NOW. Quick, off you go – run – WELL, IT'S BEEN DOUBT-FUL TODAY, HASN'T IT? IT'S NOT KNOWN WHAT TO DO . . . IS IT GOING TO RAIN? IS IT GONNA CLEAR UP – YOU JUST DON'T KNOW . . . oh, I can't keep 'em any longer – I'll see you after the interval . . . SEE YOU SOON! (applause)

----- INTERVAL -----

Well, hello again . . . I can see you've had a drink . . . You all look much more sexually attractive . . . with enhanced social skills . . . (laughter)

I've just had a little bit of a lie-down and a cup of tea, but I'm quite lazy really . . . I tend to eat just the middle section of a Mars Bar, to make me rest. Actually, I was having a little look through the *Villager* magazine and I'd never thought – before the Cats Protection League alerted my attention to it – that cat-neutering vouchers make a good gift – it's a little tip, isn't it – probably best for cat owners . . .

But I was having a little think that possibly in the first half, I've been a little bit cheeky about Sudbury – possibly suggesting that it was a little on the quiet side, perhaps suggesting that nothing usually happened that was louder than a scone being buttered . . . but I've no business to mock anyone else's town, because I come from a miserable place . . . I come from an awful place called Erith. (laughter)

Even if you've never heard of it, you can just laugh and think – oh, God. Well, it's in South-East London, stroke, Kent – it's what's known as Greater London – but to be honest, the further you get away from the middle of it . . . London doesn't really get greater – it's better where there is stuff actually – it's more Lesser London really – I'll tell you how miserable it is . . . Erith is so miserable, and depressing and dreary and soul-destroying and boring that it's not even twinned with anywhere . . . but it does have a suicide pact with Braintree . . . seems to be going quite well . . . think Marjorie put a leaflet in the library?

Now, to give you an idea of how humourless Erith is . . . I did a version of that joke on television once – I say a version because, to be honest with you, I don't always say Braintree at that point, although Swindon works anywhere in Britain . . . and parts of Europe, and the following week my Auntie Helen sent me . . . my Auntie, well, you don't strictly need to know it's her . . . promise you won't stalk her . . . just that – that's all I ask . . . my Auntie Helen sent me the local paper, the *Erith and Crayford Observer* . . . incorporating the *Kentish Times* . . .

I don't know why that doesn't have a wider circulation really . . . but anyway, she sent it to me – and I love a town . . . I love civic information generally – I just love it – gather it wherever I go . . . brilliant leaflet I picked up near Cleethorpes . . . big list of all the attractions in Cleethorpes and the slogan was . . . 'CLEE-THORPES – THERE HAS TO BE MORE' . . . so anyway, she

sent me the *Erith and Crayford Observer* and there was a headline
THAT big which read, 'LOCAL GIRL SLAMS ERITH'.

The article began, 'Erith reeled, as on national television it
was dubbed . . . boring' – they brought in a local councilor, a
Mr Valentine Muir Morgan – feel free to stalk – who was outraged
and he said, 'This is a slur on our town, it's not boring, it's interesting – and it is twinned with somewhere for her information –
we're twinned with a town in France which is quite near Paris.'
You know, Lesser Paris, I suppose, but for me the giveaway was
the final paragraph: 'THIS IS THE SECOND TIME IN ONE
WEEK THAT ERITH HAS BEEN DUBBED . . . BORING . . .
the first time was when the competition to name the Erith Leisure
Centre was won by the competitor who suggested it be called . . .
the Erith Leisure Centre.' M'lud, my case rests. (laughter)

So that's my home town and I come from a perfectly ordinary
working-class family, and in fact, I didn't really meet middle-class
people until I went to university – it was quite a shock really . . . people were saying things like, 'Well, I was always going to end up doing
English because I was brought up surrounded by books – brought
up in a house full of books' . . . and I'd think, 'yes, so was I – but they
were full of Green Shield stamps.' I suppose we could have swapped
them for books – but we had our eye on a twin tub. (laughter)

I say ordinary, but there was one thing a little bit different about
my family, in that my mum and dad were quite a bit older than people normally are when they start . . . and, as it turned out . . . finish
a family – don't know why . . . busy, I suppose – I expect my mum
had a lot of ironing to do, my dad was building a shed – years pass,
especially if you're doing a good job – two coats of creosote – so they
were quite old . . . and there was a downside to that, really . . . well,
for a start all my friends' parents were just slightly older than them
and really trendy and dressed in cool clothes, and dropping them
off at the bus and going 'Ciao!' – I used to dream of 'Ciao!'
because my mum's catchphrase on the bus was 'Thank you, driver.'
(laughter)

Proved the more enduring of the two I think, really – and that
was one thing – but the main drawback of having an older mum

was, she would KNIT – yes . . . someone, a fellow sufferer, there going, mmm yeah!, but the thing with my mum was, it wasn't recreational knitting . . . she wasn't in control of it. No – it was a kind of woolly Tourette's – it was a compulsion . . . she would be dragged round the house by the needles, with smoke coming out of them, and great tapeworms of this useless stuff – knit purl, knit purl, knit purl – consequently, every stitch I left the house in was knitted, starting off with the ever so popular . . . Crusader helmet. Ooh, I bet the Saracens were shitting themselves when the Crusaders came over the hill in those bobble hats.

Then, the twinsets – Fair Isle of course – with the pleats cunningly knitted in a fashion so bizarre . . . even Vivienne Westwood hasn't attempted it.

Socks, shoes, satchel, sandwiches – pencils, just everything . . . I looked like a time-travelling Ovalteenie on my way to school. Oh and Christ, if it rained . . . if it rained – the weight of this stuff, I would be dragged to the ground like a driftnet, honestly . . . like a little pastel beached Grimsby trawler there, trudging through the woods . . . seagulls squawk, squawk, squawk, following me all the way. To be honest, we had the EC round a couple of times asking me mum to use bigger needles – we were catching stuff that should have been chucked back . . . the Erith silver fish population has yet to recover. (laughter)

So between that and the glasses, I stayed in a lot really, watching telly . . .

Now, you see, people criticise television for children but I used to love it – it was my education . . . people think that oh, children shouldn't watch telly – they see stuff that makes them badly behaved, but I'm not sure that's true – I think violence predates television really . . . they did manage to have a war that lasted one hundred years without the benefit of *EastEnders*. I'm not saying *EastEnders* wouldn't have made it worse . . . 'SORT IT, CHARLEMAGNE' . . .

Well, I suppose people have always used that as an excuse, that seeing violent things – images – have made them behave badly . . . I bet, in fifteenth-century Bruges, there was probably some wretch in the dock, standing there going, 'Well, in mitigation, my lord, I have been looking at a lot of Hieronymous Bosch paintings lately, and I think that's maybe what gave me the idea of shoving a flute up the cat's arse really – that's the only thing I can think of – it's just lucky I didn't have any bagpipes in the house, 'cos that's a more serious charge altogether.' (laughter)

No, but I used to like sitcoms . . . suburban sitcoms, things would happen in them that would never happen in our lives – I mean, things like the vicar coming round to tea . . . I don't know, some of you – you might live in dread of the vicar always coming round on the ear'ole . . . 'Oh God, it's the vicar again – don't let him near the kettle.' No, that never happened to us, but the one thing . . . the main thing . . . that always . . . that I couldn't suspend my disbelief for, only ever happened in sitcoms, never in life . . . the boss comes round for dinner – WHO has their boss round for dinner? You don't do that, do you? In *The Good Life* it would happen all the time and for a start . . . who is your boss? Who knows these days – if you trace it right back, for 97 per cent of us it will be Bill Gates. You're not having him round your house, are you? Little freak, sat on the computer all night . . .

So in *The Good Life* Gerry would come bounding in – 'Darling, darling, Sir's coming round tonight – he wants to discuss the new contract and if he likes what I've got to say, there could be a promotion in it for me, so rustle up something marvellous, Margot – I know you can do it . . .' and I'd think, well, how would that play in my house?

Let's see – well, who was my dad's boss? Well, my dad worked for British Rail – remember that?

On track maintenance . . . remember that?

So he'd come in – 'Darling, darling, the chief civil engineer for the southern region wants to pop round tonight and he needs to discuss the upsurge in vandalism when Charlton play at home. If he likes my initiative, there could be a new deck of Waddington's finest for me and the lads at the hut, so spare no expense . . . crack open a tin of Carnation milk, in fact, go mad with the tin opener . . . I know it's not Sunday . . . crack open a tin of Trout Hall grapefruit segments!'

I used to think that Trout Hall things were called that because they were tinned in an old people's home – fifty-nine, sixty . . . lid!

Now that is something in Britain that has changed out of all recognition – the way we eat, really – from when I was a kid, totally transformed . . . because at one time we were very cautious, very conservative – always had the omelette – didn't like anything too spicy . . .

That's all changed now, for example, the way we used to treat vegetables, our attitude to vegetables . . . God, I think there is a pan of sprouts my mum put on to cook at Christmas 1973 that's just about ready . . . because we were frightened that – well, we thought that they weren't done unless they could safely be eaten by someone in a deep coma . . . . If an unconscious person couldn't get them down their neck, then they weren't done . . . but now, that's all changed – we're adventurous eaters and . . . ooh, Vienetta is the new Arctic Roll, isn't it?

Consequently, lots of old foods that have been around for ages have been repackaged as trendy . . . you know – snazzy adverts like Tango fizzy orange – it's been around since I was a kid, but now it's got wacky adverts, got a new image. Pot Noodles, got a funny advert – those lovely Pot Noodles – something new for the youth . . . Lucozade! – formerly a drink for the bedridden, an invalid food . . . now knocked back by youths out on banging all-nighters . . .

But it doesn't always work . . . now they tried it with jammy dodgers, jammy dodger biscuits – now you have to watch as much UK Nazi Gold as me really to remember this campaign, because it was last year and it lasted about three weeks – 'cos it didn't really take off, and they thought, well, we'll have these wacky Tango-type adverts and they had all these chaps in shorts running about, having vats of jam thrown all over them . . . you know, it was all sort of mad but didn't really work – and the reason was, I think, that there was no truth in the ad . . . because anyone who has ever eaten a jammy dodger, or attempted to eat one, will know immediately . . .

You couldn't pour that jam over anyone.

Not a pouring jam – is it?

Really, jammy dodger jam is, in fact, 30 per cent Lycra, never loses its shape – you could put it in a hot wash and that jam would come out – it's a stretch jam really, it's a sports jam . . . you get a full upper-body workout with a jammy dodger – wouldn't you?

Of course, I say it's show business now, but there are those who, over the years, have tried to keep the flame of boredom alive of course – Delia Smith! Yes – now, you don't seem to mind a bit of mockery of Delia – some audiences don't, but last night they were a bit iffy about it – ooh, well, I don't know . . . Delia? Mmm? Oh yes, I'm broadminded – I don't mind jokes about the Royal Family . . . but Delia! Draw the line somewhere! Easy to mock her but her recipes WORK! That is such faint praise for a recipe isn't it? IT WORKS . . . you know if it doesn't work, it's nothing – it's just a set of instructions, a recipe, at the end of the day . . . if you make a cake according to one of Delia's recipes, and it doesn't work, you'd have cause for complaint. If you made it according to the fifth chapter of *Middlemarch* it would be your own fault really, wouldn't it? (laughter)

I can't help feeling that there is something about Delia that is totally . . . evil. Have you not picked up on that? There's something about that . . . there's a sort of aggressive blandness – a touch of the Mary Archers – do you not think? You never see them together, do you? I get the idea that Delia would always be ten degrees cooler than any room she's in.

Actually, I suppose that's why she's so good at pastry . . .

Now, before she retired to do the football, someone bought me . . . oh, and her fingers, those freckly, podgy fingers, there's something a bit sinister about them, isn't there?

I always think that the freckles, if you joined them up, would spell 666. But, before she retired, that last series – ooh, that exciting last series . . . what was it called? 'How to Recognise Water' – someone bought me the book of that – so I thought, I'll give it a go – did this recipe, chilli con carne . . . so there's all the ingredients – 'meat, onions, kidney beans, chillies – brackets, OPTIONAL' – 'NOTE: English cooks may like to substitute a sponge cake at this point.' (laughter)

Of course your polar opposite of Delia . . . Ainsley Harriott! I must admit, I tend to think, with Ainsley, if you're that happy, you haven't really understood the world. You see, I think that cheeriness is all very well – beyond a certain point it becomes quite offensive. And how many versions of what is, basically, your dinner, can Ainsley do? How many versions of it can there be? There must be executives stalking the corridors of White City thinking, 'We need a new idea for Ainsley. He's so jolly – what can we have? We've had him doing *Can't Cook, Won't Cook*, *Ready Steady Cook*, *Barbecues* – we've had people coming round his house . . . we need something new, different – edgy . . . how about this, we like this – *Ainsley's Death Row Dinners*.' Yes . . . *Ainsley's Death Row Dinners* – yes, the jolly chef . . . tours the condemned cells of the United States . . . cheering up the condemned man with a last supper to remember . . . till eight o'clock the next morning. We can have the recipes in the *Radio Times* – Ainsley's Humanely Fried Chicken – with a lethal injection of butter! – guaranteed to make the governor say pardon. I imagine most of it will be Tex Mex, won't it? (laughter)

Aah! It's a bit macabre, but I get sick of those lifestyle things . . . estate agents now on the television – if it's not the estate agents it's decorating . . . when did decorating become a leisure pursuit? When did we decide in Britain – that we need to repaint our houses every fortnight? I blame these programmes like *Changing Rooms* – to me this is why children can't concentrate properly any more . . . it's because the house changes constantly – it's like a flicker book, it just passes through their eyes . . . it's a wonder they're not having fits. They go off to school, while they're out their mum and dad bring in that big ponce from *Changing Rooms* – the one that looks like Margaret Lockwood in *The Wicked Lady* . . . in he comes, trails his sleeves about a bit – by the time the kids get home, their normal semi has been turned into a Moorish palace. No wonder they're all on Ritalin . . .

And if it's not that, it's gardening . . . oh, God, that bra-less gardener . . . Alan Titchmarsh! His mates, Tommy and Charlie, they go round someone's house, perfectly nice garden . . . by the

time they've finished – gravel pit. They make these gardens look like a cat litter for a lion.

You think . . . well, what next? What bizarre permutation of this next . . . *Can't Weave, Won't Weave?* Celebrity teams of Huguenot weavers teach hapless members of the public to weave bolts of damask . . . with HILARIOUS consequences! When I was a kid, I had the same wallpaper on my bedroom walls for years, you got to know it – you knew all the little shapes . . . they'd look like animals and you'd make up little stories with them, and it was a friend – till it got dark – it became sinister – unfamiliar . . . so it was a rehearsal for real relationships. (laughter)

Children don't have that now, it's all different for children . . .

Holidays – I didn't go away on foreign holidays – we went to the Isle of Wight always – which for years my mum and dad had me thinking was a foreign country till I figured out it's not so much that we're travelling through space as travelling back in time really – we used to stay in this grim bed and breakfast, run along the lines of Tenko, with stricter portion control. If we didn't go there, we'd take a little trip to Romney Marsh . . . in Kent – now, might have mentioned we lived in Kent – don't know what was going through their heads – 'Mmm, we need a break, I know, let's go deeper into Kent.' 'But, I know – as we haven't got a car, let's go to the bit of Kent untouched by public transport, that'll be an adventure.' Michael Palin could have done a whole series on our trip to the coast basically . . . . We'd leave our house in Erith, we could get a normal sort of train from there to Ashford and from Ashford you could get a Green Line bus from Ashford to Romney – then from Romney you had to get a spacehopper or something to New Romney, and from New Romney, the only way of getting to the coast was the Romney, Hythe and Dymchurch light railway. A lovely little model steam train, lovely it was, but we were going for a fortnight. We had deckchairs, suitcases, lilos, inflatable whales, water wings, rubber rings . . . cats, donkeys – my dad's six foot two – we're sat on there with our knees round our ears . . . by the time we get to Dymchurch we've all got deep vein thrombosis.

We get to Dymchurch where my mum and dad have rented a cottage off two old ladies, assuming they would leave – no, they were like two extra scary aunts – because we didn't even know them. They moved into a shed outside my bedroom window, with bunk beds and a dangerous paraffin heater and two stinky spaniels with cornflakey eyes . . .

What is it with spaniels? They let themselves go in five minutes, they make no effort at all. One minute – aah, what a cute little puppy, and then, what a rancid old dog, look at it . . . the Marlon Brando of the canine world, no effort at all . . .

So I'd be laying under this big, damp eiderdown – you could have given me dental X-rays and I'd have been totally safe . . . it was like a fortnight in Gormenghast . . . it was a nightmare.

Kids now . . . their lives are complicated in different ways, I think. For a start, people make a big fuss about children now . . . I think, in the past, people just got married, had children – didn't really go on about it – didn't give it a thought really – just did it really . . . and you were free as a child. You were sort of semi-feral, played out for years . . . played round your friends' houses – in fact you were like a cat really where you were fed at several houses in the street and no one was quite sure where you actually lived . . . freedom.

But now before they are even born there's all the reading of books, and you think, oh, God, if you can just remember one thing about babies you'll be laughing really . . . as a parent, you'll be fine – just remember, never, ever, ever put your thumb through that soft bit on top of the baby's head – can't stress that too much really – prospective parents, really very important 'cos a baby's head is like a coconut, three little holes but only one works – remember that and you'll be fine.

But no, and then once they're pregnant – oh, we're having a baby, we've got to move to a bigger house – you think, how big is this baby going to be? They're about *that* big, aren't they? Are you going to try to find a house exactly *that* much bigger . . . then of course the baby's born and you realise why they need a bigger house – all the gear that the baby has to have – all the stuff . . . they have this kind of retinue, an entourage – like the Last Emperor. (laughter)

So when they come round your house, pantechnicons draw up outside, roadies start unloading great stacks of Pampers . . . and baby swings and changes of clothes and bottle warmers and organic baby food and they come in checking the baby alarm going 'Waah, waah – yeah that works, that's fine – the baby has entered the building.'

And the parents are like the walking dead – they come in like this . . . they are like bush babies looking round as if woken from a sleep – they're totally sleep-deprived . . . they're like they've just crawled out of Guantanamo Bay, confessing to crimes they know nothing about. And you're going, 'Can I get you anything?' and they say, 'Yes, some sleep, please, we'd like some sleep . . . have you got any sleep in the house? 'Cos if you have give it to us now – WE MUST HAVE SLEEP, DON'T HOLD OUT ON US – GIVE US THE SLEEP, FOR THE LOVE OF GOD' and you say, 'Can I get you a drink?' – 'Er . . . just something herbal' – I usually give them a cup of Radox.

So there you are, sat there – a nice piping hot cup of Radox . . . all of a sudden the room fills with an ungodly stench coming from the baby . . . now what I assume will happen here is that they will put on protective clothing, like for chemical weapons, helmets and gauntlets and some sort of sterile tongs, pick the baby up, run outside with it, leave it by the wheelie bin, hose the street down with disinfectant, phone the public health authority – get everyone in the postal district inoculated against cholera . . . basic measures . . .

Oh no – with a sandwich in one hand – and they look at you as if you are mad 'cos you're vomiting – I think new parents are like soldiers in the First World War – they've seen so much squalor that they've lost all veneer of civilisation, haven't they? They don't know how to behave any more – you have to explain gently . . . no, sick isn't a brooch – not really . . .

Still, you get your own back – invited round for Sunday lunch the next week . . . take a dump in the middle of the dining room. Any complaints . . . it's just ageism really.

Of course, the baby gets bigger and they're fretting over every aspect like . . . oh, God he's six months old and he doesn't play the violin . . . think he might be Special Needs . . .

They get a bit bigger and they're toddlers – and middle-class people are the worst for this – Quorn woman from the arts centre going, 'Well, you know I really don't like my two, little Mezzanine and Flymo, I really, really don't like Mezzanine and Flymo watching the Teletubbies – because Teletubbies talk gibberish so their language skills won't be developed.'

Oh God, I was brought up on Bill and Ben – I don't consequently go, oh flobalob oh flobalob . . . mind you, I do still enjoy a little weed.

So – a bit more relaxed about cannabis back there, aren't you? A few teachers out there thinking . . . yes, well, I don't mind a jazz Woodbine of an evening sometimes when I'm marking books and going through the Grateful Dead back catalogue but . . .

Aah, the main problem with children nowadays is they're so ill – they've got so many things wrong with them, there are so many allergies and sensitivities . . . again – a new thing, a recent thing – at my primary school, every classroom had precisely ONE asthmatic – ONE chubby kid – a smattering of glasses . . . and one kid that smelled of wee.

That was it, wasn't it? It was like they were Government issue.

The head teacher would come round saying, 'Aah, Mr Jones, you appear to have two asthmatics . . . could you give one to Miss Johnson – she doesn't have any' – 'she's got to have one in her class or the ravens leave the tower . . . anarchy in the land.'

Nowadays, you talk to a child and they're the new old people really – 'cos you talk to children and you say, 'Oh hello, Mezzanine, how are you?' 'Oh, mustn't grumble.'

'Oh, that doesn't sound too good – well, it's a lovely day – don't you want to play in the garden?'

'Play in the garden! Are you mad? Play in the garden, with the air quality officially poor and the pollen count through the roof . . . I don't think so – play in the garden! Are you trying to kill me? I don't think so – I think I'll lay in a darkened room with a pint of Sunny Delight, Ventolin top, thank you.'

'Oh well, I dunno . . . would you like a biscuit ?'

'Biscuit! Biscuits? I can't eat biscuits – I'm wheat-intolerant, I'm wheat-sensitive . . . I've got wheat issues. One nibble on that Hob Nob and I'll blow up like a puff adder.'

'Well, how about a sweet?'

'Sweets! Sweets? Look at me, woman, I'm morbidly obese, I've got early onset, late onset diabetes.'

'Oh God, your life sounds miserable . . .'

'Oh well – once you're nine every day's a bonus . . . '

Children are fun but I think your best value for fun are old people – older people are fun . . . they're brilliant – they've lived a long life, they've seen all sorts of things and they don't care what they say or do – consequently life-enhancingly rude – just come out with stuff, don't they? I love to see older people in a bus queue – senior citizens' bus pass, licence to push in . . . shoving small children into the path of oncoming traffic. 'Go on – get out of it, you little bugger – go on, out of it – get out of me way.' 'What? Queue! Queue? I can't queue – I'm nearly dead. Give me that Ventolin – aah, that's good stuff . . . 'scuse me while I touch the sky . . . '

My neighbour's like this – Betty . . . she's brilliant, very feisty old lady, got a dodgy ticker these days, but she makes the best of it . . . got together with a couple of mates down the drop-in centre – putting on a little show about it – *The Angina Monologues* – doing ever so well . . . I think Jerry Hall's in it next week . . . And she goes off with her mates on these cheap holidays in coaches – pac-a-mac'd into coaches – smoking like beagles, all the windows closed. They get to the South Coast – they open the doors, it's like Guns 'n' Roses coming out – honestly, billowing smoke, they appear – 'Hey, Eastbourne, good to see ya!' – swaggering round the streets there . . . rebels without a short-term memory. What are ya rebelling against, Betty? 'Have I had my dinner?' Saga louts – that's what they are. That's the way you want to end up – Saga louts . . .

No, but she does have a bit of a morbid streak though – I've noticed this in quite a few older people . . . they just want to mess with your head with it – so she will always try to insert a reference to her own, imagined, imminent death – into any conversation you might be having – doesn't matter how innocent or how unpromising – so she'll say something like, 'If you're going to the shops, dear – will you get me some bin bags – not twenty-four, twelve will see me out, with one left over for me personal effects.'

God, and she will insist on shopping for her shopping at Argos – why? You probably haven't got one here but if you did it would probably be a lovely little pink-washed one, with all pargetting on the outside, wouldn't it? Oh, the nightmare, if you've ever shopped in Argos, it's madness, you start off, you view the catalogue . . . so it's like home shopping – but you use the catalogue in the shop . . . so it's home shopping . . . plus a walk . . . which is . . . shopping – but you've had to pick up a catalogue in the first place, so you've done a pre-shop and a home shop . . . and a shop, before you're ever close to buying anything. By then, you're actually in the shop and you're faced with a system now whereby you have to get another look at the catalogue just to make sure you've got the right number – queue to buy your item . . . then you queue again!

Thrice you queue! – to pick the thing up!

This is the system of shopping that brought down communism. This is the system of shopping that brought down the Eastern Bloc. People had enough of it . . . why do we have it in Britain? And that is because of the unrivalled queuing facilities. We love a queue – that's what it is . . . and this also explains to me the popularity of line dancing. What else explains it? 'Cos what else is a line dance if not a queue possessed of a demon? 'Help me, Jesus, help me, Jesus, doh-zee-doh . . . '

And she drags me to funerals with her . . . 'cos she's an A-list mourner – she's invited to them all – loves to see her picture next week in *Goodbye* magazine – drags me there . . . I'm not invited, I'm wearing trainers, but she blags me in – and she's only there, really, to get something from a house really, 'cos her own home is furnished almost entirely in funeral souvenirs, 'cos she always gets her little bit of gear from a house – she's like David Dickinson honestly, appraising, going, 'Clarice Cliff? – possibly . . . I don't know,' and she's looking at it and a grieving widower comes up –

'Oh, hello, Harry – sorry for your loss.'

'Thank you for coming, Betty – now I'd like you to have a little something, a little trinket of Eileen's . . . '

'Oh no, no, I . . . well if it will ease your grief . . . I don't want much, Harry, just a little something, you know, just to keep her in my heart – something that will remind me of Eileen . . . that boiler's quite new, isn't it?'

And the flowers . . . she goes to so many the flowers get very expensive, so here's a tip . . . this is what she does – shameless, utterly shameless – goes to a petrol station, buys a cheap little one-ninety-nine bunch of spray carnations . . . leaves them at a roadside notorious for accidents . . . goes off for a few hours . . . comes back – it's covered in floral tributes. No one knows what it is – they just put 'em down . . . There you go – a few teddies if you're lucky . . . Franklin Mint items . . . whole set of thimbles in a box . . .

We've got Princess Diana to thank for that one . . .

I think as you get older, your sense of humour gets a bit darker really – I think you get a bit more macabre . . . and you start thinking about more spiritual things – I mean, I'm not religious at all – I tend to get on with most people really . . . I personally don't believe in God – I tend to think – if God wanted us to believe in Him, He'd exist . . . but I am very interested in religion – I find it a very interesting thing . . . fascinating, the things people believe in – and where I live in East London – every religion under the sun . . . but even just the Christian churches – thousands of them, all different kinds – the Church of the Seventh Day Adventists, the Church of Christ the Redeemer, the Church of the Cherubim and Seraphim – I don't even know what Seraphim are . . . I suppose they're allied to Cherubim – I dunno – bit slimmer? – I dunno – but . . . the Church of the Cherubim and Seraphim – the Church of Christ the Graphic Designer. There's even a church for Quorn woman and her mates, who don't actually believe in God; called – the Church . . . of the Vague Sense That There Must be Something More Than This.

All do pretty well, apart from the Jehovah's Witnesses, very, very unpopular . . . problem there, is with the word witness . . . sounds a bit too much like a grass and that doesn't play well in East London really – one thing you don't do – you don't grass . . . so the poor bloke comes to your door: 'Hello, Jehovah's Witness.' 'No, mate – I've never heard of him. He don't live round here – he don't live round here, does he? No, she hasn't heard of him – you haven't heard of him either – if you know what's good for yer, all right?' I think they'd do better if they called themselves Jehovah's Alibi, and if the Watchtower said, when did evil come into the world? 'Well, whenever it was, Jehovah was round his nan's all night – on my baby's life.'

Satanism gets a bad press, doesn't it? Possibly not round here, I don't know . . . nice little Satanist cheese and wine nights – I don't know, but I love that film *The Wicker Man* – that's one of my favourite cult movies – *The Wicker Man*, great cult British horror movie – I always wonder when I watch it . . . what on earth gave those Scottish islanders the idea that Edward Woodward would burn well? – lucky guess, I suppose.

No, like most people with no particular belief in God, I tend to put C of E down on forms – really, just 'cos it fits the space – and the religious duties aren't too onerous really, are they? . . . Sweet sherry of a Christmas – could manage that – and it is quite a harmless Church – quite a gentle Church – apart from all that nasty nonsense about gay bishops and everything – I mean, what's that all about? Where do they get off really, the Church of England, pretending that there aren't loads of vicars who are in it for the frocks? (laughter)

What's the problem? I would have thought gay bishops and vicars were the ideal kind really – God, they could really *run* a jumble sale . . . (laughter) It would be brilliant . . . Queer Bishop for the Straight Congregation. It could be a show with five of them, you know – at jumbles – advising you what you should wear and everything – it would be brilliant.

But generally it is quite gentle . . . you can't really imagine a Church of England Jihad – there's not enough home-made cakes in the world to pay for it really, is there? Can't really see the little thermometer outside the church . . . 'We need this much THIS MUCH for Semtex'.

But on the other hand, there is a smugness to the name – Church of England. It's a sort of little England, sort of pleased with itself . . . Church of England – there's a sort of insular – I don't know what it is – there's a vague implication that Jesus might have been English – I think it's implied . . . 'Oh yes, English chap, from down Taunton way . . . bit of a beardy – sandal-wearer but very sound, yes . . . Jewish? I shouldn't think so . . . Mind you, I've never seen him at the golf club . . .' (laughter)

You can look at any painting ever done of Jesus over the centuries and you can spot immediately that he's not English, 'cos he's very often shown wearing sandals – but never with socks.

I think that would be an English Messiah's look, wouldn't it? – socks, sandals, khaki shorts skimming the knee, little Fair Isle slip-over – in case it turns, 'cos it's deceptive, the desert – ooh, it can turn – and I think, being English, instead of all that camp and rather beautiful 'Oh Lord, why hast thou forsaken me?' business – instead of all that – I think he'd be up there trying to make the best of it – 'cos moping doesn't help, does it? I think he'd be up there going, 'Cor, here's a pretty pickle . . . No, I didn't do it either, but you don't like to say, do you?'

'You can see their point of view, can't you – Roman soldier couldn't have been more helpful – oh well, looking on the bright side . . . been lucky with the weather! Ooh, it can be shocking . . . of a Bank Holiday.' (laughter)

I don't know, we get a very mixed message in society about age and ageing, don't we? On the one hand there's this brilliant idea about middle youth . . . you know, this idea that no one's ever middle-aged any more – they just move into their middle youth – brilliant – it's a nice idea and then they die and everyone's shocked to find that they're eighty-seven – thought they were thirty-three. It's a good thing, because I think that in the past people in this country could not wait to get old and miserable, could they? It was their ambition – to just get old and die . . .

But now we've got middle youth – but it's not across the board, 'cos on the one hand there's this idea that you can dress young and you can be young and all this – but that's not the message you get from the pension industry. They don't want you to think that you're in your middle youth – your June Whitfields, your man who used to be James Herriott, all that lot . . . your Frank Windsors – they want you panicking about your twilight years when your age hits double figures! And you start getting those nasty little letters from pension companies and insurance funds and everything – on your birthday . . . horrible, isn't it?

They start off quite promisingly: 'Dear Miss Smith, happy birthday – now . . . now that you're nearly dead, perhaps we could interest you in our "not fade away" pension scheme. Or perhaps you like the smell of wee and cabbage? Is that it? Is that it, Miss Smith? Is that the aroma in which you want to live out the twilight of your years? For the sake of fifty notes a week . . . is that it, eh? Is that how you see your future? Living in the city in a rat-infested slum . . . feeble little bed with a threadbare blanket, pulled up in terror round your ears 'cos the wardens keep beating you up – with a dangerous paraffin heater just near enough for you to fall on and burn – but not near enough to keep you warm – and two stinking spaniels with cornflakey eyes sat next to the bed – God, they let themselves go in five minutes – they are like Marlon Brando – car alarms going off outside, all hours of the day and night, driving you bloody mental – is that what you want, you feckless idiot? Well, laugh now while you can 'cos you won't be laughing then – you make me sick to my stomach!

Your obedient servant, Mr Wilkinson' (laughter)
MIXED MESSAGE!

The thing that really worries me about getting old is music . . . popular music – that's what bothers me – 'cos at the minute I like anything really – I'll give it all a go – anything that comes along . . . you know, Dizzee Rascal – the Streets, whatever . . . I'll give it a listen, but this isn't going to last for ever, is it? Obviously not – why should I be different to anyone else in the world? Quite clearly, there comes a point in everyone's life – it's happened to everyone who's come before – there comes a point in their life when they wake up one morning and they think . . . right . . . I like all the music that's happened up till now . . . and nothing that's going to happen in the future. I know I haven't heard it yet – I don't care, I know it's rubbish, I know it's a racket – I only like the stuff up to this point in my life.

And of course it will happen to all of us 'cos it's happened to every generation – like fifties fans who are stuck in the Elvis era, who only like that . . . don't like anything since.

Beatles fans who only like the Beatles – jazz fans who only like music written up to 1961 . . . November of 1961 (laughter)

So it's going to happen, and it could be today – for all of us. Today could be the day when we decide – that's it, no more – I'm turning off my ears – I'm not listening to any more – and what would that mean to us? If we do take out that pension scheme, what would that mean for our retirement? Let's imagine we're in our retirement home on the South Coast – well, it would look very much like this, I think . . . wouldn't it? Similar cheery décor – wouldn't it be? This would be the sunshine lounge. The Stephen Hawking sunshine lounge, this would be – and we'd be . . . and all the armchairs in that depressing way that they are all shoved round the walls, with a great wilderness, a great empty space in the middle – it's like centrifugal force has spun them out – I think they must stop building these places in vortexes. (laughter)

And we'd all be sat there, sucking Werther's Originals to points, spitting them at each other like Ninja stars . . . going, 'Do you remember? That was a lovely film, wasn't it? . . . KILL BILL . . . Kill Harry . . . Kill Mabel' . . .

And we'll be sat there, and it will be old time musical night – our favourite night, Friday night – and there'll be a volunteer at the piano plinking out all our favourites – come on everybody, old time musical night, take you back to the time when tunes were tunes –

I want you all up and dancing – never mind the centrifugal force . . . fight it! It builds bone mass! Up you get, on your toes . . . We'll kick off with, oh, here's a favourite – he was lovely – all of us love 'im . . . who remembers him – you all do – so up on your feet and dancing – to the fabulous . . . Eminem! – two, three, four . . . will the real Slim Shady please stand up, please stand up . . . I'll be going, 'Knees up, Eminem, knees up, Eminem, knees up – knees up, slap my bitch up – knees up, Eminem!' 'Ooh . . . that was love-ly – I tell you what, you won't believe me – that Slim Shady – ooh, that Eminem . . . you could hear EVERY word he sang . . . EVERY word he sang.'

And that's just about every word from me really – you've been an absolute delight – thank you so much for coming, I must say – well, you are the difference between a performance and an afflic-tion. If I'd gone through this on my own here . . . they'd be upping my medication no end, I can tell you . . . a bit more tin foil in my shoes, but no – you were here – perfect timing that it should hap-pen like this – I'd like to thank the theatre here and Steve the techie and all the staff in the box office – and if I could ask you just one little favour before I go . . . if you could just have a little rummage under your seat – have a good look round – look underneath there before you go – if you could find ANY weapons of mass destruc-tion . . . please just send them to the Government – they've looked everywhere. I begin to think they'll never find them . . . well, they'll be in the last place they look, won't they, eh?

I'm like that with scissors.

It's a farce, isn't it really – if they really wanted to know what he had . . . they really should have kept their copy of the invoice, don't you think?

That's all from me – thank you so much – GOODNIGHT!

(Applause)

(Linda returns to the stage)

You're very kind . . . but you'll notice, I didn't push that encore . . . On like a shot, wasn't I? Really the main reason for that is you can . . . push it a bit, sometimes, with an encore – a bit of hubris creeps in – and . . . come back on – everyone's gone!

From my point of view, a bit of a downsy end to an otherwise charming evening – plus sometimes – probably not here – people are locked into very punitive park and ride schemes.

That's another thing . . . it can happen, it can be nasty – you can go outside to find the car clamped – it's not very nice, is it? But no . . . that is the end, really.

To be honest, I do tend to arrange it that way, with the end at the end – I just feel the extension is not in keeping with the rest of the show somehow – I didn't get planning permission for the extension, but no, you're a very nice audience and you're a very mixed audience – quite a mixture of age and . . . well, you're all the same species obviously – mammals, mainly, aren't you out there? – yes . . . on the whole – a smattering of others . . .

I'm getting that there might be quite a lot of radio listeners out there . . . I would imagine – ooh er . . . rather more than I was thinking . . . A rare outing away from the crystal set! It's all right, the outside world, isn't it? I know we're not wearing tiaras and dinner jackets and enunciating properly, but it's not too bad, is it? No, I myself, I'm a huge radio fan – I love Radio 4 – but not every programme . . . not keen on *You and Yours* – how long does that programme last? You turn on the radio – it's on ALL day . . . It's like being in Cuba with the speeches of Castro – only it's all about dolls that don't reach British safety standards – how many can there be, for God's sake?

Here's a little tip for the more Bohemian quarter out there – if you do some ecstasy, right . . . and listen to *You and Yours* . . . it doesn't sound any better, really!

That's all – thank you, GOODNIGHT!

(Applause)

AFTERWORD
Sandi Toksvig, writer, comedian and broadcaster

I don't know why, but I feel it would please Linda enormously that *Afterword* is the name of *Canada's National Paper For The Young Jewish Scene*. Canadians are not universally noted for their ability to alter the world's axis, so it won't surprise you that their *Afterword* is mainly awash with cheap deals to Israel via Prague and a gripping article entitled 'Humentuschens: A hidden miracle in a cookie'. Indeed, I could imagine an entire riff from Linda on the paper's revelation that Ralph Lauren's real name is Lipschitz and wondering how that would market on a designer sweater.

Words and their manipulation are my daily currency yet 'Afterword' is causing me to come more than a little unstuck. I should be fine for I have at my disposal the English language which, for the comic, is the greatest resource in the world. It has an unparalleled history and scope for, not content with an array of prose purloined from Latin and French, the English spent generations heading out on daytripper tickets nicking bits of language from anyone prepared to be impressed by their willingness to rule even in hot weather. The trouble is, even this available breadth of expression seems poor when it comes to the one woman who was entitled to wear the Black Belt of communication.

I was once talking about a free gift of condoms and a condom measurer that had been sent to me in the post. Linda shook her head and complained, 'All I ever get is catalogues from the RSPB.' It was the perfect choice of condom antithesis. Linda's humour didn't lie in set-piece jokes but in pointing out things you felt you should have noticed yourself. It was with an apparently casual air that she would ask why old people sit in retirement homes in 'the armchairs in that depressing way that they are all shoved round the walls – it's like a centrifugal force has spun them out – I think they should stop building these places in vortexes'.

I first met Linda in a café waiting to go to a recording of Radio 4's the *News Quiz*. I was eating a yoghurt when she slipped on to the stool beside me. 'I knew you'd be very rock and roll,' she said quietly. There is a terrible tendency for some comedians to never 'be off'. They feel as though they must entertain at all times, and the old adage that if the fridge light goes on they'll do twenty minutes is often true. That was never the case with Linda. Offstage you had to listen carefully because she was often funny under her breath and seemingly without meaning to be.

The world of comedy is ninety-nine per cent male, and women who make their mark often either spend a great deal of time decrying their own looks or making off-colour remarks that might let them into the boys' club. Linda did neither, and indeed the greatest compliment that old buffer Alan Coren ever paid her was that he 'forgot she was a woman'. I didn't, because I think she had a very female take on life.

I know that the real reason I have trouble with the word 'Afterword' is that it is a slightly absurd concept for a writer. There is nothing after words except silence and I am uncomfortable with that. It suggests that something is over and that is a loss that I may never be prepared to deal with. I have Linda's recordings and the memories of being allowed to play verbal tennis with a champion as sustenance, but I know it will not be enough. She was a remarkable, kind and generous woman and her loss is incomprehensible. If anyone would like to get together for old times' sake, I have this great recipe for a Jewish biscuit.

Sandi Toksvig, 2006.

ACKNOWLEDGEMENTS

This book was researched, compiled and edited in three months. The core team of two could not have turned this project around in such a short period of time without the involvement and assistance of many other people. Our heartfelt thanks must go to:

All the comedians, writers, cartoonists, producers, journalists, and broadcasters who contributed to the book. Very special thanks must go to our gang of four – Gail Elliman, Andy Hamilton, Libby Asher, and William Shaw, who burned the midday and midnight oil transcribing from various formats, helping to select and edit Linda's wonderful material.

Thanks to Nick Davies at Hodder and Stoughton who has been a pleasure to work with. To the following people at BBC radio for being so lovely and co-operative; Lucy Armitage, Amy Buscombe, Sally Heaven, Claire Jones, Cathie Mahoney, Simon Nicholls, Jo O'Leary, Julie Pearce, Karl Phillips, Kate Rowland, Paul Schlesinger, Maria Simons, Jeffrey Smith, Kyla Thorogood, Katie Tyrell. The same sentiments go out to independent producers Jon Naismith, John Rolph, Hat Trick Productions, Paul Merton, Maureen Lipman, Arthur Smith, agents Kate Haldane and Annette Parnell at Amanda Howard Associates, Joe Norris at Off The Kerb Productions, and our super literary agent Jonny Geller and his assistant Doug Kean at Curtis Brown. Our trusty graphic designer Andy Smith at Swordfish Communications; Ruth Huntman at *Radio Times*; photographers Martin Jenkinson, Sharron Wallace and several others. Garden designer Anna Wardrop for inspiration. Hanne Stinson and Caroline Black at the British Humanist Association. John Murdoch of Murdochs, Solicitors.

And all those brilliant people who provided food, shelter and support during the production of this book: Jane Baker, Katie Barlow; Carol Benjamin, Margaret Bennett, Gurpreet Bhatti, Tina and Leigh Borrett, Sarah Broughton, Dave Cohen, Hattie Coppard, Liz Cousins, Graham Downes, Austin and Mandy Giles, Scott Giles, Sue Harper, Alan Hayling, Patrick Hehir, Tony Lakin, Sheila Lakin, Mike McCarthy, Jane McMorrow, Chris Meade, Bindy Mellor, Karen Merkel, Will Merkel-Downes, Julie Pearn, Suzanne Phillips, Araya Reddah, Sandi Russell, Jennifer Reay, Angela Smith, Janet Staplehurst, Sam Stoyan, Kerrie Thomas, Martin Yarnit, Jess York.

Two audio CDs of Linda Smith's live performances are available from Hodder & Stoughton Audiobooks:

I THINK THE NURSES ARE
STEALING MY CLOTHES

is available as a two hour audio CD – a collection of previously unheard recordings of Linda's performances from throughout her career, introduced by Hattie Hayridge.

LINDA SMITH LIVE

is a classic recording of Linda's live stage show on two CDs.

DRIVING MISS SMITH:
A biography of Linda Smith

by Warren Lakin

Forthcoming from Hodder & Stoughton
Autumn 2007